The Intelligible Ode

The Intelligible Ode
Intimations of Paradise

Graham Davidson

The Lutterworth Press

The Lutterworth Press

P.O. Box 60
Cambridge
CB1 2NT
United Kingdom

www.lutterworth.com
publishing@lutterworth.com

Hardback ISBN: 978 0 7188 9643 0
Paperback ISBN: 978 0 7188 9644 7
PDF ISBN: 978 0 7188 9645 4
ePUB ISBN: 978 0 7188 9646 1

British Library Cataloguing in Publication Data
A record is available from the British Library

First Published by The Lutterworth Press, 2023

Copyright © Graham Davidson, 2023

All rights reserved. No part of this edition may be reproduced,
stored electronically or in any retrieval system, or transmitted
in any form or by any means, electronic, mechanical,
photocopying, recording, or otherwise, without
prior written permission from the Publisher
(permissions@lutterworth.com).

To
my wife, Perdita,
('With thee conversing...')
and
our daughters Hatty, Lydia and Agnes

> let my lamp at midnight hour
> Be seen in some high lonely tow'r,
> Where I may oft out-watch the Bear,
> With thrice great Hermes, or unsphere
> The spirit of Plato, to unfold
> What worlds, or what vast regions hold
> The immortal mind that hath forsook
> Her mansion in this fleshly nook:
> And of those dæmons that are found
> In fire, air, flood, or under ground,
> Whose power hath a true consent
> With planet, or with element.
>
> Il Penseroso

Reader, this is to let thee understand that when I was in my earthly garden, a-digging with my spade, with my face to the east side of the Garden, I saw into the Paradise of God, from whence my father Adam was cast forth.

Roger Crab, Dagons-Downfall

Contents

Abbreviations ix
Acknowledgements xi

Introduction 1

Part I. Patterns

1. A Philosophical Framework: Understanding the Intelligible 13
2. Expostulation and Reply: The Tables Turned 29
3. Lines written a few miles above Tintern Abbey 40
4. Geometry, Poetry and the Sublime of Man 64

Part II. Principles

5. Intimations 79
6. Recollections 101

Part III. A Crisis: The Poems of 1802

7. Several Kinds of Poem 127
8. Heaven and Earth 138

Part IV. Reading the Ode

9. Origins 155
10. Verse, Grammar and Imagery 162
11. Competing Forces 179
12. Stanzas I-IV: The Statement of Loss 186
13. Stanzas V-VIII: The Analysis of Loss 197

	14.	Stanzas IX-X: Recovery	206
	15.	Stanza XI: Resolution	216
Part V.	**Looking Forward into History**		
	16.	Poems Published and Unpublished	227
	17.	What if? A Counterfactual Reading	242

Bibliography   253
Index of Wordsworth's Work   259
General Index   263

Abbreviations

1798-9	*The Prelude, 1798-1799* (ed. Parrish)
1799	*The Two Part Prelude* (ed. Abrams, et al.)
1805	*The Thirteen Book Prelude* (ed. Abrams et al.)
1850	*The Fourteen Book Prelude* (ed. Abrams et al.)
5BP	*The Five-Book Prelude* (ed. Wu)
AP	*The Poems of T.S. Eliot, The Annotated Text* (cited by vol. and page no.)
AR	Coleridge, *Aids to Reflection*
BL	Coleridge, *Biographia Literaria*
Centuries	Thomas Traherne, *Centuries of Meditations*,
CL	*The Collected Letters of Samuel Taylor Coleridge* (cited by vol and page no.)
CN	*The Collected Notebooks of Samuel Taylor Coleridge* (cited by vol. and entry no.)
CS	Coleridge, *On The Constitution of the Church and State*
DCMS	The Dove Cottage Manuscripts
DS	*Descriptive Sketches*
DWJ	*Dorothy's Grasmere Journals*, cited by date.
EFL	*Early Family Letters*
Experiments	Jared Curtis, *Wordsworth's Experiments with Tradition*
EY	*The Letters of William and Dorothy Wordsworth: The Early Years*
F	Coleridge , *The Friend*
FN	*The Fenwick Notes*
FQ	T.S. Eliot, *Four Quartets:*
	BN Burnt Norton
	EC East Coker
	DS Dry Salvages
	LG Little Gidding
GMH Letters	*The Collected Works of Gerard Manley Hopkins: Correspondence*

HG	*Home at Grasmere* (cited either by MS and line number, e.g. HG D 123, or by page number, e.g. HG 345)
Inducements	Thomas Traherne, 'Inducements to Retirednesse'
LB	*Lyrical Ballads*
Logic	Coleridge, *Logic*
LHP	Coleridge, *Lectures on the History of Philosophy*
LL	Coleridge, *Lectures on Literature 1808-19*
LPR	Coleridge, *Lectures 1795 on Politics and Religion*
LS	Coleridge, Lay Sermons
M	Coleridge, *Marginalia* (cited by vol. and page no.)
Memoirs	*Memoirs of William Wordsworth*
MW	William Wordsworth, *The Major Works* (ed. Stephen Gill)
MWL	*The Letters of Mary Wordsworth 1800-1855*
MY	*The Letters of William and Dorothy Wordsworth: The Middle Years*
OM	Coleridge, *Opus Maximum*
P2V	*Poems in Two Volumes, and Other Poems* (ed. Jared Curtis)
Prose	*The Prose Works of William Wordsworth*
PW	*The Poetical Works of Samuel Taylor Coleridge* (Reading Text cited as *PW* and poem no.; Variorum Text by vol., part, and page no.)
RC	*The Ruined Cottage*, cited by MS and line no., e.g. *RC* E 168; or page no., e.g. *RC* 373
Reed	Mark L. Reed, *Wordsworth: The Chronology of The Middle Years, 1800-1815*
SP	*The Salisbury Plain Poems*
SWF	Coleridge, *Shorter Works and Fragments*
TA	Tintern Abbey
TPW	Thomas Traherne, *The Poetical Works*
TWC	*The Wordsworth Circle*
VL	Coleridge's Verse Letter to Sara Hutchinson
VMP	T.S. Eliot, *The Varieties of Metaphysical Poetry*
Woof	*William Wordsworth: The Critical Heritage*
WPW	*Wordsworth's Poetical Works in Five Volumes*

Acknowledgements

'Alone I did it' boasted Coriolanus, just before he was cut down by his indignant peers. There are moments, I imagine, when all authors are tempted to echo his words. However, Coriolanus was isolated by the 'execration and contempt' underpinning his heroism, and found himself an outcast, like the lonely subject of Wordsworth's Lines left upon a Seat in a Yew-tree. Much as I admire the Coriolanian spirit, to claim a sedentary imitation would belie my experience. Specific debts are acknowledged in the text, but over the years I have received considerable encouragement from many people, offering the hope that makes the work worthwhile – work without hope 'draws nectar in a sieve'. If some of those listed here are not conscious of having offered me that hope or encouragement, then they have overlooked some little nameless act of kindness. Not all are still alive, but my gratitude lives on. To those who feel they might have expected to appear here, and have not, I apologize and say that only my memory is at fault, not my thanks. The order is alphabetical.

Reggie Watters, Pamela Woof, John Powell Ward, James Vigus, Anya Taylor, Justin Shepherd, Nick Roe, Michael Raiger, Jim Mays, Peter Manning, Greg Leadbetter, Peter Larkin, Gerry Janzen, Felicity James, William Horsted, David Hopkins, Jeff Hipolito, Douglas Hedley, Richard Gravil, Bruce Graver, Eric Gill, Stephen Gill, Marilyn Gaull, Tim Fulford, Samuel Fitzgerald, David Fairer, Paul Cheshire, Adrian Brink, Jeff Barbeau.

Thank you all.

Introduction

ALTHOUGH 'THE LURE OF a general theory appears too tempting to resist', this reading of Wordsworth's poetry tries to avoid that temptation.[1] From critics who have adopted other methods I have gained insights that I would have been happy to consider.[2] But had I thus engaged, I would have written something nearer a history of Wordsworth criticism than a book on his poetry. I also know that the principle or method I have tried to adopt may be considered a theory.[3] If so, it is this: that poems will provide most of their pleasure, as well as share most of their insights, principally by reading and reflection, by establishing connections between different poems – not only by the same author – and by listening to what the author says, if anything, about their own poetry and that of others. Nevertheless, there are many poems for which we have little more than the poem itself, and which must therefore stand by themselves. In short, I am wary of importing theories derived from other disciplines.

In this book there are two principal exceptions to my use of this renewed method.[4] It depends, in some measure, on biographical sources that tell us of the states of mind that might have informed Wordsworth's poems. For instance, it would be difficult to realize all the implications of Resolution and Independence without knowing something about his relationship with Coleridge in 1802, and their wholly different attitudes to the impasse that both then faced.

[1.] Seamus Perry, 'Coleridge, the Return to Nature, and the New Anti-Romanticism: An Essay in Polemic', *Romanticism on the Net*, Vol. 4 (November 1996), # 26.

[2.] Like the devil, these theories are legion; but unlike those that possessed the sufferer in St Mark, they are not coexistent, but serial, and each requires a separate act of exorcism, the next usually trying to push the previous over the cliff.

[3.] Christopher Ricks discusses the distinctions between theory and principle in the *LRB*, Vol. 3, no. 7 (16 April 1981).

[4.] In effect, practical criticism, resurgent in respect of more recent theory: 'New Historicism is considerably dated now and some revival of interest in close reading, of formalism and prosody for poetic meaning, is more up to date' (Peter Larkin, in an email, 9 March 2022).

More importantly, the premise of this reading is that Wordsworth and Coleridge wanted to reunite what they perceived as divided – the power of mind and the power of nature – a division Coleridge attributed to Descartes. Wordsworth came to realize that in his childhood and youth he had had some experience of that unity, subsequently lost. To recover a power reinstating that union was the principal impetus of his work, and of the *Ode* in particular.

Thus a reading of no more than the poems is modified by reference to a biographical and cultural history.[5] As Coleridge said of Newton, any system of thought dependent on the passivity of mind, that is, originating principally from the information of the senses, is likely to be false in itself (*CL* II 709). Independently of the impressions of sense, Wordsworth, like Coleridge, believed that the mind has its own truths, which he considered powers not concepts. Methods of interpretation that forget this are unlikely to do his work full justice.

A Philosophical Framework

What I take as the foundations of Wordsworth's thinking, and the primary impetus of his poetry, are set out in the first chapter, beginning with the particular importance he attached to the words 'intelligible' and 'unintelligible'. Aristotle's works bequeathed to European culture the notion that nature could be fully understood not primarily by observation, but through certain general principles – which he described as the four causes.[6] Doubts about the validity of Aristotle's methods grew throughout the fifteenth and sixteenth centuries, coming to a head in the work of Copernicus, Descartes, Bacon and others – who, in essence, all proposed that the physical world should be understood by observation, not through the conception of causes and categories. An old word, reason, was put to a new purpose, quite different from the syllogistic logic inherited from Aristotle. The empirical laws thus discovered challenged the Aristotelian premise that intellectual conceptions could explain the physical world. This was the beginning of the soul and body, mind and nature distinction formalized by Descartes. The new method

---

[5.] For a discriminate evaluation of New Historicism see the Introduction to Nick Roe's *The Politics of Nature* (Basingstoke, 2002). For an example of its discriminate use, see Tim Fulford's *Wordsworth's Poetry, 1815-1845*, Chapter 2, 'The Politics of Landscape' (Pennsylvania, 2019). For a subtle dismantling of New Historicism, see Seamus Perry's 'An Essay in Polemic'.

[6.] For a succinct resumé of the four causes, see https://plato.stanford.edu/entries/aristotle-natphil/.

was exciting – it promised to understand 'the great automaton of the world, by observing how one part moves another'[7] – something we still believe. A group of theologians, the Cambridge Platonists, initially took up Cartesian methods, but soon spotted a serious flaw, evident in Patrick's remark: separating the mind from the workings of nature, it led to a mechanical view of nature wholly at odds with the powers and ideas they attributed to God – wisdom, grace, justice and freedom among others. God thus became the maker of a world extraneous to his being, which functioned perfectly well in his absence. Theists were untroubled, satisfied with God as creator, asking no more. But God *ab extra*, set apart from his creation, not *ab intra*, or the power by which his creation lived, disturbed the Cambridge Platonists. Yet they were not willing to abandon the reason that was proving itself such a success in understanding the material world.

They therefore posited a deeper function of that power which, perhaps deliberately, they did not distinguish by a separate term. They asserted that reason was also the root of spiritual truths and in accord with divine revelation, claiming it was continuous with Cartesian reason, and therefore the life of the mind (or God) had a potential presence in nature. Then, by various modes of mediation, of which Cudworth's 'plastic nature' is the best-known example, God was understood as a power in the created world, not left outside twiddling his thumbs – or, as my wife put it, playing on his Xbox.

The principles behind this massive and confusing claim were wholeheartedly adopted by Wordsworth and Coleridge. On the one hand there is deductive and inductive reason, ratiocination, the kind of logic we use daily, which applied to the observation of phenomena educes what we now call the laws of nature. On the other is the belief that the laws of nature are at one with the qualities of mind we associate with God, that the truths or ideas of that mind in some manner inform the being of nature. That now seems barely comprehensible to us, and we are astonished when we hear Wordsworth remembering that he gave a moral life to stones, saw them feel or linked them to some feeling (*1805* III 124 ff.). What possible link can there be between the ratiocination that Coleridge called the Understanding, and the Reason that he, Wordsworth and the Cambridge Platonists all associated with God?

The answer lies in mathematics, specifically geometry. It works something like this: the mind can intuit the theorems of geometry without

---

[7] Simon Patrick, *A Brief Account of the new Sect of Latitude-Men together with some reflections upon the New Philosophy* (London, 1662), p. 12.

beginning with observation or reliance on the senses. Once formalized, those intuitions are unalterable and permanent truths. Derived *from* the mind, or what Wordsworth called 'pure intelligence', they are truths *of* the mind. They are also truths that help predict or explain the behaviour of natural bodies. So the intuitions of the mind may reveal, at least in part, the laws of nature. Wordsworth speaks of meditating 'Upon the alliance of those simple, pure / Proportions and relations, with the frame / And laws of Nature' (*1805* VI 143-46). If that alliance holds good for one mode of intuition, why not of another? Why not look in nature for 'the ideas of ... eternity, freedom, will, absolute truth, of the good, the true, the beautiful, the infinite' – 'the *peculia* of our humanity'? Partly because theorems are not ideas, though Coleridge acknowledged that he initially conflated the two (*F* I 177). Partly because it was simply a step too far, although Wordsworth's willingness to find morals in stones and sermons in everything was an indication of how far he was willing to go.

They both retreated a little, and instead of searching for exact relations between mind and nature, they looked to the idea of a common power, probably not dissimilar to the search that took Cudworth to plastic nature. However, a key feature of the highest Reason, as Wordsworth called it, by which it differs fundamentally from intuitive reason, is that it is a power existing only in the moment of disclosure – that it is always a power and never a state – never an argument won or an intuition verified. Although Wordsworth imagined it might be a continuous power, his experience of it was always momentary. Nor is it a power fully within the voluntary control of the individual. It must be willed in some sense, but requires a patient waiting for 'the vision and the faculty divine', and if it comes at all it comes athwart our consciousness at surprising moments, and is habitually suppressed by the dominance of the senses. Like all power, it is known through its effect, principally experienced as feeling – or the lack of it, as Wordsworth so plangently put it in the *Ode*, 'I see, not feel'. And for Wordsworth, as for Coleridge, the world is intelligible if imbued with that power, and unintelligible if not – 'blank' or 'barren' as they separately said. To both of them there was no power greater than Reason, and Imagination was but 'reason in her most exalted mood' – a phrase quoted several times in this book.[8]

If that power lives in nature, then one might expect it to be expressed by nature. To what degree was a matter Coleridge and Wordsworth debated. Nevertheless, how a more or less singular power informs the

---

[8] *1805* XIII 167-70.

infinite variety of sense impressions is one of the principal questions that Wordsworth's poetry asks. He constantly looked for that unity, and was distressed when he saw the reasoning of 'minute analysis' looking not for the single power common to all phenomena, but 'still dividing, and dividing still / Break down all grandeur'.[9] On several occasions, Wordsworth characterized that grandeur or singular power as 'infinity' – a remarkable assertion in itself – but astonishing when he declared that in its absence there is no poetry.[10] The chapter closes with a consideration of how the idea of the infinite and the existence of the phenomenal might relate.

Patterns

With the framework of Wordsworth's thought in some measure established, the rest of the book can be summarized more succinctly. The debate between the powers of the mind, the powers of nature, and the value that can and can't be attached to sense impressions, is the essence of Chapter 2, which looks at Expostulation and Reply and The Tables Turned. I have taken these two short, even apparently slight poems as primary exemplars of Wordsworth's quarrel with himself because I think they epitomize the problems he faced. He affirmed their importance by presenting them as the opening poems of the two-volume *Lyrical Ballads,* 1800. Stephen Gill noted that The Tables Turned 'is so central that reference from it could be made to almost all of Wordsworth's mature works' (*MW* 691). Such authorities are good enough for me.

Chapter 3, on Tintern Abbey, follows the deepening of this debate, finding what was tentative in The Tables Turned now more clearly espoused, and also delineates some patterns of thought structural to Wordsworth's poetry: the belief that love of nature leads to love of man; that there is a human form sublime, and also 'something more sublime', transcending mortality; that, paradoxically, suppression of the senses is essential to seeing into the life of things; that the memories of childhood represent an ideal condition to be recovered; and less evident, that his assertion of belief or experience is followed by doubt, which is then followed by a re-expression of faith in similar but less assertive terms.[11] This is a

---

[9.] *RC*; additions to MS D, pp. 373-74.

[10.] *The Diary, Reminiscences and Correspondence of Henry Crabb Robinson* (London, 1869), vol. II, p. 22.

[11.] See Alan Rawes's reference to Susan Wolfson's *Questioning Presence* in his 'Romantic Form and New Historicism', in his *Romanticism and Form* (Basingstoke, 2007), pp. 99-100.

pattern central to the Ode. And as Wordsworth felt it was written in that spirit, Tintern Abbey is discussed as a five-part ode.

Chapter 4 pauses to find the pattern beginning with love of nature, through the sublime of man, to something more sublime, in several other poems. As mentioned above Wordsworth asserts that the truths of geometry, and of intuitive reason, are the laws of nature; and yet they also pass beyond nature, surpassing life, to a world out of space and time, an independent world created by 'pure intelligence'. Euclid's *Elements*, truths not limited to space and time, provide the 'purest bond' for the wedding of man to man. These truths are the foundation of every act of nameless, unremembered kindness. How the beauty of nature, or 'Such stores as silent thought can bring', arising from a 'wise passiveness', leads to compassion for our fellows, and may then pass through all nature to rest with God, is traced out in three of Wordsworth's archetypal figures: the Discharged Soldier, Simon Lee and Margaret. Finally, the Lines left upon a Seat in a Yew-tree warn of the tragedy ensuing if this intermediate stage towards something more sublime is bypassed.

Principles

The next two chapters first consider how the *Ode* gained its 1815 subtitle – 'Intimations of Immortality from Recollections of Early Childhood' – and then the nature of those intimations and the validity of the recollections. Wordsworth's idea of immortality cannot be understood unless one understands his attitude to mortality – which is pretty ruthless – for him there was no resurrection of the body or of the self. One must take his hints – not a declaration of what immortality is, but 'intimations', suggestive only, not assertive or dogmatic. Despite the heaping of much critical doubt upon them, past and present, Coleridge included, Wordsworth hung on to the value of his recollections – indeed, in their absence one might wonder what else he could have hung on to. They are usually regarded as idiosyncratic, something few others if any have experienced. Yet they are forcefully substantiated by the work of Thomas Traherne, a poet Wordsworth could not have read as his poems were only discovered and published early in the twentieth century. Traherne's thinking was closely allied to that of the Cambridge Platonists, further evidence of their otherwise untraceable influence on Wordsworth. Chapter 6 outlines how Traherne's progress – from childhood recollections, to a subsequent loss of vision, to a proposed means of recovery, and so a return to Paradise – matches and supports that of Wordsworth.[12] Perhaps stemming from a lost tradition, that progress is much more substantial than any parallels with Vaughan.

The Poetry of Crisis

In 1802, the year of his marriage, Wordsworth had a crisis, or several crises, the most serious of which is epitomized in the first four stanzas of the *Ode*, written in late March. He could not find in himself the power that he believed was the life of nature; equally, nature appeared beautiful but powerless. He could see the beauty but could not feel the power. His long-hoped-for marriage of mind and nature had become a divorce. Paradise was as lost as ever it was. After a brief discussion of the preliminary crises, and the grouping of the poems of 1802 in relation to each – of which his impending marriage and his relationship with Dorothy was the most important – this chapter reads the apparently modest poems about flowers, birds and butterflies as Wordsworth trying to reconcile, or find a relationship between, the divine and the terrestrial, between heaven and earth – an analogy of the mind and nature debate. These poems are much more than a rest and a 'refreshment' from his long labour on The Recluse. They are his struggle with profoundly conflicting impulses that will both inform and find a degree of resolution in the *Ode*.

Reading the Ode

The chapters in this section are more or less self-explanatory. That on origins begins with the first mention of the *Ode*, an entry in Dorothy's journal, its relationship with Coleridge's Verse Letter and the debate the two men had about how to cope with the impasse both faced. Chapter 10, on verse, grammar and imagery, discusses how surface simplicity belies profundity of intent, that we should not be deceived into thinking that the high rhetoric is only bombast or marvellous, meaningless music. The mostly plain declarative sentences almost always present plain, uncomplicated images – for instance 'I hear the Echoes through the mountains throng' – which gain their significance in relation to their use elsewhere in Wordsworth's poetry – something considered in more

---

[12.] A re-creation of or a return to Paradise is a vision central to the works of both poets, a vision embedded in seventeenth-century thought, as evident in Milton's two epic titles, *Paradise Lost* and *Paradise Regained*. A brief survey of the pervasiveness of the idea in all circles of seventeenth-century life can be found in Richard Wilmott's *The Voluble Soul*, chapter 3, (Cambridge, 2021).

detail in Chapter 11. The chapter on competing forces first discusses Wordsworth's conflicting attitudes to the notices of sense in the *Ode*, reiterating some of what was discussed in 'Patterns', then the syncopated rhythms of lamentation and celebration, finally outlining what I take as the tripartite structure of the poem – loss, analysis and recovery – discussed separately in the three following chapters. The last chapter of this section considers the last stanza of the *Ode*, and how its resolution follows the suggested patterns of Wordsworth's thought.

Looking Forward

This is a speculative section, a sketchy potted history, which looks forward from the completion of the *Ode* and of *The Prelude* to Wordsworth's Victorian reception, and thence to his influence on twentieth-century poetry. It first considers Wordsworth's wayward publication record and the peculiar organization of his poems, and its influence, or lack of it, on the next generation of poets; then suggests a method of reading his poetry based on the patterns and principles earlier established, and how differently his work might have been received had he coordinated composition and publication; finally proposing that that failure, via the Victorians, led to Eliot's serious misreading of Wordsworth, and so to his writing of neo-romantic odes. That brief conclusion may be developed in a future book, which will focus on the idea of the Word in the writings of Wordsworth, Coleridge, Hopkins and Eliot.

A Note to the Reader

I doubt that many readers of academic books begin at the beginning and work through to the end. Each section of this book will more or less stand alone, and therefore I have permitted myself some repetition of quotations and ideas across the sections. There are also repetitions, principally of ideas, within chapters – largely the result of my own struggle with those ideas, but perhaps useful as a form of reinforcement.

A very long and careful examination of the *Ode*, and several other poems, may help reveal layers of latent meaning, but it also destroys elusive qualities that can only come from the reading or recitation that make a poem the poem it is. Therefore I advise readers to take away as much as they find valuable in this book, then let it sink into the mind forgotten, returning to the poems. And if on listening to the *Ode* they weep as Philip Larkin wept – dangerously – while driving down a motorway, then the poem is doing the work it should.

The titles of poems are not in inverted commas, a convention I don't feel necessary. Very occasionally there might be a confusion – as between

The Leech-gatherer, and the leech-gatherer, or the ancient mariner, and The Ancient Mariner, but they can usually be thus distinguished. On the other hand, I have decided to italicize the *Ode*, so as not to confuse it with other odes. Inverted commas are retained where first lines are titles.

Much of this book was written during the 2020-22 lockdown, without access to a library. So references are not always to standard works, and quite often to online sources. As long as readers can find the quotation, then I think, whatever the mode of reference, it has served its purpose. Poems are given solely by their titles, Dorothy's Grasmere journal by date, and the Fenwick Notes simply as *FN*.

* * *

Overall, what do I think I have done? Many attempts have been made to ground Wordsworth's thought in one kind or another of philosophy or religion. None has been entirely convincing, but in what follows I begin by offering one more: that of the Cambridge Platonists. Unique in fighting the Cartesian division between mind and nature (that deep wound Wordsworth's poetry sought to heal), they were soon dismissed to the backwaters of cultural history, and there is no evidence that Wordsworth read or was aware of any of them. Nonetheless, their apparent influence not only on his thought but also on the structure of his poetry is remarkable.

I also hope I have shed some light on the substance of Wordsworth's continuous debate with himself – what is owed to the senses, what to Nature, what to the mind, how they connect across the grand Cartesian rift and how they relate to the patterns and pains of human life – expressed through an unmatched variety of poetic form and style. Having followed that debate through a selection of his major and minor poems, concluding with the *Ode*, I sketch out how his poetry failed to have the influence it could have had, and consequently how that failure affected the history of English poetry.

That at best. At worst, I have presented studies of several of Wordsworth's best known poems, which whether successful or not, more or less free of literary theories, could furnish material for essays and classroom discussion.

Finally, I know that some of the chapters that follow involve quite close reading – particularly that on Tintern Abbey. Any struggle the reader may have reflects the struggle I had in the writing.

Things semireal such as Love, the Clouds &c ... require
a greeting of the Spirit to make them wholly exist

(Keats to Bailey, 13 March 1818)

Part I
Patterns

Chapter 1

A Philosophical Framework: Understanding the Intelligible

'a superb piece of verbiage' T.S. Eliot[1]

WORDSWORTH'S ODE was first published in 1807, the last poem in his collection, *Poems, in Two Volumes*. It was greeted with very little praise and various degrees of incomprehension, descending into ridicule. Francis Jeffrey, a spirit as mean as he was witty, declared it 'illegible and unintelligible' (*Woof* 199). If by 'illegible' he meant that its irregularity and obscurity made it unreadable as poetry, then the world quickly proved him wrong: there was music in it, even if, then as now, some of the grand rhetoric was felt to be vague and bombastic. As T.S. Eliot also said, 'The first question about a poem is not whether it is intelligible but whether it is readable' (*AP* I 803). It proved then as it proves now, very readable. But 'unintelligible' hit home harder. How was it to be understood? What was its subject matter? The lack of any description in the title, against the grain of Wordsworth's frequent practice, suggested he wasn't sure himself, and the epigraph *Paulò majora canamus* (*Let us sing of things a little greater*) didn't help: what was this greater theme? That question puzzled Wordsworth's advocates as much as his enemies. Thus Henry Crabb Robinson urged Wordsworth to give it a subtitle when it was republished in 1815.[2] Unfortunately that subtitle – 'Intimations of Immortality from Recollections of Early Childhood' – proved a hostage to fortune. Where in the poem was the proposed 'immortality'? Did the 'recollections' have any validity?

---

[1] *The Dial*, 83 (September 1927), pp. 259-63; *AP* I 529. My thanks to Christopher Ricks for the reference.
[2] Henry Crabb Robinson, *Correspondence of Henry Crabb Robinson with the Wordsworth Circle* (Oxford, 1927), vol. II, pp. 838-39.

Neither Coleridge, friend, nor Hazlitt, foe, believed they did. Such doubts have haunted the poem ever since, even though Wordsworth consistently regarded it as a summation of his work, the 'master light' of all his seeing, placing it last in all his collections bar *The Excursion*, and expecting readers to draw on earlier poems to understand it.

By 'intelligible' Jeffrey meant what is open to rational explanation. For Wordsworth and Coleridge, that was one meaning, but it also meant something quite different. In Tintern Abbey we meet its negative – 'unintelligible'. Wordsworth speaks of a mood

> In which the burthen of the mystery
> In which the heavy and the weary weight
> Of all this unintelligible world
> Is lightened: –

Wordsworth then describes not what he means by 'unintelligible', or 'mystery', or 'burthen' – emphasized as 'the heavy and the weary weight' – but turns to the conditions by which 'that serene and blessed mood' may be realized, partially relieving the burden. We are left to wonder why he finds the world unintelligible, why the burden is a such a mystery and how the two clauses relate. Our difficulties are complicated by the encompassing 'all'. It may mean all the world is unintelligible, or that there is a distinct or specific world – 'this' – which is separately unintelligible from another world more intelligible. That still leaves us with the question 'What world?' The nearest we get to its identification is in what the blessed mood achieves – seeing 'into the life of things'. There is one life and there are many things. Whatever those things are, they are discrete phenomena, existing, we presume, according to whatever law or system governs their being. It only requires the discovery of those laws to understand the existence of any particular phenomenon, or group of phenomena, and so all 'things' become intelligible – we understand their life – we do not need any mystical power to see into what constitutes their mode of being. Thus we are puzzled as to why Wordsworth should find the world, an assembly of 'things', such an enormous burden that had to be lightened or resolved.

It was not ever thus. The rational investigation of the phenomenal, the very groundwork of our relationship with the world in which we now live is, in historical terms, a relatively recent achievement. We presume that, although our bodies, as all bodies sensible and insensible, are governed by material laws, our minds are not, that we have a life that we call variously, psychological, moral or spiritual, and that this life is peculiar to us, both generically and individually; and that it is not the life of the physical or material world. Thus there are at least two distinct forms of life. However self-evident it may now seem, that distinction did not always exist, or not with the clarity that has in effect become a division. Until the sixteenth century, it was by and large presumed that the mind and the physical world had common powers, or if there was a difference, it was not of kind. On the one hand, there was a greater sense of one world and one mind, giving rise to such concepts as the *anima mundi* – espoused by Plato. On the other, Aristotle's corralling of all forms of being into generic categories (e.g. substance, quantity, quality, motion), composed of variations of the four elements – air, earth, water and fire – explained the particular nature of phenomena by the imposition of mental concepts rather than by a progressive or rational investigation. That is, classical and medieval thinking tended not to distinguish powers of the mind from their insights into the structures of the physical world.

Openly expressed dissatisfaction with Aristotle's methods is sometimes dated to Copernicus's *De revolutionibus* (1543), and over the next hundred years his approach was taken up, for example, by Tycho Brahe, Francis Bacon, Galileo, Johannes Kepler and formalized by Descartes in *Discours de la Méthode* (1637). If not a new power, a new method of using a known power was established. What is now called reason had escaped the limited and sometimes syllogistic logic of medieval thought and would eventually lead to the continuing discoveries of modern science, now taken for granted. It was also a power whose systematic results are considered more or less irrefutable – at least until further investigation reveals another level of 'truth'. The classic example is the modification of Newton's law of universal gravitation by Einstein's theory of general relativity.

What we now take as an unquestionable relationship between mind and phenomena by no means immediately disposed of the intellectual methods attributed to Aristotle. Late in the seventeenth century, in *A Free Inquiry into the Vulgarly Received Notion of Nature* (1686), Robert Boyle was puzzling over aspects of Aristotle's ideas, still then considered sufficiently important to be addressed. Aristotle's principles have never been entirely dismissed. Eliot thought that what he called the 'Copernican revolution' was the 'real abyss between classic scholastic philosophy and all philosophy since' and had been 'impressed on the world by Descartes' (*VMP* 80). He took it as not much less than a European tragedy, one consequence of which he called the 'dissociation of sensibility'. Eliot's thought remained classical and Aristotelian, an example of which is his decision to identify each of the *Four Quartets* with one of Aristotle's four elements.[3]

The newly focused power, perhaps inevitably, came to be termed reason. Its boundaries took longer to determine. It is sometimes associated with Bacon's *lumen siccum* ('dry light'), which has been defined as 'the objective light of rational knowledge'.[4] That fits quite well with our understanding of the term 'reason', and our capacity for induction and deduction. Yet in that form Coleridge relegated reason to 'the reflective faculty', subject to any one of Bacon's four idols. For him, as for Bacon, the *lumen siccum* was also a greater and intuitive power. It did not begin with the notices of sense, nor depend upon inductive or deductive processes. He distinguished it as 'the purest reason, the spirit of true light and intellectual intuition'. He believed this power anticipated and guided empirical discoveries, because the pure laws thus intuitively revealed would 'be found to correspond to certain laws in nature' (*LHP* 487-88).

'Reason' was therefore a complex power of uncertain definition. In its simpler form, its ability to relate one phenomenon to another, to deduce causes and produce chains of causes, it became evident that it might lead to a full understanding of how the universe functions. If all causes relate, then something or someone has to be the first cause, *causa causarum* – or, for Christians, God. The office of this new philosophy, declared one adherent, must be

> to find out the process of this divine art in the great automaton of the world, by observing how one part moves another, and how those motions are varied by the several magnitudes, figures, positions of each part, from the first springs or plummets … and Descartes hath proceeded farthest in the like attempt, in that vast machine, the universe…[5]

It was a short step from there to the paradigm of God's relationship to the world as of clockmaker to clock, or the maker to the made, which dominated the next two centuries, and has yet to find a replacement fit for the pulpit. In sum, God set the world a-going, and on it went – tick-tock.

[3.] Wordsworth noted the continuing influence of Aristotle: 'the English, with their devotion to Aristotle, have but half the truth: a sound Philosophy must contain both Plato and Aristotle' (6 October 1844).

[4.] *The Oxford Essential Dictionary of Foreign Terms in English*: www.oxfordreference.com /view/10.1093/acref/9780199891573.001.0001/acref-9780199891573-e-3977.

[5.] Patrick, *Brief Account*, p. 12.

Beginning with the notices of sense, with the observation of phenomena, this form of reason necessarily deals with what is material. Consequently, British materialism also went steadily marching on, hugely successful in its own terms, meeting occasional but always defeated resistance, unwittingly marching into the philosophical and poetic impasse from which it has yet to escape.[6]

This did not bother most theistic thinkers – God was still the author of the universe – but a group of theologians and philosophers, collectively known as the Cambridge Platonists, saw consequences that diminished their enthusiasm for Descartes. God would stand outside nature and take no part in its working. There would be no ongoing relation of maker and made, their modes of being heterogeneous, as a clock functions quite differently from the mind that made it. Ralph Cudworth saw this as potentially undermining even theism. He posits the idea of 'plastic Nature' as an intermediary between God and the world, without which 'either God must be supposed to Doe all things in the world Immediately, and to Form every *Gnat* and *Fly*', or else 'the whole *System* of this *Corporeal Universe*, must result onely from *Fortuitous Mechanism*, without the Direction of any *Mind*; which *Hypothesis* once admitted, would Unquestionably, by degrees, *Supplant* and *Undermine* all *Theism*'.[7] A prescient remark: fortuitous mechanism is still the generic answer of the godless. However, for the godly there is another, perhaps more serious consequence: Cartesian reason as described by Simon Patrick would 'make God to be nothing else in the World, but an *Idle Spectator*... and render his Wisdom altogether Useless and Insignificant, as being a thing wholly Inclosed and shut up within his own breast, and not at all acting abroad upon anything without him'.[8] God is isolated from his creation and mind is divorced from nature, a divorce that, like the Platonists, Coleridge attributed to Descartes, who was 'the first man who made a direct division between man and nature, the first man who made nature utterly lifeless and Godless' (*LHP* 565). The world is thus meaningless in relation to the distinct powers of the mind – exemplified by

---

[6.] British, and American, idealism had a brief flowering in the late nineteenth and early twentieth century, in figures such as Josiah Royce, T.H. Green and F. H. Bradley; more loosely in R. G. Collingwood and Owen Barfield. It is a surprising feature of all these idealists, except Barfield, that they never connect their work with that of Coleridge or the Cambridge Platonists.

[7.] Ralph Cudworth, *The True Intellectual System of the Universe* (London, 1678), p. 147.

[8.] Ibid., p. 149. There is an echo of this thought in Eliot's lectures, *The Varieties of Metaphysical Poetry*: under the influence of Descartes 'Mankind suddenly retires inside its several skulls' (*VMP* 80).

Patrick as 'Wisdom' – but elsewhere identified with other ideas by both Wordsworth and Coleridge, for example, 'eternity, freedom, will, absolute truth, of the good, the true the beautiful, the infinite', ideas derived from intuitions independent of sense.[9] In that respect, the world has become unintelligible, for it is unrelated to these ideas. However, reason as a tool – empirical, rational and reflective – proved itself such a force that it left behind all the worries of the Platonists who, though flourishing in their own time, are now regarded as having made little or no impression on the subsequent development of theology or philosophy in England.

Nevertheless, they appear to have made a deep impression on Wordsworth's poetry and Coleridge's thought. Coleridge, according to Lamb, declaimed Iamblichus and Proclus in the cloisters of Christ's Hospital, and he read Cudworth when only 23 or 24, never veering far from what he called 'the Plotino-platonic Philosophy', the principal virtue of which was 'that it never suffers, much less causes or even occasions, its Disciples to forget themselves, lost and scattered in sensible Objects disjoined or *as* disjoined from themselves' (*CN* III 3935). In this mode of thinking, the objects of sense – things, phenomena – are, ideally, joined to us, part of what we call self, and that self is all that one discovers if one follows Coleridge's principal dictum, 'Know thyself'.[10] The implication is that the beings of those who examine sensible objects detached from self – the very principle of rational investigation – are lost and scattered through those objects. And for those who would have it otherwise, objects detached from self lie like a dead and unintelligible weight on the soul.

What is more surprising, as there is no indication Wordsworth ever read them, is how closely many of his beliefs and assertions, particularly as recorded in *The Prelude*, match the opinions of the Cambridge Platonists.[11] His thought is too deeply and too early embedded with Platonism, and particularly this form of Platonism, for him to have taken it from Coleridge. If a principal concern of the Platonists was the divorce of mind and nature, the consequence of Cartesian methods, Wordsworth both felt the presence of mind in nature – 'while yet a child'

[9.] *CS* 47; see also *AR* 351, where Coleridge describes these ideas as 'the *peculia* of our humanity … *congenera* of Mind and Will'.
[10.] *BL* I 252.
[11.] See 'A Track Pursuing Not Untrod Before', in Douglas Headley and David Leech (eds), *Revisioning Cambridge Platonism: Sources and Legacy* (Heidelberg, 2019), pp. 215-40.

> ... in the hollow depths of naked crags
> He sate; and even in their fix'd lineaments,
> He trac'd an ebbing and a flowing mind,
> Expression ever varying.[12]

and saw his principal task as their reunion, outlined in his soaring Prospectus to *The Excursion* – originally the conclusion to the most optimistic of his poems, *Home at Grasmere*. He begins with mind: 'the Mind of Man, / My haunt and the main region of my Song'.[13] This mind, which he also calls 'the discerning intellect of Man', is to be 'wedded to this goodly universe' – no mere marriage but a 'great consummation' – which his 'spousal verse' would celebrate. He believed it a match made in heaven, or a heaven-making match, his 'voice' proclaiming 'How exquisitely the individual Mind /.../...to the external World / Is fitted; and how exquisitely, too – / ... The external World is fitted to the Mind'. The outcome of this 'blended might' of mind and nature is 'creation (by no lower name / Can it be called)'. That creation is self-evidently not of the phenomenal world because that world exists prior to this marriage.[14] The nature of that creation is considered below.

The Cambridge Platonists did not refute or refuse the achievements of reason as understood by Descartes and Bacon. They began there, and then hoisted the flag a good deal higher:

> For reason is that faculty, whereby a man must judge of every thing; nor can a man believe anything except he have some reason for it, whether that reason be a deduction from the light of nature, and those principles, which are the candle of the Lord, set up in the soul of every man, that hath not wilfully extinguished it; or a branch of divine revelation in the oracles of holy Scripture.[15]

The Platonists saw the various forms of reason as continuous, from simple deduction to the principles constituting the soul to its supporting

---

[12.] *RC* E 153-56. Wordsworth is speaking as the Pedlar. In a manuscript, he also wrote 'In all forms of things / There is a mind' (*RC*, p. 123).

[13.] Cf. his belief that 'the mind of man can become / A thousand times more beautiful than the earth / On which he dwells' (*1805* XIII 446-48).

[14.] Cf. 'there is nothing in the course of religious education adopted in this country ... that appears to me so injurious as perpetually talking about *making* by God' (*MY* II 188-89). God is a power in nature, not a material being creating a material world.

[15.] Patrick, *Brief Account*, pp. 5-6.

the truths of revelation. Whether they were able to demonstrate that continuity is less certain. There is little doubt that Wordsworth and Coleridge inherited those attitudes to the forms of reason, and developed and defined their relations. For instance, Coleridge, as noted above, described inductive and deductive reason, the reflective faculty, as the Understanding, working with the notices of sense. He spent much of his life distinguishing it from Reason as an intuitive power. To achieve expression, the truths or ideas of Reason must inform the Understanding, and Coleridge always declared their relationship reciprocal, however often he stated the limitations of the Understanding. What is also clear is that that power, as it must always be considered, was very closely associated with other nominated powers – meditation, contemplation, imagination, the philosophic imagination, the philosophic mind, and even faith are instances.[16] The very variety of terms suggests a sense of discovery, that whatever its true nature, that power was gradually revealed in many different circumstances and through various modes of expression.[17] In an early poem, The Destiny of Nations, 'Fancy' functions just as the Imagination later would. Moreover, in Coleridge's view, Wordsworth was still conflating the two powers in his Preface of 1815: 'I am disposed to conjecture, that he has mistaken the co-presence of fancy with imagination for the operation of the latter singly. A man may work with two very different tools at the same moment' (*BL* I 294) In the same Preface, however, Wordsworth identified another form of imagination, and all but rehearsed Coleridge's distinction between the primary and secondary imagination, conflating, as Coleridge complained, the latter with fancy:

> the Imagination is conscious of an indestructible dominion; – the Soul may fall away from it, not being able to sustain its grandeur, but, if once felt and acknowledged, by no act of any other faculty of the mind can it be relaxed, impaired, or diminished. – Fancy is given to quicken and to beguile the temporal part of our Nature, Imagination to incite and support the eternal.[18]

[16.] What is the Pedlar's 'meditation' in *The Ruined Cottage* will become Margaret's 'faith' in *The Excursion*.

[17.] Wordsworth connected Reason and Imagination much earlier than Coleridge. He had established or at least asserted the connection in the conclusion of the 1805 *Prelude*. Coleridge tried but failed in the *Biographia* (1817).

[18.] Cf. 'the eternal act of creation' of the primary imagination, akin to what Wordsworth means by 'creation' when mind and nature are wedded.

Wordsworth and Coleridge also distinguished two modes of intuitive Reason, the principal examples of which are found in mathematics, particularly geometry. Wordsworth describes the Pedlar's pleasure in 'books that explain / The purer elements of truth, involv'd / In lines and numbers' (*RC* E 242-44), and in *The Prelude* he shares John Newton's experience of 'that clear synthesis built up aloft / ... / ... an independent world / Created out of pure intelligence' preserving 'the mind / Busy in solitude and poverty' (*1805* VI 182-87). Although at first conflating the two, in *The Friend* (1818), when defining 'pure Reason' as the power by which we become possessed of ideas, Coleridge noted that 'In the severity of Logic, the geometrical Point, Line, Surface, Circle etc. are Theorems not Ideas' (*F* I 177). The difference between the two resides in the function of the will. Once realized, no act of will can alter the truths of mathematics – and that form of intuitive reason is in some measure continuous with the Understanding. Yet the 'principles, which are the candle of the Lord, set up in the soul of every man', can be 'wilfully extinguished'.[19] Paradoxically, it is not a candle that can be lit by a simple or deliberate act of the conscious will. Wordsworth thinks of Reason as 'A crown, an attribute of sovereign power, / Still to be courted – never to be won' (*The Excursion* V 502-4). Coleridge speaking of 'the highest and intuitive knowledge', which he believes one with Wordsworth's 'The vision and the faculty divine', reminds us that according to Plotinus we should 'watch in quiet till it suddenly shines upon us' (*BL* I 241). This is a power that comes upon us, or rises up within us, only when the will is attentive but not deliberative. And its arrival is often a surprise.

That there is a mind in Nature, and that Nature and Reason are co-ordinate powers, are two key principles underpinning Wordsworth's poetry. In *Home at Grasmere,* as he draws towards 'This small abiding-place of many men, / A termination and a last retreat', he knows that 'On Nature's invitation do I come / By Reason sanctioned' (*HG* D 71-72). As the poem closes, his arrival is celebrated as Nature's achievement in exactly the same terms: 'That which in stealth by Nature was performed / Hath Reason sanctioned' (*HG* D 733-34). In both instances, Nature works to draw him back to his better self; in the first, putting behind him 'the Realities of Life – so cold', which nonetheless have been 'Bold and bounteous unto me'; and in the second, taming his 'wild appetites and blind desires, / Motions of savage instinct' that gloried in such tales as those of 'Of two brave Vessels matched in deadly fight' – the

---

[19.] 'The spirit of man is the candle of the Lord', from Proverbs 20:27, was first the mantra of the Cambridge Platonists, and then taken up by George Fox.

'desperate course of tumult and of glee'. Nature working 'in stealth' suggests some kind of guardian angel gently guiding an errant spirit back to their proper course. In turn, Reason says to Nature, 'Well done'.

That what 'is an Idea in the Subject, i.e. in the Mind, is a Law in the Object, i.e. in Nature' (*F* I 497) is the premise with which Wordsworth and Coleridge began; in other words, the ideas that individuals must realize within themselves are 'essentially one with germinal causes in Nature'. Throughout his works Coleridge offers examples of the ideas of Reason, but to see how these are also Nature's 'germinal causes' is a much harder, even impossible, task. Insight into the laws of nature was and is the work of reason, but we cannot imagine how the ideas of 'eternity, freedom, will, absolute truth, of the good, the true, the beautiful, the infinite' – 'the *peculia* of our humanity ... *congenera* of Mind and Will' – are co-ordinate with nature's 'germinal causes'.

That proved to be a route neither poet actually took. If Aristotle and Plato are 'the two classes of men, beside which it is next to impossible to conceive a third', it is their attitude to reason that distinguishes them: 'The one considers Reason a Quality, or Attribute; the other considers it a Power. I believe Aristotle could never get to understand what Plato meant by an Idea'. Nonetheless, Coleridge admired Aristotle, who 'was and is the sovereign lord of the Understanding' (*TT* I 173; 2 July 1830). In naming ideas as above, there is the risk of considering them attributes rather than powers, and Coleridge gradually moved from the naming of ideas to considering words inadequate to their expression. In the *Biographia* (1817), he wrote that 'The ideas themselves [Plato] considered as mysterious powers, living, seminal, formative, and exempt from time' (*BL* I 97); and in the *Opus Maximum* he declared that 'All pretense, all approach to particularize on such a subject involves its own confutation: for it is the application of the understanding ... to truths of which the reason, exclusively, is both the substance beheld and the eye beholding' (*OM* 215). All we are finally allowed to know is that 'the *Ideas* (living truths – the living Truths,) ... may be re-excited but cannot be expressed by Words, [they are] the Transcendents that give the Objectivity to all Objects, the Form to all Images, yet are themselves untranslatable into any Image, unrepresentable by any particular Object' (*CN* V 6742).[20] Coleridge felt that his mind had been prepared to receive these powers in his 'early study of Plato and Plotinus ... of Proclus' and Bruno, later

---

[20] '"Philosophy is fundamentally prosaic" insisted Kant ... This censure is consistent with the restriction Kant places on speculative Reason. Unlike Coleridge and much of Plato, Kant denies that human Reason can have access to the noumenal realm': James Vigus, *Platonic Coleridge* (London, 2019), p. 6.

catalysed by the mystics Fox, Boehme and Law, all 'keeping alive the *heart* in the *head*' (*BL* I 144/152). His was nevertheless a journey of discovery, demonstrated by the subsequently muddled and wandering progress of the *Biographia*.

If Wordsworth took Reason as the principal power of the mind, and 'Imagination /.../ ... reason in her most exalted mood' (*1805* XIII 167-70), he made no attempt to delineate any specific forms, only distinguishing 'the grand / And simple reason' from 'that humbler power / Which carries on its no inglorious work / By logic and minute analysis' (*1805* XI 123-27).[21] But he did associate that power with the power he found in Nature. Therein rose his principal difficulties, as it was in the appearances of nature that he sought expression of that power – that appearance must be some measure of reality. That again is a tough ask. What is the relationship of discrete appearances to a power essentially singular, that power which is the power of the one life? This became the question he had to answer as soon as he discovered that his youthful sense of the union of power and appearance had faded away. Yet if he believed that a singular power sustains nature through all its forms, he also believed that power was a power in him, common to humanity and to nature, and thus that, if he could find the power in himself, he would find the power in nature. Where did Wordsworth finally locate that power?

Paul Davies, describing the Baconian process of 'vexing' nature that links one cause to another, creating a set of causes, which then rest upon some laws or physical principles, asks 'Where can such a chain of reasoning end? It is hard to be satisfied with an infinite regress', a dissatisfaction he illustrates by the tale of the turtle.[22] A woman interrupts a lecture on the universe to declare that it is 'a flat plate resting of the back of a giant turtle'. The lecturer asks what the turtle rests on and she replies, '"It's turtles all the way down!"' (p. 223). Faced by the necessity of interrupting that infinite regress all one can do is draw a line in the sand: 'God' – or 'a "superturtle" that stands at the base of the tower, itself unsupported'. Davies then takes the reader through three versions of 'turtle trouble' as he calls it, and concludes that the 'search for a closed logical scheme that provides a complete and self-consistent explanation for everything is doomed to failure' (p. 226). But that is not the end of the story. He suggests that we can make at least some sense of the universe if

---

[21.] Cf. 'I had been taught to reverence a Power / That is the visible quality and shape / And image of right reason' (*1850* XIII 20-22).

[22.] Paul Davies, *The Mind of God* (Harmondsworth, 1990), p. 223.

we are willing to venture 'outside the road of rational scientific inquiry and logical reasoning'; that it is possible that 'the reason for existence has no explanation in the usual sense', and that 'an understanding of its existence and properties' may lie beyond 'the usual categories of rational human thought' (p. 224). Thus Davies, an atheist, turns to mysticism to escape the various forms of infinite regress and the limitations of rational thought: 'mystics claim that they can grasp *ultimate reality* in a single experience, in contrast to the long and tortuous deductive sequence (petering out in turtle trouble) of the logical-scientific method of inquiry' (p. 227). Davies's examples of mystical experience are not drawn from traditional sources, but from scientists, and eminent scientists at that – from people who have come to or seen the end of their rational road, and know their journey is not done. What is curious from a romanticist's point of view is the strong sense of déjà vu, of having heard it all before – in other words.

Russell Stannard, a particle physicist, 'writes of the impression of facing an overpowering force of some kind, "of nature to command respect and awe ... There is a sense of urgency about it; the power is volcanic pent up ready to be unleashed"' (p. 227). One is reminded of the apocalyptic power that Wordsworth experienced after losing his way through the Simplon Pass. David Peat, a solid state physicist, speaks of

> a remarkable feeling of intensity that seems to flood the whole world around us with meaning ... We sense that we are touching something universal and perhaps eternal, so that the particular moment in time takes on a numinous character and seems to expand in time without limit. We sense that all boundaries between ourselves and the outer world vanish, for what we are experiencing lies beyond all categories and all attempts to be captured in logical thought. (p. 227)

That experience has its clearest counterpart in Eliot's moments in and out of time, but the sense of boundaries dissolving, of all life being present in one moment, is also at the centre of Wordsworth's experience. The Pedlar looking on the world around him finds that

> All things there
> Breath'd immortality, revolving life,
> And greatness still revolving; infinite.
> There littleness was not; the least of things
> Seemed infinite;   (*RC* E 216-20)

The idea of the infinite pervades Wordsworth's poetry, epitomized in his remark to Henry Crabb Robinson in which he spoke of 'that infinity without which there is no poetry', a remark as difficult to understand as it is significant.[23] What Wordsworth's idea of the infinite and Peat's kind of experience have in common is that they begin with or go on to reach the *ne plus ultra*. There is a sense of completeness, of having no more questions to ask.

It is not self-evident that mystical experience involves the infinite, but that is the step that Davies takes.[24] If one allows, as did Coleridge, that the infinite and the absolute speak of the same truth, then the kind of experience which permitted Wordsworth to believe that the infinite underpinned all life – 'the one thought / By which we live, infinity and God' (*1805* XIII 183-4) – may be considered the inverse of Rudy Rucker's, a mathematician:

> The central teaching of mysticism is this: *Reality is One* ... No door in the labyrinthine castle of science opens directly onto the Absolute. But if one understands the maze well enough, it is possible to jump out of the system and experience the Absolute for oneself ... But, ultimately, mystical knowledge is attained all at once or not at all. There is no gradual path ... (*Mind of God*, p. 228)

In Rucker's view, one must get to the end of the road before one is fit to jump; but jump one must if not to be faced with the meaningless prospect of an infinite – in the sense of endless – regression.

Out of all this, I have but one point to make: if one begins with the phenomenal, and in order to reach conclusion one must make the leap to the infinite or absolute, then if one begins with the infinite, might it not be possible to make the leap in the opposite direction, jumping back into the phenomenal; from a singular power, to a power endlessly diversified? There may be a question whether the two forms of consciousness are harmonious or heterogeneous; but that may be answered by the connection between reason and Reason.

[23.] Robinson, *Diary*, Vol. II, p. 22; cf. Robinson, *Correspondence*, Vol. I, p. 401. This is no casual remark of Wordsworth's: 'in poetry it is the imaginative only, viz., that which is conversant with or turns upon Infinity, that powerfully affects me ... but all great Poets are in this view powerful Religionists' (Letter, 21 January 1824).

[24.] Davies's argument is more complex than my presentation of it, but Wordsworth would surely have agreed with Davies's conclusion that that power 'can only be known through a flash of mystical vision' (p. 231), even though he hoped it might be continuous.

So, were one to follow the maze in the opposite direction, one might find a continuous and reciprocal relationship between the phenomenal and the infinite. It is an act of trust, of faith, and I make no claim that this was a conscious act on Wordsworth's part. However, he had a belief in, and some experience of, what he took as the infinite; and he had an equal belief that the appearances of nature were substantiated by the same power, and always hoped that each could speak to the other. It is a happy exemplification of Coleridge's adage ('extremes meet') to think that beginning from opposite poles rational thinkers could meet poets and philosophers coming the other way, and in their passing agree that 'physical existence surely cannot be rooted in anything finite' (*Mind of God*, p. 230) – that all begins and ends in the infinite.

Remembering his early years, Wordsworth declares 'I sought not then / Knowledge, but craved for power – and power I found / In all things' (*1805* VIII 754-56). That power as a continuous presence soon deserted him, and he recognized that as a man he could only see by glimpses (*1805* XIII 338). As soon as he ceased to experience that power, to feel its presence, the relationship between mind and nature broke down, and nature became unintelligible, no more than a series of objects 'dead and spiritless ... // ... a barren picture on the mind', such as that subject to rational investigation.[25] But what is 'the creation' – which cannot be called by any 'lower name' – that the 'blended might' of mind and nature may yet 'accomplish'? Those lines are almost a rehearsal of some just preceding – 'For the discerning intellect of Man / When wedded to this goodly universe / In love and holy passion' (*HG* D 805-6) then 'Paradise, and groves / Elysian, fortunate islands' are 'the growth of common day', that which, had we the power to see it, is around us all the time – for 'Earth [is] nowhere unembellished by some trace / Of that first Paradise whence man was driven' (*1850* III 112-13). When mind and nature are perfectly integrated, when the world has become wholly intelligible, Paradise is regained. But this power was – inevitably in the light of the discussion above – a rare and fleeting visitor, and Wordsworth only ever saw by glimpses, fearing he would cease to see at all.

Thus he celebrated whatever intimations of Paradise he saw around him, or found in himself. Grasmere, seen for the first time from Loughrigg Terrace, looked like 'paradise before me' (*HG* B 12). The poem beginning

---

[25.] *RC*; additions to MS D, pp. 373-74. More of the passage containing this core belief closes the Introduction, followed by lines from Eliot's *The Waste Land*. Stephen Gill emphasizes its importance by quoting it at full length as appendices both in *William Wordsworth: A Life* and in *The Major Works*.

'Who fancied what a pretty sight', in which he sees a rock encircled with snowdrops, concludes, 'The device / To each or all might well belong. / It is the Spirit of Paradise / That prompts such work, a Spirit strong' (*MW* 303). Recovering from an illusion that he had been 'falsely taught', he describes himself as having 'the eyes of Adam, yet in Paradise / Though fallen from bliss' (*1805* VIII 818-19). Beside this must be set his willingness, only 160 lines earlier, to dismiss 'all Arcadian dreams, / All golden fancies from the golden age' (*HG* B 829-30), dreams and fancies hardly distinguishable from Elysian groves and fortunate isles. This is not a unique paradox in Wordsworth's poetry: we find our happiness in 'the very world' or not at all; yet our home is with infinitude and only there. How this kind of paradox might be resolved is discussed principally in Chapter 9.

* * *

In this introduction I have tried to present a clear if simplified account of the background of Wordsworth's poetry, clearer than Wordsworth himself could ever have expressed because he was *in media res*, and the critic has the advantage of the complete works to consult. His was a journey of discovery, of loss and of at least partial recovery, often uncertain what direction he was taking, what he was struggling with. The chapters that follow trace something of that struggle, and the various forms his search for power took, that power which would make the world intelligible. Understanding what he and Coleridge meant by the words 'intelligible' and 'unintelligible' makes it possible, paradoxically, to offer a rational and progressive account of the Great Ode, not only countering Jeffrey's condemnation, but also the repeated refusal by some of every generation to read it for anything but its music and emotional power, a refusal typified by Eliot's thoughtless remark.

* * *

> *For was it meant*
> *That we should pore & dwindle as we pore*
> *Forever dimly pore on things minute*
> *On solitary objects still beheld*
> *In disconnection dead and spiritless*
> *And still dividing, and dividing still*
> *Break down all grandeur still unsatisfied*
> *With our unnatural toil while littleness*
> *May yet become more little waging thus*
> *An impious warfare with the very life*
> *Of our own souls. Or was it ever meant*

That this majestic imagery, the clouds
The ocean, and the firmament of heaven
Should lie a barren picture on the mind?

On Margate sands.
I can connect
Nothing with nothing.

Chapter 2

Expostulation and Reply: The Tables Turned

'I will in the light of my soul show you the Universe'[1]

'The noblest gift of Imagination'

THE LIFE THAT BOTH Wordsworth and Coleridge believed was in nature they sought to experience as power – a word much more frequent in *The Prelude* than either Reason or Imagination. Perhaps because it was impossible to define or discuss, to reduce to the categories of the understanding, the principal evidence that such a power existed was experience, expressed as feeling. However, the premise or article of faith that in nature there was a mind, grounded in Reason, akin to the human intellect, involved the necessary corollary that nature thus empowered could act on the mind just as the mind could act on nature. That is, the experience of power in relation to nature could either originate in nature or in the mind. In that belief both poets began their careers. In his early years, Coleridge was particularly optimistic. Long before he met Wordsworth, still only 21, he declared he could 'weep for the deadened and petrified Heart of that Man' wandering 'among fields in a vernal Noon or summer Evening' who could not see the manifestation of the power and intelligence of the Deity: 'The Omnipotent has unfolded to us the Volume of the World, that there we may read the Transcript of himself. In Earth or Air the meadow's purple stores, the Moons mild radiance ... we see pourtrayed the bright Impressions of the eternal Mind' (*LPR* 94). Although Coleridge says 'we may read' and thus nature's revelation requires an act of observation, that is assumed as almost passive – nature exists, we observe and there in the

---

[1] *Centuries* III 6.

visible world we see the mind of God. It's a tad simple. However, in the same year, he gives the imagination the principal role in the reading of nature; he does not concentrate on appearance, or what he calls 'effect', on the aesthetic, but on underlying cause, presenting the imagination as that power which, depending on an intelligent first cause, enables our reading of God's written language – 'the other great Bible of God, the book of nature' (*LHP* II 541) – making intelligible what is otherwise a 'blank' – a significant idea in his and Wordsworth's poetry:

> The noblest gift of Imagination is the power of discerning the *Cause* in the *Effect*, a power which when employed on the works of the Creator elevates and by the variety of its pleasures almost monopolizes the Soul. We see our God everywhere – the Universe in the most literal sense is his written Language. If we could suppose an Atheist educated in the total disbelief of an intelligent first Cause, all this magnificent work would be a blank.   (*LPR* 338-39)

To seek the '*Cause*' in the '*Effect*' (many effects and a single cause) is an early version of the distinction between 'germinal cause' and appearance. On the other hand, the ability of nature to act, and to reveal the immanence of 'the Almighty Spirit' is at the heart of This Lime-tree Bower my Prison, just as in Frost at Midnight, 'The lovely shapes and sounds intelligible / Of that eternal language, which thy God utters', teach 'Himself in all, and all things in himself'. Whichever takes the lead, intelligibility depends on the interaction of mind and nature. Yet those shapes and sounds are only intelligible to those who can read God's language by means of their imagination, whose hearts are not dead and petrified, not rattling winter twigs.

Wordsworth shared and probably reinforced Coleridge's belief that nature could both act and by acting, teach. The *locus classicus* for this belief is a stanza from The Tables Turned:

> One impulse from a vernal wood
> May teach you more of man;
> Of moral evil and of good,
> Than all the sages can.

Really? we might say: how literally can we take that? A fine piece of rhetorical verse, but can nature really teach *moral* evil or *moral* good? In Tintern Abbey, he thought that Nature would be the guardian of his moral life. Nowadays we have no sense that any form of morality pertains to nature; thinking rather that what we might term good is accidental, and the idea of evil inapplicable to what has, in our minds, no consciousness. We have to suspend our judgement because, believing that there was a mind in nature, the context in which Wordsworth thinks is very different. For instance he also said, reversing the direction of his thought, that 'To every natural form, rock, fruit or flower, / Even the loose stones that cover the highway, I gave a moral life' (*1805* III 124 ff.) and Coleridge in some measure agreed with him when he wrote, 'We cannot conceive even the merest *thing*, a stone for instance, as simply and exclusively being, as absolutely passive and *actionless*'.[2] Both men believed, though ultimately in very different ways, that the life and mind in man is of a kind with the life and mind in nature. Nonetheless it remains remarkable to find Wordsworth asserting that nature can know more of man than man can know of himself, can be his teacher or guardian, especially in respect of his moral life. It is consistent with his being surprised by nature, enabling him to realize the power of and a language for the imagination when he saw, through the 'unfather'd vapour', the apocalyptic features of an Alpine landscape as the 'workings of one mind', or in 'the homeless voice of waters' rising through 'a blue chasm', an image of the mind that informs all being. For Wordsworth, nature is nothing if not mind. And yet …

'The eye it cannot chuse but see'

The two poems of this chapter title are one work with two voices – a debate. In the first four verses of Expostulation, Matthew encourages William to stop dreaming, and go back inside to his books – 'the spirit breathed / From dead men to their kind'. Given Wordsworth's willingness, like Coleridge, to see the appearances of nature as the language of an active mind, his initial response to Matthew's cheerful exhortation is surprising:

> The eye it cannot chuse but see,
> We cannot bid the ear be still;
> Our bodies feel, where'er they be,
> Against, or with our will.

[2.] *Logic*, 21. Of *The Pedlar* Wordsworth wrote that 'many a legend, peopling the dark woods, / Nourish'd imagination in her growth / And gave the mind that apprehensive power / By which she is made quick to recognize / The moral properties and scope of things' (*RC* E 159 ff.).

There is no indication in these lines that the senses are in any way providing an insight into or a language for the life of the mind or 'an intelligent first Cause', no indication that they are bequeathing a light 'to beings else folorn and blind!' On the contrary, they seem to justify Matthew's assertion that Wordsworth is time-wasting: the senses do their work at all times and in all places to no stated purpose, incapable of direction by the will, and so dreaming all day achieves nothing. Or, as Coleridge put it, all the magnificent work of nature draws a blank.

Wordsworth is uncomfortable with the work of the senses alone, and the next verse implies that there are other kinds of power:

> Nor less I deem that there are powers
> Which of themselves our minds impress,
> That we can feed this mind of ours,
> In a wise passiveness.

Whatever these powers are, they are 'of themselves', the 'Nor less' suggesting that they are different from the ineluctable notices of sense, and feed the mind by deliberate inaction – a choice – unlike that of seeing and hearing. Thus, dreaming, a turning inward, away from externalities of sight and sound, ignoring both the immediate appearances of nature and the 'light bequeathed' by books, permits the growth of whatever constitutes these powers, and may be an embryonic version of Tintern Abbey's 'laid asleep / In body'. Thus Wordsworth justifies his indolence through the growth of powers only possible under the conditions of 'wise passiveness'. His doubt that the senses do all the work is the ground of his denial that he is dreaming his time away sitting on an old grey stone.

The very next verse complicates that reading:

> Think you, 'mid all this mighty sum
> Of things for ever speaking,
> That nothing of itself will come,
> But we must still be seeking?

The two final lines are consistent with the intentions of 'wise passiveness'. Something will come even if we do not seek, if we just wait, attend upon a power not wholly within our voluntary control. To seek is to look outward, to nature or to books, and implies a dependence on what can be found outside ourselves, a disbelief that there is anything inward that will rise up of its own accord – a disbelief that there are any powers, discoverable by dreaming, which 'of themselves our minds impress'.

The first two lines do not at first appear to tally with this reading. The mighty sum of things is now speaking, is articulate, has something to say, though what is not yet evident. Wordsworth seems to distinguish the things themselves, the plural, from their singular sum: the parts – the 'things' – have become a whole – the 'sum'. That whole is 'mighty' or powerful, as intentional as the involuntary notices of sense are unintentional. It is a power that gathers all the 'things' together, and gives them the power of speech. However, if that mighty sum is a power, so too is whatever will come of itself, and it rises up ''mid' – through the middle of – the sum of things, of which it is therefore implicitly a part. There are now, apparently, two powers, interacting, which enable all the things or appearances of nature to speak. So, in this, the third of the three verses that constitute the substance of his reply to Matthew, there is the outline of a resolution to the conflict inherent in the first two: Wordsworth simultaneously focuses his attention inwardly on the growth of powers and outwardly on the sum of things: the two powers find a means of expression and the 'things' have a potential meaning.

If that resolution is by no means obvious, to us or to Matthew, nonetheless in the last stanza of Expostulation Wordsworth deems he has answered Matthew conclusively:

> – Then ask not wherefore, here, alone,
> Conversing as I may,
> I sit upon this old grey stone,
> And dream my time away.

Even this stanza contains, if not a conflict, then a paradox: one cannot converse without an interlocutor. At one point he talks to Matthew, but that exchange is not part of the dreaming state in which he converses throughout the day. So with whom or what is he having a conversation in his dream-like state? It seems likely that the powers rising up in Wordsworth, impressing themselves on his mind, are conversing with the power expressing itself in nature. If Wordsworth finds his source of power in 'wise passiveness', it is not 'a thing wholly Inclosed and shut up with in his own breast', where 'his Wisdom' would remain 'altogether Useless and Insignificant', but in this conversation 'acting abroad', in nature, as Cudworth thought God's power should (*True Intellectual System*, p. 149).

'Come forth into the light of things'

The Tables Turned can be read as an expanded rehearsal of the pattern traced in Expostulation. Wordsworth begins by reversing Matthew's exhortation, encouraging him to quit his books – 'a dull and endless strife'.[3] The next three verses provide examples of the beauty, language or songs of nature – various 'things'. The sun spreads 'His first sweet evening yellow' across 'the long green fields'; the woodland linnet sings his sweet music, imbued with wisdom; and the thrush sings out of sheer happiness – and consequently is 'no mean preacher'. The attractiveness of these verses lies in the images themselves and the lightness and simplicity of their expression, coupled with some almost doggerel rhymes – 'woodland linnet' / 'wisdom in it'; 'no mean preacher' / be your teacher' – and occasional colloquialisms – 'surely you'll grow double' / 'on my life'. There is a lot of fun in the verse, but although these examples are delightful in themselves, it is difficult to say what we can learn from the sun on the fields, or specify as the linnet's wisdom or the throstle's preaching. They are all separate 'things' that Wordsworth notices.

But the last two lines of the fourth verse introduce the singular power. Wordsworth urges Matthew to 'Come forth into the light of things', the one light illuminating many things. That light Wordsworth identifies as 'Nature' and is comparable to the 'mighty sum of things' as both express one power underpinning a variety of 'bright Impressions'. It is also comparable to 'We see into the life of things' of Tintern Abbey'; again, a singular life and many things. That vision is only possible when 'we are laid asleep / In body' which, as noted above, is probably of a kind with the dreaming and 'wise passiveness' of The Tables Turned.

This pattern, of the singular informing the plural, is repeated in the following stanza. The light of Nature will be Matthew's teacher, but the appearances of nature are 'a world of ready wealth', and it is that combination which blesses both our minds (because a multitude of appearances are underpinned by a singular power) and our hearts (because they are gladdened by that union). 'Truth' is a form of power and 'chearfulness' a modest form of joy. Nature has a power which breathes upon, or inspires, 'spontaneous wisdom' and 'Truth' in the willing recipient. Wisdom is twice attributed to the works of nature: here, and to the 'sweet music' of the woodland linnet. Neither Wordsworth nor Cudworth particularize wisdom: for Cudworth it epitomizes all

---

[3.] In the Advertisement of the 1798 *Lyrical Ballads* Wordsworth notes that Matthew 'was somewhat unreasonably attached to modern books of moral philosophy'. In approximately 1796, Wordsworth had 'Yielded up moral questions in despair' (*1805* X 874 and note).

God's powers, and for Wordsworth the powers inherent in Nature. Nevertheless, they work in much the same way, and to the same ends.

A particular end is identified in the next verse. God, Nature and Reason are interconnected powers for Wordsworth, as they were for the Cambridge Platonists,[4] who believed that one of the prime tasks of Reason or Nature was to demonstrate or determine the laws of morality. Benjamin Whichcote asserted that 'as to the great *Notices* of Reason and Nature; the Measures of Vertue and Vice; the Grand Instances of Morality; there can be no allowance, no Variation; because they are matters unalterable, unchangeable, indispensible ... by Reason of the thing' (Whichcote, 1753, pp. 80-81). Wordsworth was almost as absolute. In discovering that Cambridge was not the place to offer him the education he wanted, nonetheless he believed that 'hither I had come / endowed with holy powers', one of which was the power 'of Reason and her pure / Reflective acts to fix the moral law / Deep in the conscience'.[5] This reverses the 'impulse of the vernal wood', in which Nature is teaching man about 'moral evil and of good' – 'the Measures of Vertue and Vice'; the impulse in *The Prelude* derives from the pure reflective acts of Reason, a power issuing from the mind, undistracted by the notice of sense. Both powers point to the same end, a moral life as fundamental. This interplay of the two powers of Nature and mind, a 'blended might' (*HG* D 823), the one always capable of informing the other, and the impossibility of discerning an indubitable precedence (to Coleridge's consternation) is the ground of Wordsworth's thinking.

The penultimate verse begins 'Sweet is the lore which nature brings' and we should probably read 'lore' as of a kind with the earlier 'light of things', a singular power out of which all the varieties of nature's expression develop. Therefore, if there is any remaining doubt, the 'vernal impulse' is not the impulse of sense, but that which comes from within nature, a germinal cause, the reality behind appearance, at one with the powers that impress the mind. Wordsworth does not want to know how that lore is discovered, how its singularity is determined by tracing the way back through a maze of phenomena, only that it is, that it is a knowable and experiential power. As soon as it is subject to Cartesian analysis by the 'meddling intellect', its power is lost, mis-shaping 'the beauteous form of things', murdering by inevitable dissection. Take it apart – destroy the power. Use it whole or lose it wholly.

[4.] 'Reason is from God, and God *is* reason, *mens ipsissima*' (*SWF* II 1281).

[5.] *1850* III 83-88. The moral law is singular for Wordsworth; for Whichcote it permits 'no Variation'.

Having invited Matthew in the fourth stanza to 'Come forth into the light of things', Wordsworth repeats that invitation in the concluding lines of the poem: 'Come forth, and bring with you a heart / That watches and receives'. He has chosen his words carefully: not the eye, not the ear – both hopelessly subject to sense impression – but the heart, distinguishable from the random input of the senses and from the 'meddling intellect' of 'logic and minute analysis', is to watch and to receive.[6] That is, another power is involved, not sense perception, not the rational thought found in the 'barren leaves' of science and art, but whatever Wordsworth means by the heart.[7] The two principal impetuses of the poem, the power of 'lore' or 'light' offered by nature, and the power arising from the heart, can only be known in relation to each other.[8] Nature cannot teach an unreceptive heart; and an unreceptive or joyless heart will not see a world of ready wealth, of the spontaneous wisdom that such wealth may offer, but only a series of disconnected, unintelligible things. One cannot come forth into the light of things unless one is open to the powers that impress our minds, powers for which we wait quietly, dreaming hearts open, willing to watch and receive, to give and be given.

'Creator and receiver both'

Therefore there is always a potential division between the senses informed and the senses uninformed by the power common to man and nature. It is a division that grows in Wordsworth, becoming more apparent in Tintern Abbey, and elsewhere it becomes a distinction between freedom and slavery – 'Whose mind is but the mind of his own eyes / He is a Slave; the meanest we can meet!' (*MW* 269) – and even life and death: in *The Prelude* he recollects a time 'In which the eye was master of the heart' and as 'The most despotic of our senses, gained / Such strength in me as often held my mind / In absolute dominion' (*1805* XI 171-75).[9] The

---

[6.] Benjamin Whichcote, a Cambridge Platonist, wrote that 'Reason discovers what is Natural; and Reason receives what is Supernatural' (*Moral and Religious Aphorisms* (London, 1753), Aphorism 99).

[7.] For the inadequacy of books of moral philosophy, see the 'Essay on Morals' in *Prose* I 103-4: such books don't have sufficient power to be incorporated into 'the blood & vital juices of our minds'. The distinction is perhaps between thoughts – dead and complete – and the living, continuous work of thinking and feeling.

[8.] That the Cambridge Platonists considered nature a light in itself, not a subject on which a light need to be shone, is evident in Nathaniel Culverwell's *An Elegant and Learned Discourse of the Light of Nature*.

[9.] However, years later, Coleridge was still worried about Wordsworth's subjection to sense impression. In 1803, addressing him, he wrote, 'surely always to look at the superficies of Objects for the purpose of taking Delight in their Beauty, & sympathy with their real or

phrase 'the eye was master of the heart' clearly identifies the distinction latent in these two poems. It also indicates that this is an inversion of the ideal order – the heart should be master of the eye. Elsewhere, he speaks of habit enslaving the mind, oppressing it 'by the laws of vulgar sense' so substituting 'a universe of death, / The falsest of all worlds, in place of that / Which is divine and true' (*1805* XIII 135 ff.).[10] The laws of common sense, of passive perception, supplant transcendent truth far too easily. On the other hand, the mind is capable of discovering its own powers, proving itself in opposition to the falsest of all worlds. Speaking of geometry, he declares 'Mighty is the charm / Of those abstractions to a mind beset / With images ... / an independent world / Created out of pure intelligence' (*1850* VI 158 ff.). That 'pure intelligence' is of a kind with the 'purer mind' of Tintern Abbey, and the truths of geometry are continuous with powers of Reason, derived from that which 'is divine and true'.

The ambiguities found in these two poems are indicative of the difficulty, and probably the impossibility, as suggested above, of finding a hierarchy of mind and nature in Wordsworth's poetry. Together they open *Lyrical Ballads* (1800), which may be an attempt to advise the reader of the debate he was having with himself. Whether sense speaks to mind, or mind speaks to sense, the ultimate end is consciousness of a power unifying discrete objects, 'else detached / And loath to coalesce' (*1805* II 249-50). In whom that power lives is

> An inmate of this active universe
> For, feeling has to him imparted power
> That through the growing faculties of sense
> Doth like an agent of the one great Mind
> Create, creator and receiver both,
> Working but in alliance with the works
> Which it beholds.   (*1850* II 254-60)

The phrase 'creator and receiver both' is at least a partial echo of the 'heart / That watches and receives'. Watching may only be the first step to creating, but both phrases are expressions of the two-fold activity of 'one great Mind / .../Working but in alliance with the works / Which it beholds'. Anyone imbued with that power is an agent of that Mind – an

---

imagined Life, is as deleterious to the Health and Manhood of Intellect, as always to be peering & unravelling Contrivances may be to the simplicity of the affections, the grandeur & unity of the Imagination' (*CN* I 1618). This is a more forceful assertion of 'in our life alone does nature live'.

[10.] The editors note that 'the universe of death' describes Hell in *Paradise Lost* II 622, and that Wordsworth is taking issue with 'purely habitual perception'.

'inmate of this active universe'.[11] As evident in the concluding epigraph, Wordsworth would have happily endorsed Traherne's confident assertion, 'I will in the light of my soul show you the Universe'.

If there is no hierarchy of mind and sense in Wordsworth's poetry, it is also true that all resolves itself into mind. He may have been anxious about sense oppressing mind, but he is also willing to assert that sense leads mind, even if it has taken years of reflection or meditation to come to that conclusion. That is, the appearances of nature, if informed by a universal and active power, cannot be entirely random or fortuitous – mind can make itself evident in the appearances of nature. As we have seen, Coleridge also started out with this belief, and on one occasion at least – in This Lime-tree Bower my Prison – he tackles the problem of how appearance and power relate in a way Wordsworth rarely did, or lost confidence that he could. Instead of a shutting down Coleridge imagines an intensification of sense – 'richlier burn, ye clouds! / Live in the yellow light, ye distant groves! / And kindle, thou blue Ocean!' – and thus Lamb

> Struck with deep joy may stand, as I have stood,
> Silent with swimming sense; yea, gazing round
> On the wide landscape, gaze till all doth seem
> Less gross than bodily: and of such hues
> As veil the Almighty Spirit, when he makes
> Spirits perceive his presence.

Each sense intensifies, and as they do so they induce a joy that dematerializes its original objects into a single 'swimming sense. . . / . . . Less gross than bodily', which, in a phrase omitted from the published poem, transforms the landscape into 'a living Thing / That acts upon the mind' (CL I 335). This is a reciprocal relationship in which the intensified landscape induces joy in the poet, and that joy makes the landscape not just a series of objects but a power that in return acts on the mind, creating the diaphanous veil through which 'the Almighty Spirit' is visible. That singular and all-powerful spirit is not passive, just there to be seen, but acting, for it *makes* human spirits perceive his presence. It is a power mediated through the appearances of nature fused into one by Coleridge's gazing, a singular power perhaps comparable to

---

[11.] Hazlitt reported Coleridge as saying of Wordsworth that 'his soul seemed to inhabit the universe like a palace, and to discover truth by intuition rather than by deduction'. Cited from Stephen Gill, *William Wordsworth: A Life* (Oxford, 2020), p. 150.

Cudworth's 'plastic nature'. The act of gazing is much like Wordsworth's 'wise passiveness' – a form of attention very different from deliberate looking. To all intents it is an act of the imagination, fusing the many into one, 'discerning the *Cause*' (the almighty spirit) 'in the *Effect*', the multi-hued veil of the transformed landscape.

Whatever doubts one may have about Coleridge's method – and by omitting 'a living Thing / That acts upon the mind' it would seem Coleridge himself had doubts – he clearly hopes that Lamb will be able to follow the process he has outlined, a vicarious transferring of power frequent in Coleridge's poetry. The capacity of nature to induce joy, the implicit change of bodies into spirits – 'laid asleep / In body, [to] become a living soul' – is key to the process by which the power in nature is both manifested and experienced, how nature is made intelligible. If nature acts, it is to reveal the powers of the mind or the human spirit, as it did for Wordsworth on the top of Snowdon, powers ultimately of divine origin; if the mind acts it is to reveal the intelligence immanent in nature. Either way, the information derived from the senses alone does not present us with an intelligible world, and the presence of an intelligible world is a paradise regained.[12]

* * *

> *There is an active principle alive in all things:*
> *In all things, in all natures, in the flowers*
> *And in the trees, in every pebbly stone*
> *That paves the brooks, the stationary rocks*
> *The moving waters and the invisible air.*
> *All beings have their properties which spread*
> *Beyond themselves, a power by which they make*
> *Some other being conscious of their life;*
> *Spirit that knows no insulated spot,*
> *No chasm, no solitude, – from link to link*
> *It circulates, the soul of all the worlds.*
> *This is the freedom of the universe;*
>
>   *yea plants, yea stones detest,*
> *And love; all, all some properties invest;*

[12.] The two epigraphs are from *LB* 309 and John Donne, A Nocturnal upon St. Lucy's Day.

Chapter 3

Lines written a few miles above Tintern Abbey

> *And never for each other shall we feel*
> *As we may feel till we have sympathy*
> *With nature in her forms inanimate*
> *With objects such as have no power to hold*
> *Articulate language. In all forms of things*
> *There is a mind.* (RC 121-23)

THE AMBIVALENT PROCESSES that Wordsworth sketched out in Expostulation and Reply and The Tables Turned took a more definitive form in the lines written a few miles above Tintern Abbey, midway through the year of his collaboration with Coleridge. Although not formally an ode, Wordsworth felt that 'the transitions, and impassioned music of the versification' gave it the spirit of an ode.[1] The major transitions are marked by five verse paragraphs, termed sections here, each of which can be considered as having a distinct function. The relationship between these sections is indicative of the structure of Wordsworth's thinking – the gradual revelation of an intellectual process, a method, by which he, and Coleridge, attempted to reorientate the relationship between mind and nature.

This chapter follows some of the ways in which Wordsworth expressed the reciprocal relationship of power and appearance, and the first indications of how social relationships would relate to that vision, more fully developed in the next chapter. It is a poetry moving towards the metaphysical, in that appearance is revisioned by a power independent of appearance, a process that might be compared, for instance to the metaphysical poetry that opens the first sections of the *Four Quartets*, especially *The Dry Salvages* and *Little Gidding*. On the surface that

---

[1.] Both comments taken from *LB* 357.

poetry may seem little more than descriptive, and to prevent this both Wordsworth and Eliot, on occasion, add an explanation – 'a meditation rose in me that night', 'The river is within us, the sea is all around us'. In both instances what might have been little more than description is suddenly given another kind of meaning alive within the appearance, derived from a different source. Yet the desirable end of the union of mind and nature is that the thought should not be separated, even if separable, from the image – that it is incarnational. What might be just a picture, the moon rising above a mountain mist, is illuminated by the imagination, so we see images apparently accidental becoming significant and even sacramental, building up 'greatest things / From least suggestions' (*1805* XIII 98-99). The known or remembered is revisited and illuminated by the light of another power, often much later, as it took Wordsworth many years to realize what he had seen from the top of Snowdon; or as he put it in relation to his childhood memories, 'objects and appearances, / Albeit lifeless then, and doomed to sleep / Until maturer seasons called them forth / To impregnate and to elevate the mind' (*1805* 1 621-64).

If there is a question that Tintern Abbey seeks to answer, it is by what method can we 'see into the life of things'; how do we, as he urged us in The Tables Turned, 'Come forth into the light of things'? The duality of his vision is expressed as a light shining into and a light shining out of things. How is appearance imbued with power? The definitive solution closing the second section produces another question: can that power be known only by reflection or meditation on the past, through images remembered; or immediately, in the present, gazing on the landscape? That question also lies at the heart of the *Ode*.

Section 1: 'Thoughts of more deep seclusion' (ll. 1-24)

The opening section of Tintern Abbey divides into two parts, separating at line 8. The first part is the experience of return, the principal effect of which is to inspire the hope of a deeper seclusion. The second part is a description of what he sees having returned, which ties in with what he remembers from the earlier visit. How long ago it feels is apparent in the first part through the repetition of '*Five* years have passed; *five* summers, with the *length* / Of *five long* winters!' The exclamation mark implies that it has been an absence hard to endure – pent, as he later says, in the unreal city, 'amid the many shapes / Of joyless daylight'. The gladness, even relief, he associates with his return is carried through both parts by another repeated word – 'and *again* I hear, 'Once *again* / Do I behold',

'I *again* repose' and 'Once *again* I see', all hinting at a recovery of something vital. The rich and detailed painting of the second part, of the scene he observes below him, describes the sources of that revival, uncluttered by thought or reflection. Here is 'a world of ready wealth / Our minds and hearts to bless', images yet unused.

In the opening lines, Wordsworth first notices not what he sees but what he apparently hears, the waters of the Wye 'rolling from their mountain-springs / With a sweet inland murmur'.[2] This is most unlikely, as only very near a river will one hear anything, and usually, however close, nothing. The second part of this section suggests he is some way above it, a wide prospect before and below, and so no such sound could possibly reach him. If these lines are not quite literal, that suggests they arise from an internal feeling as much as an external impression, and that the relief of returning has initiated some specific form of revival in him. The implication is that he saw himself situated somewhere between the mountain source of the river and the sea as its destination – some midway point in the life of the Wye.[3]

Rivers running from their unknown source to the open sea, from an 'abyss', through life's temporal countryside, to eternity or infinity, is a primary metaphor in his work: structural in *The Prelude*, explicit in the Essay on Epitaphs and the *Ode*; and present even in less-read poems. The River Duddon sonnets open with 'I seek the birthplace of a native Stream. – / All hail, ye mountains!', and close with the hope that the Wanderer will 'advance like Thee; / Prepared, in peace of heart, in calm of mind / And soul, to mingle with Eternity!' Being inland, but still in contact with that heaven or infinity which is our home, enables the process of recovery in the *Ode*: 'Though *inland* far we be, / Our souls have sight of that immortal sea / Which brought us hither' – the reversal of metaphor, the sea as origin not destination, but a variation of the idea. And at the mid-point of the Wye, he is similarly distant from his childhood, but still able to hear its murmurings, as in the *Ode* he still able to 'hear the mighty waters *rolling* evermore'. It is far from certain, even unlikely, that the image is used consciously in Tintern Abbey, but equally unlikely that the idea is not latent in the image. Therefore intimations of a barely articulate power coming to life may explain why

---

[2.] Cf. *1805* XIII 172 ff. 'we have traced the stream / From darkness, and the very place of birth / In its blind cavern, whence is faintly heard / The sound of waters'.

[3.] Wordsworth's footnote – 'The river is not affected by the tides a few miles above Tintern' – suggests that the idea of the continuous outward flow of the river – not reversed by tides – matters to him.

the river's imagined murmur – hesitant, hardly heard, half-created – first draws his attention.[4]

He is then drawn to 'these steep and lofty cliffs', which 'on a wild secluded scene impress / Thoughts of more deep seclusion; and connect / The landscape with the quiet of the sky'. This is almost as curious as the murmuring of the Wye because the valley was then much more industrial than it is now, with several furnaces, many charcoal burners and iron works less than half a mile from Tintern. There was also a busy quay at Lydbrook, not far from Symonds Yat Rock – from which Wordsworth very likely saw the landscape he describes in the second part. The sense of seclusion may have arisen from his escaping both urban life and industrial Tintern, and finding a quiet part of the river before reaching Lydbrook. The point is that Wordsworth is half-creating the seclusion he feels. If not as secluded as he would have it, neither is it 'wild', but as his description goes on to demonstrate, very much pastoral; though again, probably not quite as pastoral as he supposed; for the wreathes of smoke rising 'from among the trees' are likely to have been those of charcoal burners supplying the local iron furnaces. The bare rugged cliffs seem to occupy one part of his consciousness, and the homely pastoral landscape another. High on his rock, Wordsworth sees what he wants to see: he is half-creating the landscape he perceives.

If the seclusion of the lofty cliffs is part-invention, what is the nature of the 'Thoughts of more deep seclusion' that the cliffs 'impress' on him? It seems unlikely that he is thinking simply of a more remote landscape, further from the habitations of men; for when his reflections on seclusion end, he turns back to describe with pleasure a landscape not in any sense remote, nor which he wishes to leave in search of another. The difference between isolation and seclusion is more of feeling than of fact, but Wordsworth makes the isolation he felt 'in lonely rooms, and mid the din / Of towns and cities' almost the antithesis of the 'Thoughts of more deep seclusion' that impress themselves on him as he 'beholds' the lofty cliffs – for it is in this immediate experience and the deeper seclusion he sought that he finds his freedom. That is, for Wordsworth, seclusion is freedom. The sense of escape from the isolation of a populous city to a reclusive freedom is matched in the opening lines of the *Prelude*, in which 'coming from a house / Of bondage, from yon city's walls set free', the burden of his 'own unnatural self' was 'shaken off, / As by miraculous gift 'tis shaken off, / ... / The

---

[4.] Cf. 'I hear thy voice, / Beloved Derwent, that peculiar voice / Heard in the stillness of the evening air, / Half-heard and half-created' (*LB* 274).

heavy weight of many a weary day / Not mine, and such as were not made for me'.[5] He is free of the unreal, unintelligible city.

His escape is the beginning of his journey home to Grasmere, where he would remain free, he and Dorothy 'seceding from the common world' (*HG* B 249), secluded from 'the fretful stir / Unprofitable and the fever of the world'. As a boy, looking down on Grasmere, he was 'overcome / At sight of this seclusion', and watching shadows, butterflies, birds and even angels – all 'Lords / Without restraint of all that they behold' – he 'seemed to feel such liberty was mine, / Such power and joy' – again, liberty in seclusion. It is however a very particular kind of seclusion. In the Wye valley, he does not seek seclusion from society or community, for along with the imagined hermits and vagrant dwellers there is also an unseen human presence in the 'plots of cottage grounds', 'orchard tufts', 'pastoral farms / Green to the very door' – the marks of an unkempt cultivation all green set amidst green. The landscape, and the presence of a community in that landscape, is prescient of what he will find and love in the paradise of Grasmere – 'a small community of many men', not suffering penury or 'cold and hunger's abject wretchedness' (*HG* B 445-46).

Yet there could hardly be a deeper seclusion, for he would find in Grasmere 'a termination and a last retreat', providing the conditions allowing him to speak, hermit-like, 'Of the individual Mind that keeps her own / Inviolate retirement, subject there / To conscience only, and the law supreme / Of that Intelligence which governs all' (*HG* D 772-75) . Conscience only, the governing intelligence, is partially secluded even from the light of sense, which is turned down if not quite put out. Wordsworth's ambivalent attitudes to the notices of sense may allow an additional reading. The 'impress' of 'there are powers / Which of themselves our minds impress' might be comparable to the 'impress' by which the lofty cliffs create thoughts of a deeper seclusion. There is a tacit barrenness in the steep and lofty cliffs, at odds with the rich and various landscape subsequently described, a barrenness perhaps comparable to the passiveness advised in Expostulation, the seclusion from sense, which would permit the growth of a power or powers that will allow the landscape to become intelligible. The steep and 'lofty' cliffs suggest that Wordsworth is looking above or beyond that part of the landscape which is the 'mighty sum / Of things for ever speaking'. The cliffs also 'connect / The landscape with the quiet of the sky'. That

---

[5]. *1805* I 1-25; cf. his view of Cambridge: 'A feeling I was not for that hour / Nor for that place' (*1805* III 81-82).

might be taken as no more than an aesthetic comment, landscape and sky blended into one, although 'quiet' suggests a stillness, and might be opposed to the much busier landscape he observes below him. Perhaps the steep and lofty cliffs above and the rich pastoral landscape below represent a barely conscious blending of power and sense that makes the world intelligible. Those lines look forward to what Wordsworth was to write of the vale of Grasmere, where he found 'the sense / Of majesty and beauty and repose, / A blended holiness of earth and sky' (*HG* B 159-61), reminiscent of Herbert's 'Sweet day, so cool, so calm, so bright / The bridal of the earth and sky'.[6] The blending of heaven and earth, or their division, is a large part of the debate he was to have with himself in 1802, trying to reconcile the mortal with the immortal, the earth with the sky, intellect with sense – the bridal ambition of *Home at Grasmere*. This is an impression, which like that of the murmuring waters, points to a quality of consciousness that will gradually become linked to a metaphysical energy as Wordsworth's poetry develops.

The second part of this section, lines 9-23 has few complications bar what place the vagrant dwellers and the hermit have in Wordsworth's consciousness. Only recently installed in Alfoxden, Wordsworth was aware that he and Dorothy had been and probably would again be wanderers, and hence his sympathy for the 'vagrant dwellers in the houseless woods' – Mary Hutchinson's uncle once called Wordsworth 'a Vagabond' – and 'houseless' is what he and Dorothy felt themselves to be, longing for a home of their own.[7] On the other hand, the modestly housed hermit sitting alone by his fire more or less defines Wordsworth's domestic ambitions, to sit in a long barren silence before his half-parlour, half-kitchen fire – or, outside, dreaming on his old grey rock. These two types, vagabond and hermit, may point to different aspects of Wordsworth's nature.[8]

[6.] Virtue. Cf. Wordsworth's response to 'The minstrel of our troop' who 'blew his flute / Alone upon the rock': 'oh, then the calm / And dead still water lay upon my mind / ... and the sky, / Never before so beautiful, sank down / Into my heart like a dream' (*1805* II 174-80).

[7.] *MWL* xxv, and John Worthen, *The Life of William Wordsworth* (Chichester, 2014), p. 251. Cf. Pamela Woof, *The Grasmere Journals* (Oxford, 1993), p. x, lists Dorothy's many and frequent changes of abode, and her longing for a home.

[8.] These figures were a focus for political interpretations by new historicists. Nick Roe points out that Wales 'was significant for Wordsworth's generation as a last retreat from political defeat. It is in this context that "Tintern Abbey" appears as a poem carefully situated to address contemporary political issues, some of which had come to be associated with the Wye valley' (*The Politics of Nature*, p. 173). Is Tintern Abbey a politically focussed poem? As early as 1796 Wordsworth had given up his attempts 'To anatomise the frame of social life, / Yea the whole body of society' and 'turned to abstract science, and there sought /

Other than those two figures, Wordsworth simply presents us with a picture, making no more of the images than the fact of their being; for they appear to do no work, posit no problems, ask no questions, promise nothing, by contrast with the opening section. In his 'sense of present pleasure' we feel a world of ready wealth lying all before him. Lines echo through our minds – 'hedge-rows, hardly hedge-rows, little lines / Of sportive wood run wild' – but to no identifiable purpose except for the pleasure we find in them. That is, the images have yet to be 'used', Eliot's strange, and mistaken, complaint about the imagery of Kubla Khan. What he means is that they point to nothing beyond themselves, they are not underpinned by any kind of metaphysic; that, as Wordsworth put it, they have yet to gain a power 'called to life / By after-meditation' (*1805* III 647-48). Both poets agree that images have work to do, and do not finally stand alone, self-sufficient. As the next section suggests, by circumstance rather than by design, returning to the Wye after five years, he had during that time secluded himself from the impressions of immediate sense and so discovered how he could imbue those images with power. He had, in Coleridge's words, eloigned himself from nature in order 'to learn her unspoken language'.[9] And in his words, knowing he had made nothing of them so far, he was also filled 'with pleasing thoughts / That in this moment there is life and food / For future years' – 'a world of ready wealth'. Wordsworth lives in a metaphysical landscape.

Section 2: 'These forms of beauty' – 'time past and time present'

A meditation is the substance of the second section (ll. 24-49) and begins by his looking away from the scenes in front of him, from the present back to the past, to those images arising from his first visit, images that remained present to him even in his absence – unlike 'a landscape to a blind man's eye'. The past will prove the only way back to the present. The first stage of the metamorphosis of the remembered images into power goes almost unnoticed in the opening phrase, 'These forms of beauty', which suggests that the various discrete images have

---

Work for the reasoning faculty enthroned / Where the disturbances of space and time – / ... find no admission' (*1850* XI 328-33). Then follows the passage in which he describes Dorothy preserving him a poet. Politics and poetry are set in opposition, and he turns from one to the other.

[9.] *LL* II 222 and *CN* III 4397-98. The process Coleridge outlined is followed by the Pedlar in *The Ruined Cottage*: speaking of the deep feelings that had from boyhood 'impress'd / Great objects on his mind', the narrator records that the Pedlar 'as he grew in years/ With these impressions would he still compare / All his ideal stores, his shapes and forms' (*RC* E 138-40).

become representations of the idea of beauty, more than just images standing alone. In 1827 Wordsworth changed 'These forms of beauty' to 'These beauteous Forms', rearranging the word order, so that that phrase opens the section, and perhaps deliberately reminding readers of 'the beauteous forms of things' of The Tables Turned (*LB* 117), and so in this instance sense leads mind to the idea of beauty.[10]

Through a process of intellectual digestion – from blood to heart to mind – Wordsworth takes sustenance from these 'sensations sweet', the many forms of nature infused with the singular idea of beauty. They become a power in him, the power known because it is felt (twice) in the blood and in the heart. They are the power that guides 'a good man's life' towards 'His little, nameless, unremembered acts / Of kindness and of love', and that generates that sublime and blessed mood which lightens the burden of the unintelligible. All that happens is 'owed' to these forms, which can be distinguished from the idea of beauty – inherent in the distinction of nature and mind – but their integrated life is the power of this section.

This independence, and yet the one as the language of the other, is evident in the concluding lines of *Home at Grasmere*, probably written some two years later. He identifies 'Beauty' as 'a living Presence of the earth, / Surpassing the most fair ideal Forms / Which craft of delicate Spirits hath composed / From earth's materials'. In the earlier MS B, 'Beauty' is described not as 'a living Presence of the earth' but as a quality 'whose living home is the green earth'. The revision indicates that Wordsworth wanted to distinguish 'home' from 'Presence', suggesting that whatever it is that is present is not necessarily at home, not 'composed / From earth's materials' – which is consistent with his belief that 'We come / From God who is our home', foster children on this earth. The distinction acknowledges the transcendence of a power often presumed only immanent and therefore pantheistic in Wordsworth's poetry. Implicit in the word 'Presence' is the idea of a personified power.

The lines from *Home at Grasmere* describing 'Beauty' and its relation to earth's materials are parenthetical: the main sentence reads, 'Beauty ... waits upon my steps, / Pitches her tents before me as I move, / An hourly neighbour'. Remonstrating with the Hebrews for abandoning their God, Moses asks, 'Who went in the way before you, to search you out a place to pitch your tents, in fire by night, to show you by what way ye should

---

[10.] That one leads to the other is explicit in *1805* VIII 119 ff.: 'Beauteous the domain / Where to the sense of beauty first my heart / Was opened – tract more exquisitely fair / Than is the paradise of ten thousand trees / Or Gehol's famous gardens'.

go, and in a cloud by day' (Deuteronomy 1:33). Wordsworth's use of the image is allusive, perhaps only half-remembered; but Beauty waits upon his steps as God waited upon the wanderings of the Hebrews, occupying a place in his consciousness comparable to that which God occupied for Moses – the ultimate source of power, another aspect of 'that Intelligence which governs all'.[11] The subliminal image is of Wordsworth guided by the power of beauty wandering through this world in search of his Canaan, his Promised Land, or as the idea is not limited to a particular image, the 'Paradise and groves / Elysian' of the next line. And if God attended upon the Hebrews moment by moment, step by step, in *Home at Grasmere* Wordsworth describes the power of 'Beauty' as an 'hourly neighbour' – an odd phrase in relation to a quality but fitting in respect of a 'Presence' or a person, and therefore also befitting the 'affections' that 'gently lead us on' in Tintern Abbey towards a vision of truth.

The forms of beauty, fully digested, pass into his 'purer mind' – that mind willing to be impressed by powers 'of themselves', not derived from sense – and induce a feeling of 'tranquil restoration', presumably from the 'weariness' of urban life. This is the first hint of the union of mind and nature that will finally lighten the burden of the unintelligible.[12] That restoration achieved, there begins a progress of growing intensity, and the pattern of that progress is indicative of the structure of Wordsworth's thinking, for it is repeated in section four, and is also found in other works, notably *The Prelude*.

If those 'forms of beauty' pass into his mind to create a sense of 'tranquil restoration', they also generate feelings of 'unremembered pleasure': that may appear a paradox – how can one feel pleasure in what one cannot remember? If not easily explicable, it is a foundational experience to which Wordsworth regularly returns. He speaks of the 'pleasure and repeated happiness / … Of obscure feelings representative / Of joys that were forgotten', and a few lines later of his 'weakness of a human love for days / Disowned by memory' (*1799* I 434 ff.). A sudden

---

[11.] In a late notebook, Coleridge connects the idea of Beauty with God: 'in the word BEAUTY! in the intuition of the Beautiful! – This too is spiritual – and the Goodness of God … Beauty is implicit knowledge – a silent communion of the Spirit with the Spirit in Nature not without consciousness, tho' with the consciousness not successively unfolded!' (*CN* IV 5428).

[12.] By his purer mind Wordsworth means many things – among which are the mind untrammelled by the welterings of passion (*1805* VI 156); a conscience that never tampered with itself (*1850* XIV 152); the individual Mind subject 'To conscience only' (*HG* D 772-75); and the mind that building up a synthesis aloft creates 'an independent world / … out of pure intelligence' (*1805* VI 182-87).

sense of well-being with no immediate cause may be a more common form of that experience, rather as, in conversation with Matthew, William feels that 'life was sweet I knew not why'. He then gives an instance of how that quality of feeling – 'no trivial influence' – affects our relationships with other people, fostering 'the little, nameless, unremembered acts / Of kindness and of love'. Again, things done but not remembered, done without deliberation or self-consciousness, the consequence of simple but universal human goodness, allowing man to move closer to man – that goodness an idea underpinning and supervening all human relationships, one aspect of the sublime. This is one gift occasioned by the forms of beauty passing into his purer mind.[13]

The next, here distinguished as 'another gift, / Of aspect more sublime', will prove a step along the same path, the end of which is an experience of the sublime transcending mortality. His description of this gift, which concludes this section, can be considered the kernel of his thought, rehearsed with a variety of emphases as his poetry developed. It is identified as 'that blessed mood', and this is the first indication that this power has an emotional component, the ability to feel the presence of that power, crucial to his confidence that it does or can exist. Although Wordsworth will – in his poetry but not in his prose – finally classify that mood as the imagination, in this poem, unbound by name or definition, it is felt as a new and vital experience, through the work of which mind and nature are suddenly felt as one, and the visible world rendered partially intelligible. He is no longer moving about in worlds unrealized, the world of discrete, separate objects.

He then describes the process by which that power develops, repeating and developing the phrase in lines that run on with a growing sense of power:

>   that serene and blessed mood,
> In which the affections gently lead us on, –
> Until, the breath of this corporeal frame
> And even the motion of our human blood
> Almost suspended, we are laid asleep
> In body, and become a living soul:

[13.] Coleridge declared that his intention in writing poetry was 'to elevate the imagination & set the affections in right tune by the beauty of the inanimate impregnated, as with a living soul, by the presence of Life' (*CL* I 397, 10 March 1798). The beauty of the inanimate setting, 'the affections in right tune', is comparable to the forms of beauty fostering little nameless acts of love.

> While with an eye made quiet by the power
> Of harmony, and the deep power of joy,
> We see into the life of things.[14]

What he calls 'the affections', comparable to 'those first affections, / Those shadowy recollections' (*Ode* 151-52), working like the idea of beauty, lead him through a series of stages that are essentially a shutting down of the senses, while allowing another power to live. This is a sleep almost of death, but this 'wise passiveness', removing the oppression of the senses, permits the growth of 'a living soul'. It is consistent with the lines Coleridge viewed with horror in the *Ode*, describing the child 'To whom the grave / … without sense or sight' is but 'A place of thought where we in waiting lie'. There, 'thought' prepares us for the later introduction of 'the philosophic mind'. Here, the passage unfolds as a progress, the conclusion of which is seeing into 'the life of things' – that is, apprehending what things are in themselves, and developing our ability to know them, to find them intelligible, to look behind appearance to find their essential power. But there has been an implicit change of tense: looking to the past, the power has been disclosed as knowable in the present. This will have a significant effect on the rest of the poem.

That end comes only through the realization of two cooperative powers, harmony and joy. The eye 'that cannot chuse but see' is 'made quiet by the power / Of harmony'. If 'there are powers / Which of themselves our minds impress', harmony is one of these – Plato's word for the power that would unite the being of man with the being of the universe.[15] Our minds are impressible because they are formed in the image of that power: 'The mind of man is framed even like the breath / And harmony of music.' (*1805* I 351-52). Undistracted by the senses, this power has grown in the living soul of the poet, permitting his ability to see mind and germinal causes, the 'life of things', as one life and the same. Moreover, joy is either a power released by this experience, or a power enabling it, and in Wordsworth's poetry, it is never quite certain which. There is no doubt that joy is at the heart of his vision of

---

[14.] For a full history of this word vital in Wordsworth's poetry, see Adam Potkay's *The Story of Joy* (Cambridge, 2007).

[15.] For Coleridge on harmony and Plato, see Vigus, *Platonic Coleridge*, pp. 13 and 19. In the final verse of a late poem, On the Power of Sound, the poet asks whether 'Harmony' is the 'destined Bond-slave' of 'Silence'? The answer is a rapturous 'No! though Earth be dust / And vanish, though the heavens dissolve, her stay / Is in the Word, that shall not pass away.'

the universe, 'the deep enthusiastic joy, / The rapture of the hallelujah sent / From all that breathes and is' (*1805* XIII 261-63). Earlier, in *The Prelude*, he rehearses the method by which this joy is experienced in Tintern Abbey:

> for in all things
> I saw one life, and felt that it was joy.
> One song they sang, and it was audible –,
> Most audible then when the fleshly ear,
> O'ercome by grosser prelude of that strain,
> Forgot its functions, and slept undisturb'd.
> (*1805* II 429-34)

Wordsworth is happy with his paradoxes – the ear hears best when the song is 'music heard so deeply / That it is not heard at all'. We see into the life of things when we have ceased to see the things themselves; shutting down the senses allows other and much greater powers to impress our minds. The intelligible is only manifest in the light of a governing intelligence.[16]

Section 3: 'If this / Be but a vain belief'

With concluding line of the second section, Wordsworth might be thought to have achieved his goal, but the opening of the third and very short section (ll. 50-58) throws some doubt on the solidity of his achievement. His words suggest that what he has described is as much a manifesto as a record of experience. Doubt rising after a proclamation is not unique in his poetry, for the lines from *The Prelude* above, recording how 'the one song' was 'Most audible then when the fleshly ear, / ... Forgot its functions', are immediately followed by 'If this be error', just as here he fears that his declaration that the deep power of joy can see into the life of things is 'but a vain belief'. Both passages recover from the implied doubt in a similar way: by first asserting the Dantean gloom of a life in limbo – 'how oft, / In darkness, and the many shapes of / Joyless daylight' and 'the fretful stir / Unprofitable and fever of the world'. This is paired by a much longer passage in *The Prelude* that can be summarized as 'this time / Of dereliction and dismay'. In Tintern

---

[16.] Cf. Thomas Traherne, Innocence: 'A Serious Meditation did employ / My Soul within, which taken up with Joy / Did seem no Outward thing to note, / But flie / All objects that do feed the Eye.'

Abbey, Wordsworth then reasserts the benign influences of nature as a power – the happy 'oft' and 'often' countering the first grim 'oft' of urban life: 'How oft, in spirit, have I turned to thee / O sylvan Wye ... / How often has my spirit turned to thee'; He turns 'in spirit', that is, to the forms of beauty that have passed into his purer mind. The joy, the exultation behind these two lines rids the world of 'joyless day-light'; if, he says in the comparable passage in *The Prelude*, he manages to retain a faith:

> That fails not, in all sorrow my support,
> The blessing of my life; the gift is yours
> Ye winds and sounding cataracts! 'tis yours,
> Ye mountains! thine, O Nature! Thou hast fed
> My lofty speculations; and in thee,
> For this uneasy heart of ours, I find
> A never-failing principle of joy
> And purest passion.   (*1850* II 447-51)

If the mountains and cataracts of his native Cumbria helped him keep his faith and fed his lofty speculations, here it is 'the sylvan Wye' and the wealth of its fondly remembered landscape that he believes has rescued him from 'the fever of the world'.

Section 4: 'And so I dare to hope'

The fourth section (ll. 59-112) can be seen as an expanded rehearsal and reassertion of the second, developing along similar structural lines, but given the upbeat conclusions to both sections two and three, the uncertainty with which this section begins is striking: 'And now, with gleams of half-extinguish'd thought, / With many recognitions dim and faint, / And somewhat of a sad perplexity, / The picture of the mind revives again'. That is, the past, the picture, is only revived through or by those confusing uncertainties – principally the gleams of half-extinguished thought. Although he has a 'sense / Of present pleasure', it does not hold the life he looks for, as he knows that he is not now seeing into life of things, but only absorbing the 'life and food / For future years', as five years earlier he had ingested scenes that five years later enabled the vision concluding section two.

For whatever reason, Wordsworth has either failed to realize or been unable to sustain his vision, and so reverts to 'the picture' rather than to the present. Yet because he knows some such picture will reform in his mind after this visit, he is confident that these images will eventually serve a purpose that cannot be presently realized. When the images of sense, a 'grosser prelude of that strain' (*1805* II 429-34), become memories they do not impinge on the working of the mind, do not suppress its powers, indeed become 'food' for it to work upon, the stuff of 'tranquil restoration'.[17] This may have some connection with Wordsworth's theory that poetry is emotion recollected in tranquillity; for if the initial emotion is what he calls an 'appetite; a feeling and a love', the recollected emotion becomes the closely associated but differently functioning 'joy'.

The cause of his perplexity, and his taking refuge in the thought that the reality looks to the future not in the present, lies in the 'half-extinguish'd thoughts', the 'recognitions dim and faint' that another form of consciousness is emerging. He is beginning to remember that in his youth he did not need to feed these images into his purer mind in order to realize their power. The childhood vision is slowly coming upon him. However, because he does believe that what he now sees will serve a future purpose, he is able to say, 'And so I dare to hope', which tacitly adds 'despite' – despite the fact that I am 'changed, no doubt, from what I was'.

The reader looks for a description of that hope, but syntactically none appears, and some 20 lines are spent remembering how 'nature then / ... / To me was all in all' before any discernible version of hope pops up, by which time the grammatical thread has been lost. Those 20 lines are rather a lament for, or a celebration of (a conflict also embedded in the *Ode*), what he was five years earlier, 'when like a roe / I bounded o'er the mountains', when 'nature then / ... To me was all in all'[18] That is, he remembers how he lived in the immediate, and rejoices that he did so, which is at odds with the method he has made his creed in the second section, and at odds with what he says about the eye and ear seeing and hearing whether we will or no, and oppressing the mind. 'I cannot paint', he says, 'What then I was', before immediately doing so with some intensity: 'The sounding cataract / Haunted me like a passion: the tall rock, / The mountain, and the deep and gloomy wood, / ... were

---

[17.] There may be a connection between 'tranquil restoration' and the 'renovating virtue' of the spots of time. Suffering the 'deadly weight' of 'trivial occupations and the round / Of ordinary intercourse, our minds / Are nourished and invisibly repaired' by those moments. That the 'deepest feeling' comes when 'the mind / Is lord and master, and that outward sense / Is but the obedient servant of her will' (*1805* XI 270-72) is also in accord with the process of tranquil restoration.

[18.] Cf. the first of 'To a Daisy' poems: 'In youth from rock to rock I went / From hill to hill in discontent / Of pleasure high and turbulent / Most pleas'd when most uneasy'.

then to me / An appetite; a feeling and a love', images of sense felt as a primal unmediated power.[19]

What he then declares is surprising, for he dismisses thought, the powers of the mind arising of their own accord, and asserts the adequacy of what was an immediate experience that 'had no need of a remoter charm, / By thought supplied, or any interest / Unborrowed from the eye'. This looks back towards infancy, when 'Those hallowed and pure motions of the sense / … seem in their simplicity to own / An intellectual charm' (*1805* I 580) – that is, to a barely conscious union of mind and sense that Wordsworth associates with childhood.[20] How good that time was is celebrated in the acknowledgement of its loss, 'That time is past, / And all its aching joys are now no more, / And all its dizzy raptures.' Wordsworth develops this idea of an intense, unmediated union with nature, and presents it in the *Ode* as the child's perception of the world apparelled in celestial light. He also recognizes that there are stages of loss, and his time of dizzy raptures in Tintern Abbey is comparable to that belonging to 'The Youth, who daily farther from the East / must travel', but is still 'Nature's Priest', attended by the fading 'vision splendid'. When any form of hope does appear it is only in the form of 'other gifts', and even if they prove an 'abundant recompence', they are only a replacement, a compensation for the near-catastrophic loss, not the revival of the power itself. In the words of the *Ode* 'the radiance which was once so bright' has now for ever been taken from his sight.

He is determined to move on, for his valediction forbids any mourning, 'Not for this / Faint I, nor mourn, nor murmur'. His declaration that he has learned to look on nature, 'not as in the hour / Of thoughtless youth' makes a direct comparison with his earlier affirmation that nature had no need of a remoter charm 'By thought supplied'. The implication is that whatever restoration takes place in this part of the poem has something to do with thought, or 'the philosophic mind', but the first of the two gifts that do follow has only a loose relationship with thought, for that

---

[19.] 'Passion' has both positive and negative connotations for Wordsworth. Here it is that passion 'which itself / Is highest reason in a soul sublime' (*1805* V 39-40). Abandoning his studies at Cambridge, conscious of other powers, he speaks of the 'visitings / Of the upholder, of the tranquil soul, / Which underneath all passion lives secure / A steadfast life.' (*1805* III 115-18) – an example of 'tranquil' as 'tranquil restoration'. It is negative in the 'welterings of passion' (*1805* V 156).

[20.] Cf. *1799* 458-64: 'need I from thee / Harsh judgements' he asks Coleridge if 'loath to quit / Those recollected hours that have the charm / Of visionary things … / … that throw back our life / And make our infancy a visible scene / On which he sun is shining?' Ironically, the harshest judgement Coleridge imposed on the *Ode* was its dependence on the visions of infancy.

gift is 'hearing oftentimes / The still sad music of humanity'. As in the second section, the initial stage of the progress from the notices of sense to the realization of the intelligible and the sublime is marked by the poet's concern for humanity. If in the first part that relationship has a potential sublimity, waking in the poet the 'best portion of a good man's life', here the music is still and sad, with 'ample power / To chasten and subdue'. None of those terms are developed, so what the ample power is, why still, why sad and what may be chastened or subdued, remain questions unanswered: some suggestions are offered in the next chapter. Moving to the second gift, nature, his verse unfolds with a declaration in which there is no sense of restraint, of anything chastened or subdued:

> And I have felt
> A presence that disturbs me with the joy
> Of elevated thoughts; a sense sublime
> Of something far more deeply interfused,
> Whose dwelling is the light of setting suns,
> And the round ocean, and the living air,
> And the blue sky, and in the mind of man,
> A motion and a spirit, that impels
> All thinking things, all objects of all thought,
> And rolls through all things.[21]

He is again seeing into the life of things, but unlike the comparable passage in section two, which concludes, 'We see into the life of things', this begins 'I have felt'. Although not clearly distinct, there is a difference of tense and tone between the two – 'I do' and 'I did'. Nonetheless here is an assertion of experience, and what he has felt is a 'presence'. Nor should we miss the 'the joy / Of elevated thoughts' – feeling issuing as power, power inspiring feeling, those thoughts comparable to the unnameable non-discursive powers that Coleridge believed were 'the *Ideas* (living truths – the living Truths,) that give the Objectivity to all Objects' (*CN* V 6742), powers or ideas that unite all modes of being.

The magnificence of the vision Wordsworth is claiming is evident in the rhetorical grandeur expressing this power, which runs equally through 'the light of setting suns', 'the round ocean', 'the blue sky' and 'the mind of man' – words reminiscent of the opening lines connecting

---

[21.] Coleridge twice took exception to this passage, in *AR* 404 and *OM* 113. He objected to the absence of a personal deity, and to an implicit pantheism. Wordsworth's idea of God was not focussed on a figure, more on a power he associated with infinity, infinitude or eternity. His thought, not his theology, is the question here.

'the landscape with the quiet of the sky', but here definitive. In that experience of 'Something far more deeply interfused', we may see the germinal causes in nature wedded to the ideas of the mind, the consummation achieved – the 'sense sublime' or 'the primal sympathy / Which having been must ever be'. In section two Wordsworth *does have* that experience: here he only claims that he *has had* it. Yet in either case, this sense of unity between mind and nature – as joy – is the point. He cannot present it as a form of knowledge, for the requisite of knowledge is murderous dissection. He has felt the singularity of an ultimate power, 'A motion and a spirit, that impels / All thinking things, all objects of all thought, / And rolls through all things.' It is a magnificent if fleeting vision of a sublime and wholly intelligible world, not dimmed by the film of familiarity. One may question particular phrases – do 'things' really 'think'? To the extent that Wordsworth believes that the power that impels them, impels us, that Nature can act on us as we on Nature, then yes.

The success of this past vision once more breeds confidence in what can be, even if its immediate presence is uncertain. Remembering the experience of this unifying power, the appearances of nature redolent with a 'governing intelligence', Wordsworth feels he can move back into the present. He has no need, for the moment, to set those images aside as future food because he has felt that there is life in all things and it is one life. With a powerfully consequent 'Therefore', Wordsworth reasserts his belief in 'all the mighty world / Of eye and ear', giving a role to sense that he had previously questioned, and would continue to question in subsequent poems in order to disclose latent power.[22] Because experience has told him that Nature can act, '*Therefore* am I still / A lover of the meadows and the woods, / And the mountains; and of all that we behold', for the life in them is alive in him. There is a comparable progress in the *Ode*. If the last line of stanza X looks to 'the philosophic mind' as a means of recovering his lost vision, the first lines of the final stanza, XI, begin:

> And O, ye Fountains, Meadows, Hills, and Groves,
> Forebode not any severing of our loves!
> Yet in my heart of hearts I feel your might;

[22.] Three well-known instances: raising a song of thanks and praise 'for those obstinate questionings / Of sense and outward things' (*Ode* 144-45), celebrating the 'conquest over sense, hourly achieved / Through faith and meditative reason' (*1850* VI 444 ff.), and rejoicing when 'the light of sense goes out'.

That is, they have power or 'might', the power, to act, to create, just as does 'all that we behold / From this green earth'. In both, there is 'the primal sympathy' that binds world and mind together, each alive, each acting on each equally.

This achievement of eye and ear is expressed in that seemingly ambiguous phrase, 'what they half-create / And what perceive'. If the senses do all the perceiving, they only do half the creating – the power of mind or imagination is the other half. Only when they are infused with the power to speak, and sense becomes the 'language' of nature, not merely a series of disconnected objects, is the perception Wordsworth seeks possible. What follows is in that spirit. Far from being beset with images, Wordsworth is:

> well pleased to recognize
> In nature and the language of the sense,
> The anchor of my purest thoughts, the nurse,
> The guide, the guardian of my heart, and soul
> Of all my moral being.

Nature, a singular power, expressing itself through the language of the sense, is that which sustains the life and integrity of all his being, teaching him 'of moral evil and of good'. One can only conceive how extraordinary this is by comparing it with what he says elsewhere of 'Reason and her pure / Reflective acts to fix the moral law / Deep in the conscience'.[23] Here Nature is functioning in the same way as Reason, thus his belief that Reason sanctions the actions of Nature. They are two powers, each working to the same end, one through the senses and one through the mind.

The derogation of sense, competing with its celebration elsewhere, is a difficult circle to square, and the resolution depends on the presence or absence of that infusive power which Wordsworth encapsulates in the term 'joy'.[24] Whether the images of sense are set aside as future food or are capable of immediate incorporation depends on the presence or absence of joy, the emotive aspect of a power that is synonymous with that Wordsworth calls intellectual. If not informed by that power, they are not intelligible, and remain discrete and disconnected. In

---

[23.] *1850* III 80 ff.

[24.] Wordsworth is conscious of nature and sense at war when he speaks of the time when the eye, 'most despotic of our senses', was 'master of the heart' and 'often held my mind / In absolute dominion'. Like that of the heart, Nature's business as a power is 'to thwart / This tyranny' (*1805* X1 171 ff.).

another formulation of his creed in *The Prelude* already partly quoted, Wordsworth looks back to a time when he felt no division between the image and the intellect, speaking of:

> Those hallowed and pure motions of the sense
> Which seem in their simplicity to own
> An intellectual charm, that calm delight
> Which, if I err not, surely must belong
> To those first-born affinities that fit
> Our new existence to existing things,
> And, in our dawn of being, constitute
> The bond of union between life and joy.
> (*1805* I 578 ff.)

In other words, the infant mind, haunted by the eternal *deep* has already 'intellectualized' the 'pure motions of the sense'. Note that 'if I err not', so characteristic of his assertion of this mode of belief.[25] Four years later Wordsworth will acknowledge that, now far beyond his 'dawn of being', this bond is broken in him, that he cannot find or create that joy in the immediately perceived world. Even then, in the *Ode*, that admission doesn't come without a struggle. However, eventual acknowledgement enables him to move forward and seek a method of repair.

Section 5: 'And this prayer I make'

Although the ideal union has had to look forward not backward for its realization – 'That time is past ... / ... other gifts / Have followed' – the revival experienced through the presence of 'something far more deeply interfused' has prevented an irremediable loss. To keep alive the hope of that union is the mark of the fifth and final section (ll. 112-60). On the other hand the suppressed conflict between that hope and his recorded experience is reflected in the convoluted structure of the first three lines – 'Nor, perchance, / If I were not thus taught, should I the more / Suffer my genial spirits to decay'.[26]

---

[25] Cf. above, 'If this / Be but a vain belief' (*TA* 50-51) and 'If this be error...' (*1805* II 435).

[26] This is a reference to *Samson Agonistes*: 'So much I feel my genial spirits droop, / My hopes all flat, nature within me seems / In all her functions weary of her self' (593-95). Samson believes that he has betrayed the purpose for which God or Providence singled him out. Wordsworth's refusal to 'suffer' his comparable powers not to 'decay', suggests that he sees his task in a providential light. Yet just as Samson would fulfil providence's expectations in an unexpected way, so Wordsworth had to allow all the pillars of his

He is aware that the power necessary to keep nature alive for him is at risk, and it is only in knowing that he has been taught that 'nature and the language of the sense' is 'the guardian of my heart, and soul' that he has found a temporary reprieve. Or perhaps not only that spirit, for we suddenly realize late in the poem that Wordsworth is not alone: 'For thou art with me, here, upon the banks / Of this fair river' – a simple statement of fact, possibly including a deliberate echo of Psalm 23, which would give Dorothy a function akin to the divine shepherd. The phrasing is probably subconscious, but 'He restoreth my soul' echoes his fear that his spirits are decaying, and he believes that Dorothy's presence may prevent that decay. However, he has been 'thus taught' – and what he has been taught is manifest in an array of active verbs – two are further echoes from Psalm 23 – which gain much of their power from their place at line endings: 'that Nature never did *betray* / The heart that loved her'; that she will therefore continue 'to *lead* / From joy to joy'; '*inform* / The mind that is within us'; '*impress* / With quietness and beauty', and '*feed* / With lofty thoughts' – 'taught' and 'impress' taking us back to The Tables Turned; 'feed' also reminding us of 'in this moment there is life and food / For future years' (65-66). This list indicates his belief in the ability of nature to act in various, fundamental ways, and not just be the subject of passive observation, so that all the ills social life is heir to will not disturb his and Dorothy's 'cheerful faith that all which we *behold* / Is full of blessings' – or, 'Surely goodness and mercy shall follow me all the days of my life'.

But had he *not* had this experience, not been thus taught, he declares that his 'genial spirits' still would not have decayed because Dorothy is with him, and in her voice he catches 'the language of my former heart' and 'in the shooting lights / Of thy wild eyes' his 'former pleasures'. Her presence is for him a living proof that an innocent and unmediated union with nature is still possible despite his experience of loss, and that she can keep him in touch with his younger self which had no need of thought – that remembered self so important in the *Ode*: 'Oh! Yet a little while / May I behold in thee what I was once, / My dear, dear Sister!'.[27]

---

hopes to collapse before he could attempt to rebuild them: the first reassertion of joy in the *Ode* fails, and the rest of the poem is a close examination of the foundations, followed by a tentative rebuilding.

[27.] The prevalence of the first person in this last section makes some readers uncomfortable – 'If *I* were not thus taught'; 'should *I* the more / Suffer'; 'in thy voice *I* catch / The language of *my* former heart'; '*my* former pleasures'; 'May *I* behold in thee what once *I* was once'. However, all those are from the first ten of some forty-five lines, and the rest do move outward, and think more of Dorothy than of himself. Mrs Humphry Ward records the Duke of Argyll's account of Wordsworth's reading of Tintern Abbey in 1847:

But that imposed or inferred simplicity could be seen as a form of intellectual imprisonment, a determination that she should represent a version of his earlier and empowered self, her independence threatened. It would have been understandable if she had rejected this restriction of her being, but all the evidence points the other way: that Dorothy wanted to see in nature that condition of simplicity just as much as her brother did, a search that is the constant subtext of their wanderings, something considered in Chapter 8.

Wordsworth is divided between hoping that nature can act immediately through the senses and believing that a power must arise within the mind to create or find a unity in the disparate images of sense. Nevertheless, the nature that acts can be distinguished, if not divided, from the nature presented to the senses via discrete images. That is, as we have seen in The Tables Turned, nature's power lies behind nature's appearances – and that power, when disclosed, is at one with the principal power of the human mind – Reason. It is not the images of nature that 'impress' or 'feed' but the power that is latent in them, the 'impulse from a vernal wood' rather than the wood or the trees themselves. Yet in the late 1790s Wordsworth doesn't fully distinguish the image from the power. There is thus a tendency to conflate the power of Reason, sometimes expressed through the idea of beauty, with the appearances of nature – a healthy conflation in terms of poetry, slightly confusing when considered analytically. As a consequence, there is another significant 'Therefore' as he imagines nature working on Dorothy's behalf:

> Therefore let the moon
> Shine on thee in thy solitary walk;
> And let the misty mountain winds be free
> To blow against thee ...

So begins a process from images to forms to potential power imagined thus, the third time round, for Dorothy. In 'after years' he says of Dorothy, perhaps thinking of the five years between his visits to the Wye, 'When these wild ecstasies ('sensations sweet') shall be matured' ('Felt in the

---

'Mrs Wordsworth was strongly affected during the reading. The strong emphasis that he addressed to the person to whom the poem is written struck me as almost unnatural at the time. "My DEAR DEAR friend!" – and on the words, "In thy wild eyes". It was not until after the reading was over that we found out that the poor paralytic invalid we had seen in the morning was the *sister* to whom Tintern Abbey was addressed.' (*A Writer's Recollections*, [London, 1918] p. 79). That 'strong emphasis' was always evident – 'thou my dearest Friend' precedes 'My dear, dear Friend' and is soon followed by 'My dear, dear Sister!'

blood, and felt along the heart') 'Into a sober pleasure, when thy mind / Shall be a mansion for all lovely forms' (passing into her 'purer mind / With tranquil restoration'), 'Thy memory be as a dwelling-place / For all sweet sounds and harmonies' ('life and food / For future years'). The security of her power thus established, Wordsworth can safely invoke the potential vicissitudes of Dorothy's life, knowing that all will be well:

> Oh! then,
> If solitude, or fear, or pain, or grief,
> Should be thy portion, with what healing thoughts
> Of tender joy wilt thou remember me,
> And these my exhortations!

This is not what it might appear to be – the egoism of a man wanting to be remembered – but rather an acknowledgement that Dorothy will suffer if she is left alone without him. His thinking of a time when 'I should be where I no more can hear / Thy voice' is an empathetic act 'of kindness and of love'. Yet he believes that her 'solitude, or fear, or pain, or grief' consequent upon that or other causes can be healed by the tender joy arising from 'these my exhortations', as the course of the poem moves through human suffering to something more sublime. That is, the joy thus realized masters the exigencies of life, of death, his words pointing gently to a happiness not confined to the conditions of mortality.

These are hints only, and the poem is on the verge of coming to a downbeat, almost inconsequential ending: after all our wanderings, together or apart, let's remember, he suggests, 'That on the banks of the delightful stream / We stood together'. However, just as earlier in the poem his concern with humanity occurs prior to a return to the sublime powers of nature, so here, after his address to Dorothy, there is one last curious flourish, that also looks to the *Ode*. Even if he later disclaimed that he was 'A worshipper of Nature', nonetheless he wants to remind us that he 'hither came / Unwearied in that service: rather say / With warmer love, oh! with far deeper zeal / Of holier love'. Those are the words of worship, but to quibble as to whether or not he is a worshipper of nature is to miss the point. Wordsworth is reminding us, or Dorothy, that he has returned to the Wye and discovered, not nostalgia, but a renewed intensity of feeling; and how intense is evident in almost every word and phrase of that final effusion – 'unwearied', 'service', 'warmer', 'holier', 'love' and 'far deeper zeal' – 'zeal' a word more marked than enthusiasm; and, in Wordsworth's idiolect, 'deep' and 'deeper' are redolent of his most hallowed ideas of non-verbal power. Of all those words, 'love' may be the most critical, not love for Dorothy, not for a person at all, but love for the natural scenes he and Dorothy are revisiting. As already noted, the final verse of the *Ode* begins 'And oh ye Fountains, Meadows, Hills and Groves, / Think not of any severing of our loves!', for that love severed, human beings are alienated from the world in which they live, from the potential paradise all around them. If there should come a time when he cannot retrieve 'these gleams of past existence' – and as he acknowledges in the *Ode*, 'nothing can bring back the hour / Of splendour in the grass' – this love, 'healing thoughts / Of tender joy', will enable the union or reunion of mind and nature, the lost condition of childhood, and thus a return to Eden. The *Ode* and Tintern Abbey point to the same end, always present in Wordsworth's poetry, but in the *Ode* there is a much deeper chasm between time past and time present, which the poem struggles to overbridge.

* * *

> *There is a creation in the eye,*
> *Nor less in all the other senses; powers*
> *They are that colour, model, and combine*
> *The things perceived with such an absolute*
> *Essential energy that we may say*
> *That those most godlike faculties of ours*
> *At one and the same moment are the mind*
> *And the mind's minister: In many a walk …*
> *Have we to Nature and her impulses*
> *Of our whole being made free gift, – and when*
> *Our trance had left us, oft have we by aid*
> *Of the impressions it has left behind*
> *Look'd inward on ourselves, and learn'd perhaps*
> *Something of what we are.*[28]

> *Then is he wise*
> *Who with unweari'd diligence repairs*
> *To Nature as to an unerring rule*
> *And measure of those ennobling principles*
> *Eternal and unchang'd – correcting thus*
> *Deformities that steal by easy steps*
> *Into the heart and raising up his thoughts*
> *From that abasement into which perforce*

[28.] *LB* 323-24; quoted by Gill, *A Life*, p. 207.

The mind must sink that hangs on its own works
With an exclusive dotage. And the man
Who has been taught this lesson will so feel
Its wholesome influence ... /...
That even the meanest object, else perhaps
Despis'd or loath'd or dreaded, as a part
Of this great whole insensibly will cleave
To his affections ...[29]

[29.] *LB* 313.

Chapter 4

Geometry, Poetry and the Sublime of Man

Geometry and Poetry

> *On poetry and geometric truth*
> *(The knowledge that endures) upon these two*
> *And their high privilege of lasting life,*
> *Exempt from all internal injury,*
> *He mused –   (1805 VI 64-68)*[1]

TWO MODES OF REASON were distinguished in the Introduction, Coleridge reminding himself and us that, distinct from the ideas of Reason – which for their realization depend on the attentive if not deliberative will – the intuitive reason of 'the geometrical Point, Line, Surface, Circle etc. are Theorems not Ideas' (*F* I 177), unalterable once understood.

In Book VI of *The Prelude* Wordsworth spends some 50 lines describing the benefits of 'geometric science' (135-88). Although he went no farther than 'the threshold' of these inquiries, he remembers that with 'awe and wonder'

> did I meditate
> Upon the alliance of those simple, pure
> Proportions and relations, with the frame
> And laws of Nature – how they could become
> Herein a leader to the human mind –

It is easy to overlook how remarkable a statement this is. He is associating the truths of geometry with the laws of nature. He describes it as an

---

[1] Cf. 'Poetry is the first and last of all knowledge – it is as immortal as the heart of man' (*Prose* I 118-65, cited from Gill, *A Life*, p. 212); and 'poetry is the blossom and fragrancy of all human knowledge, human thoughts, human passions, emotion, language' (*BL* II 26).

'alliance', but he gives no example how this relationship works – because, as discussed in the Introduction, Wordsworth could not possibly have hoped to trace that alliance step by step back to the common source of nature and geometry. Beginning with neither axioms nor theorems, there are no logical steps in Wordsworth's progress, although he did make some 'dark guesses' (*1805* VI 149). He is more attracted to the idea of geometry than geometry itself, and from this idea he drew 'a still sense / Of permanent and universal sway / And paramount endowment of the mind' – 'paramount', that is, the principal power, the 'leader' of the human mind. That process of construction he then calls

> An image not unworthy of the one
> Surpassing life, which – out of space and time,
> Not touched by welterings of passion – is,
> And hath the name of, God. Transcendent peace
> And silence did await upon these thoughts
> (*1805* VI 154-59)

He has reached the idea of infinity, what he takes as the starting point of poetry and rational research takes as the end point. A life outside or 'surpassing' life frees the mind from the constraints of space and time, thus offering a peace transcending both. The editors of the Norton *Prelude* note that these lines gave Wordsworth a deal of trouble and were among the earliest revised, at the beginning of 1807, only reaching their final shape in 1839. If a little clumsy, his revisions clarify his intentions. From the 'permanent and universal sway' of geometric proofs, he found 'A type, for finite natures, of the one / Supreme Existence, the surpassing life'. Thus he makes his readers absolutely certain that he considers that the proofs of geometry are finite representations of the infinite or 'Supreme Existence'. This vision is superior to the 'boundaries of space and time', which in 1850 he describes parenthetically as 'melancholy space, and doleful time'. A life beyond and surpassing life, 'incapable of change', is the reality to which he finally, and one might say, almost bravely, gives the name of 'God'.

The limitations inherent in the isolated study of geometry are outlined in *The Ruined Cottage*, partly quoted in the Introduction. Gazing 'upon that mighty Orb of Song, / The divine Milton', he also delved into 'Lore of a different kind' ...[2]

> books that explain
> The purer elements of truth, involv'd

---

[2] Note the use of 'lore', suggesting underlying principle, both here and in The Tables Turned.

> In lines and numbers, and by charm severe,
> Especially perceiv'd where nature droops
> And feeling is suppress'd, preserve the mind
> Busy in solitude and poverty. (*RC* E 242-47)

That sense of geometry giving comfort in adversity, when 'nature droops', is developed in the passage of Book VI of *The Prelude* where Wordsworth compares himself to the shipwrecked John Newton, slave-trader turned hymn-writer, who with only a 'treatise of geometry' and 'of food and clothing destitute' did 'oft beguile his sorrow, and almost / Forgot his feeling' (*1805* VI 174) by drawing diagrams in the sand. Both separated from the world they would inhabit by two quite different causes, Wordsworth believes they found a common relief in 'that clear synthesis built up aloft / ... / ... an independent world / Created out of pure intelligence' (*1805* VI 182-87). Although the mind is thus preserved, it is associated with the suppression of feeling, the 'drooping' of nature and 'listless hours' of 'lonesome idleness' – that is, with the failing of 'genial spirits'.

To prevent this effect, the Pedlar 'cloth'd the nakedness of austere truth' with the hues, forms and spirit of nature: 'While yet he linger'd in the elements / Of science, and among her simplest laws, / His triangles, they were the stars of Heaven' (*RC* E 258-60). By combining the laws of geometry with images of sense, nature is revived, watered by fundamental truths. Interestingly this process is reversed in Coleridge's account of his growing disconnection between seeing and feeling, the failure of his 'genial spirits', a process he called 'exsiccation': 'I look at the Mountains (that visible God Almighty that looks in at all my windows) I look at the Mountains only for the Curves of their outlines; the Stars, as I behold them, form themselves into Triangles' (*CL* I 714).

Fundamentally allied, the key difference between the works of reason and Reason, between geometry and poetry, is the presence of feeling – or passion as Wordsworth calls it. He bemoans the fragility of 'all the meditations of mankind', their inability to survive an apocalypse:

> Yea, all the adamantine holds of truth
> By reason built, or passion, (which itself
> Is highest reason in a soul sublime),
> The consecrated works of Bard and Sage,
> Sensuous or intellectual, wrought by men,
> Twin labourers and heirs of the same hopes –
> Where would they be? (*1805* V 39-44)

He then has a dream arising from that sense of fragility in which 'an arab of the Bedouin tribes' is chased by a second Deluge, carrying a stone and a shell through the desert, intending to bury them to preserve the principal achievements of mankind. The shell is poetry – 'An ode in passion uttered' – that 'was a god, yea many gods, / Had voices more than all the winds, and was / A joy, a consolation, and a hope' – in the word 'joy', passion and feeling. The stone is *Euclid's Elements*, which 'held acquaintance with the stars, / And wedded man to man by purest bond / Of nature, undisturbed by space or time' (*1805* V 97-109). Poetry is the sensuous or passionate, underpinned by the austere truths epitomized in geometry, and is one step further on from those truths, for it is the 'highest reason in a soul sublime'. The two forms of intuitive Reason are interdependent and both conclude in versions of the sublime.

The Sublime of Man

'Tis the sublime of man,
Our noontide Majesty, to know ourselves
Parts and proportions of one wond'rous whole[3]

Euclid's *Elements* wed man to man by means of the kind of truths inherent in geometry, truths free of the limitations of space or time – absolute truths. This is Wordsworth's surprising assertion.[4] In both section two and section four of Tintern Abbey, in the parallel developments towards a unity of vision (seeing 'into the life of things', and the spirit that 'rolls through all things'), the preceding steps consider either how one human being relates to others (the 'little, nameless, unremembered acts') or the general state of human life ('The still, sad music of humanity'). Each passage is only a stepping stone on the way to a vision of the sublime, which will seemingly either exclude or move well beyond his experience of the human condition. Moving from man to nature in Tintern Abbey, he says of the forms of beauty, 'To them I may have owed another gift, / Of aspect more sublime'. The comparative infers that there is a sublimity in the relations of man to man, in our social relations, as the passage above on Euclidean truths wedding 'man to

---

[3.] Religious Musings 126-28; *PW* 101 126-28.
[4.] Wordsworth has prepared for this by having imagined the destruction of the world, then adding 'Yet would the living presence still subsist / Victorious' (*1805* V 33-34). Emily Bronte says much the same in Last Lines.

man' suggests.[5] Towards the conclusion of Book VIII of *The Prelude*, Wordsworth describes his understanding of how the unity of man relates to the sublime:

> among the multitudes
> Of that great city oftentimes was seen
> Affectingly set forth, more than elsewhere
> Is possible, the unity of man,
> One spirit over ignorance and vice
> Predominant, in good and evil hearts
> One sense for moral judgements, as one eye
> For the sun's light. When strongly breathed upon
> By this sensation .../ ... doth the soul
> Rejoice as in her highest joy; for there,
> There chiefly, hath she feeling whence she is,
> And passing through all Nature rests with God.
> (*1805* VIII 824 ff.)

This might be considered the 'moral sublime'. It has the same end as the truths of geometry. The implication is that, whatever their moral condition, all people have the ability to recognize the good, 'One spirit over ignorance and vice', and it is that recognition which binds man to man; thus the nameless unremembered acts of a *good* man's life all contribute to the realization of what Wordsworth calls in the 1850 version 'a sublime *idea*' (his emphasis) – or in Coleridge's words 'the sublime of man'. Mankind's experience of unity depends on 'One sense for moral judgements', that is a single moral foundation, to all intents a moral absolute, on which all particular moral decisions are built. That unity, whether real or not, matters much less than the effect it has on the soul – forcefully emphasized in 1850 – which 'when smitten thus / By a sublime *idea* ... / ... feeds/ On the pure bliss, and takes her rest with God' (*1850* VIII 672-75). That is the idea of the unity of mankind allows the soul to move to a 'transcendent peace', (*1805* VI 154-59) because 'hath she feeling whence she is'.

[5.] Wordsworth sometimes associates strong but imperfectly remembered feeling with the sublime. E.g. 'the soul – / Remembering how she felt, but what she felt / Remembering not – retains an obscure sense / Of possible sublimity' (*1805* II 334-36). The images or forms of nature remain alive in the poet's heart as 'the feelings of unremembered pleasure', which he links to 'nameless, unremembered, acts'. It seems that in both passages 'unremembered' is repeated deliberately, almost insistently, as if pointing towards some kind of subconscious sublime, as discussed in Chapter 3.

If geometry, or *Euclid's Elements*, weds man to man, then it is not anything temporal, not the tragedies of time, nor the satires of circumstance, not the sufferings of Margaret or Michael, but something beyond their mortal lives, 'passing through all Nature', independent of time and space, the transcendent truth that 'rests with God'. Wordsworth is profoundly sympathetic to all forms of human suffering, but ultimately looks beyond the temporal for a resolution. Occasionally this leads to some lines easily misread: thus the opening of Book V, addressing mankind, 'Even in the steadiest mood of reason, when / All sorrow for thy transitory pains / Goes out' could be understood as an empathetic response to human suffering. But here it isn't, and 'Goes out' means extinguished, as in 'The light of sense goes out' describing his disorientation in the Alps.[6] And it is extinguished by reason, here Reason. What he means he clarifies when he seeks to define what it is about man's condition that he grieves for, and it is 'not for woes / Which thou endur'st – that weight, albeit huge / I charm away'. His grief is for the great fragility of mankind's intellectual and spiritual achievements, 'all the adamantine holds of truth, / By reason built, or passion', of geometric truth and of poetry, symbolised in the stone and the shell. In the light of this grief the lesser grief of human suffering he charms away. Thus he moves from one form of the sublime to a higher.

The discharged soldier (*1805* IV 400 ff.)

This barely scrutable figure places suffering in much the same order of things. Wordsworth, walking out at night on a deserted road, 'of deeper quietness / Than pathless solitudes', and finding himself 'tranquil', a key word, he received amusement despite himself 'From such near objects as from time to time / Perforce disturbed the slumber of the sense / Quiescent' – an amusement that is 'unworthy of the deeper joy / Which waits on distant prospect, cliff or sea', a distinction comparable to that between the landscape and lofty cliffs of Tintern Abbey. In both poems the immediate imagery has to be set aside, sense 'quiescent', for the mind or deeper joy to come to life, 'My body from the stillness drinking in / A restoration like the calm of sleep / But sweeter far.' The pattern found in Tintern Abbey continues, but is here more marked: the immediate and local images suppressed, the tranquil restoration achieved, then 'What beauteous pictures now / Rose in harmonious imagery – they rose / As

---

[6.] Cf. the 'conquest over sense, hourly achieved, / Through faith and meditative reason ...' (*1850* VI 458-59).

from some distant region of my soul / And came along like dreams'. They arise very far from his immediate circumstances, unlike the much closer relations of a landscape seen and remembered above the Wye. But as in Tintern Abbey, they are the first step along the road that leads beyond the temporal.

This progress precedes the story of the discharged soldier which, were it not a part of a pattern, is a strange, and one would have thought, an irrelevant introduction to his suffering, indignation at his treatment the more likely focus.[7] But for that and his own story, the soldier has a 'stately air of mild indifference', an echo of the poet's desire to free his soul from circumstance – quiescence in the poet is languor in the soldier, who is 'more than half detached / From his own nature'. He is rescued from this detachment, and his immediate suffering resolved, by the poet who finds him a home (not his) for the night. The soldier's gratitude is not effusive – there are no kindly exchanges between him, the poet and the host, no warm thanks, nothing we might habitually expect. All he says, after being ticked off by the poet for not seeking succour 'at the door of cottage or of inn', is, 'My trust is in the God of heaven, / And in the eye of him who passes me.' This is also curious – on the one hand trust in a timeless and transcendent being, and on the other believing that in the fortuitous passing of another person he will meet a temporal version of that trust. For a man so destitute, so dependent on others, these words seem to hover between the confident and the arrogant. It might be that in the soldier's indifference to his own suffering, telling his tale as if 'Remembering the importance of his theme / But feeling it no longer', he is charming away all sorrow for his transitory pains, and turning to the sublime for his source of comfort; but the sublime as mediated by the human, not in this instance nameless or unremembered, but an act of kindness from a chance acquaintance, an act which unites God and man with man in 'a sublime *idea*'.

This is an early exploration of how the soul 'passing through all Nature rests with God' (*1805* VIII 824 ff.) and Wordsworth is a little puzzled by the soldier's behaviour. He might well have asked him, as he later asked himself, 'But how can He expect that others should / Build for him, sow for him, and at his call / Love him, who for himself will take no heed at all?' (41-43, *MW* 261).[8] Indifference to the immediate has its

---

[7.] Stephen Gill cites '*Prelude*, ii 545-6' (*MW* 687), for another account of the soldier, 'Neglectfully and ungratefully thrown by / Even for the service he [had] wrought'. He kindly informed me that the correct citation is '*Prelude*, i 545-6'.

[8.] Wordsworth is much like the soldier: his legs are long, he desires solitude and he has uneasy thoughts.

own flaws, and the poet's kindness, if not unremembered, is rewarded by the soldier's thanking him, 'in a voice that seemed / To speak with a reviving interest, / Till then unfelt'.

Simon Lee

Are the closing words of that 'poor unhappy man' the still, sad music of humanity? Those two adjectives suggest a condition either incapable of, or never reaching, a resolution. Wordsworth's poetry has many examples of tales where the reader half-expects a development that will offer some relief for the suffering protagonist – Margaret's story in *The Ruined Cottage*, for instance – but the relief never comes, the suffering never resolved except in death. Wordsworth understands that he risks disappointing the reader, saying in Simon Lee, 'My gentle reader / I perceive / How patiently you've waited, / And I'm afraid that you expect / Some tale will be related.' Though the stubborn tree stump will be removed by a single blow, the conditions of Simon Lee's life will not change, and he will till the land he can barely till for the 'Few months of life he has in store' – even though 'the more he works, the more / His poor old ancles swell'. If this too is the still, sad music of humanity, it is not the whole story. Had you in mind, the poet tells the reader, 'Such stores as silent thought can bring' (the reward of 'wise passiveness'?), 'you would find / A tale in everything'. The two penultimate verses of this thirteen-verse poem describe the removal of the stump, but the real 'tale' or point of the poem only appears in the last verse, when the poet is overwhelmed by Simon's gratitude, and even that is only given its context by the last two, enigmatic lines, when noting how kind deeds are sometimes coldly received, Wordsworth adds, 'Alas! the gratitude of men / Has oftener left me mourning.' In a word, after telling Simon Lee's story at some length, a story that has no mitigation, the poet is left chastened and subdued by Simon's reception of his very brief and simple act – an act that will in practice change the huntsman's life very little, just as arranging accommodation for the discharged soldier, by whom he is also left puzzled and subdued, will help him for that night only. Simon's gratitude has perhaps left the poet mourning that he can do nothing more to relieve the huntsman's suffering. Nevertheless, that good man's nameless act of kindness has evoked the spirit of humanity, the moral sublime, and the poet finds a community of being with the tearful Simon, whose gratitude has bound man to man, partially superseding the huntsman's suffering. However, in this tale, there is no passing from that suffering to a transcendent peace.

Margaret

The soldier and Simon are left alive at the end of their stories. The conclusion of *The Ruined Cottage* is very different. Margaret is dead and the last words of Pedlar are 'I turn'd away / And walk'd along my road in happiness' – hardly the words of a man chastened or subdued.⁹ But Wordsworth has divided his responses between the poet and the pedlar. The poet is more or less overcome by his grief:

> The Old Man ceas'd …/… rising instinctively,
> I turned aside in weakness, nor had power
> To thank him for the tale which he had told.
> I stood, and, leaning o'er the garden gate,
> Review'd that Woman's sufferings, and it seem'd
> To comfort me while with a Brother's love
> I bless'd her in the impotence of grief.   (*RC* E 838-45)

That impotence may be of a kind with the mourning the poet feels when unable to do any more for Simon Lee.¹⁰ But in what might be a kind of preparation for the Pedlar's declaration, the poet also traces that 'secret spirit of humanity' which survives 'the calm oblivious tendencies / Of Nature' – nature in this instance the relentless cycle of life and death. He doesn't say *where* he traces that secret spirit, though it can hardly be other than in himself, and his sympathy for Margaret's sufferings. Because it survives the 'silent overgrowings' of nature, the implication is that this secret spirit is superior to mortality; and might be described as the sublime of man.

The Pedlar tries to relieve the poet of his grief, and turn him to the recognition 'of another gift, / Of aspect more sublime'. What the Pedlar tells the poet is first that 'enough to sorrow you have given' and then 'Be wise and chearful, and no longer read / The forms of thing with an unworthy eye.' To do so, the Pedlar implies, is a 'weakness'. The form of things is death, and to read its apparent finality is 'unworthy' of the poet: after life's fitful fever, 'She sleeps in the calm earth, and peace is here'. The Pedlar then attempts to explain this platitude by offering an

---

⁹· For a full account of the genesis and history of *The Ruined Cottage* see Stephen Gill's *Wordsworth's Revisitings* (Oxford, 2011), chapter 2.

¹⁰· David Fairer believes that the 'distinctive character of the poem can be found in the way in which pastoral tragedy is embraced by a kind of georgic stoicism': *Organising Poetry* (Oxford, 2009), p. 284. This certainly characterizes Margaret's sufferings, but the Pedlar takes one further, vital step which changes the final intention of the poem.

instance of the ultimate sublime, beyond the human: 'the high spear-grass on that wall, / By mist and silent rain-drops silver'd o'er', supplants his uneasy thoughts, so

> That what we feel of sorrow and despair
> From ruin and from change, and all the grief
> The passing shews of being leave behind
> Appear'd an idle dream that could not live
> Where meditation was: I turn'd away ...

Meditation is the key word – Reason, Imagination, Contemplation and Faith are others – which not only makes the world intelligible, infuses all forms of being with one life, but also looks through death to a life not this life. Just as Wordsworth had charmed away the woes mankind endures, the Pedlar turns away from the suffering that had ended only in death.

The Pedlar is given the ruthless task of asserting that temporal life is 'an idle dream' that cannot live in the light of meditation. This is by no means a dismissal of the lives that suffer as exemplars of the 'passing shews of being'. The music of these poems, of relentless, unremitted suffering, is very carefully orchestrated, far from being a biting condemnation of the futility of human life, and is given ample power to chasten and subdue the reader's feelings, especially if they are looking for some life larger than that presented. Wordsworth does not dismiss human sufferings; quite the contrary, he makes them a stage upon a journey.

That journey is usually undertaken by the protagonist alive, who thus has some chance to experience the sense of human sublimity, of the unity of mankind, as do Simon Lee and the discharged soldier. But for Margaret it is a vicarious process, performed by the Pedlar on her behalf, without any indication that she herself ever arrived at such happiness, just as she had no knowledge of the secret spirit of the poet's fraternal love. Wordsworth cherished a hope that 'Once taught to love such objects as excite / No morbid passions, no disquietude', we can obtain a power that 'Shall link us to our kind'. Then,

> No naked hearts
> No naked minds shall then be left to mourn
> The burthen of existence   (*RC* 373)

Because of that lack of power in Margaret herself, not living in 'the eye of Nature', her inability to relieve or look through her sufferings, she remains in our consciousness as unable to do anything other than mourn the burden of her existence. Hers remains a naked heart, and she trails through life in utter nakedness. She is not saved from her burden either by the Pedlar's regular visiting or by the poet's sense of brotherhood. The final 40 lines of *The Ruined Cottage* are an extraordinary, almost brutal transition from the impotence of grief to a happiness transcending mortality, but they are a happiness in the Pedlar. Wordsworth recognized the problem and in *The Excursion* gave Margaret faith – meditation by another name. In context it is unconvincing, because, by contrast with the Pedlar, there is no suggestion of that gift in the narrative of her life – her faith does not develop from her experience. If soothing thoughts do arise out of human suffering, they can only do so in those who, while alive, have developed a faith strong enough to find a limited relief in the experience of the human form sublime, or in whom the years have brought a philosophic mind able to look through death – as had the discharged soldier. After life's fitful fever she may sleep well, but to give Margaret peace through death is nonetheless a betrayal, even if kinder than that which disposed of Duncan. What is presented as her vicarious salvation leaves the reader sceptical of its success.

Lines left upon a Seat in a Yew-Tree

The substance of these lines is that a recognition of the suffering of mankind is a necessary stage towards a transcendental vision, by which the beholder would otherwise be alienated from society. The young man 'who own'd / No common soul … by genius nurs'd, / And big with lofty views', went forth into the world, prepared to face anything but neglect. However, neglect he got, and 'with rash disdain he turned away', pride 'sustaining his soul / In solitude'. In the sights immediately before him, his eyes downcast, he nourished a 'morbid pleasure', an 'emblem of his own unfruitful life'. There follows a process very like that of Tintern Abbey, which concludes with one distinctive and telling exception. He first lifts up his eyes to 'gaze / On the more distant scene' until 'it became / Far lovelier, and his heart could not sustain / The beauty still more beauteous';[11] then, the consequence of that failure unexplained, his thoughts turn to those 'warm from the labours of benevolence' (little nameless acts of kindness and of love?) for whom 'The world and man

---

[11.] In This Lime-tree Bower my Prison, such gazing is the means by which Coleridge believes that God will make spirits reveal his presence. And 'beauty still more beauteous' echoes Tintern Abbey's 'forms of beauty', the variant 'beauteous forms' and 'the beauteous forms of things' of The Tables Turned.

himself, appeared a scene / Of kindred loveliness'. So he turns in the right direction, but he sighed 'to think that others felt / What he must never feel' – not suffering with those whom he saw suffer – and so becomes a 'lost man'. Wordsworth defines precisely what is lost, and how: 'he, who feels contempt / For any living thing, hath faculties / Which he has never used; that thought with him / Is in its infancy' – a moral not dissimilar to the conclusion of The Ancient Mariner. Wordsworth knew himself capable of that destructive contempt, fought against it, and found the remedy in a process that threads through all his work, compassion replacing contempt, and human suffering not just a casualty as he realized his vision of Paradise.

It is always the forms of beauty or the beauteous forms that come first in this process. In Book VI of *The Prelude*, for instance, when speaking of Nature, he writes, 'With such a book / Before our eyes, we could not choose but read / Lessons of genuine brotherhood, the plain /And universal reason of mankind, / The truths of young and old' (*1850* VI 552 ff.) The unity of man with man, and of man with nature, resides in 'universal reason' or 'the grand / And simple reason' (*1805* XI 123-24). In the penultimate book, he describes how Nature (here 'a Power') teaches reverence for 'right reason', which then:

>Disposes her, when over-fondly set
>On throwing off incumbrances, to seek
>In man, and in the frame of social life,
>Whate'er there is desirable and good
>Of kindred permanence, unchanged in form
>And function, or, through strict vicissitude
>Of life and death, revolving.   (*1850* XIII 33-39)

First looking to the forms of beauty revealed in the appearances of nature, Wordsworth then looks for 'a kindred loveliness', a 'kindred permanence' in 'the world and man himself', in 'the frame of social life'. Qualities desirable and good are 'undisturbed by space or time' (*1805* V 107) or 'out of space and time' and survive the 'strict vicissitude / Of life and death'. All the potential sufferings of mankind lie in the word 'vicissitude', beyond which, so Wordsworth declares, there is transcendent peace (*1805* VI 143-59), in which the soul 'takes her rest with God'.

As noted above, the forms of beauty always begin the process sketched out here, and the corrective that Wordsworth offered the young man looking over Esthwaite Lake is modest compared to that of 1799, and

eventually published in *The Excursion*. Here they are presented as a concluding epigraph, summing up the initial stages of the pattern of thought traced in this chapter. The beauties of nature first soften down the poet's 'the execration and contempt' – for human life other than his own – so enabling him to feel compassion, and act in the little numberless ways which reveal the sublimity of mankind.

* * *

> *Not useless do I deem*
> *These quiet sympathies with things that hold*
> *An inarticulate language for the man*
> *Once taught to love such objects as excite*
> *No morbid passions no disquietude*
> *No vengeance and no hatred needs must feel*
> *The joy of that pure principle of love*
> *So deeply that unsatisfied with aught*
> *Less pure and exquisite he cannot chuse*
> *But seek for objects of a kindred love*
> *Accordingly by degrees he perceives*
> *His feelings of aversion softened down*
> *A holy tenderness pervade his frame*
> *His sanity of reason not impaired*
> *Say rather all his thoughts now flowing clear*
> *From a clear fountain flowing he looks round*
> *He seeks for good and finds the good he seeks*
> *Till execration and contempt are things*
> *He only knows by name and if he hears*
> *From other mouth the language which they speak*
> *He is compassionate and has no thought*
> *No feeling which can overcome his love.*[12]

[12.] *RC* 372. Stephen Gill (*MW* 686) thinks that Lines Left upon a Seat in a Yew Tree may also have Coleridge in mind, who spoke of himself 'as less *contemptuous*, than I used to be' (*CL* I 334); and perhaps he is that 'other mouth' in the passage above. Coleridge's belief that the affections are set in right tune by 'the beauty of the inanimate impregnated, as with a living soul' describes the same process (*CL* I 397). So strong is this pattern in Wordsworth that possibly *Descriptive Sketches* preceding *Salisbury Plain* indicates its first subconscious workings.

Part II
Principles

Chapter 5

Intimations

The Epigraphs, the Subtitle and Coleridge's Reading of the *Ode*[1]

1807: *'Paulo majora canamus'*

THE *ODE* WAS FIRST published as the concluding poem in the 1807 collection, *Poems, in Two Volumes*. The epigraph, taken from Virgil, can be translated as 'Let us sing of things a little greater', thus separating it from the preceding poems, asking readers to give it particular attention. It might also be considered as a provisional keeping of the promise made in the Latin epigraph to both volumes: *'Hereafter shall our Muse speak to thee in deeper tones, when the seasons yield to me their fruits in peace'*.[2] In addition, by placing the poem last in this and all subsequent collections Wordsworth indicated that it was the culmination of the poetry that both preceded and succeeded it, closing his canon.[3] Therefore it is best read in the light of his other works, rather than in the isolation afforded by its reputation. The placing of the *Ode* also has another purpose, explained in the 1815 Preface: 'the following Poems have been divided into classes', in order, as far as possible, to 'correspond with the course of human life', and to exhibit 'the three requisites of legitimate whole, a beginning, a middle, and an end'. Therefore, Wordsworth arranged them 'according to an order of time, commencing with Childhood, and terminating with Old Age, Death, and Immortality'. Bar *The Excursion*, there at the end of all his collections stood the Immortality Ode. The poems are often thus in an order very different from the chronology of their composition, and of the experience underlying

---

[1.] A version of the two following chapters was first published in the *Philological Quarterly*, vol. 96, Spring 2017, no. 2, (Iowa), pp. 239-268. My thanks to Eric Gill for permission to re-use the material.
[2.] Translated in *P2V* 26.
[3.] Peter J. Manning, 'Wordsworth's Intimations Ode and its Epigraphs', *Journal of English and Germanic Philology*, Vol. 82, no. 4 (1983), p. 540.

them. The *Ode* was completed in 1804, when Wordsworth was 34; he had another 45 years to live, and much poetry to write. His experience of the intimations of immortality came to him as a young man, but even then the *Ode* was a struggle to recover a vision already almost lost; soon the hiding places of his power would close and his later years were characterized by a gentle stoic despondency. However, in making the *Ode* the conclusion to all his work, Wordsworth remained faithful to what he saw as the truth of a vision no longer available to him. He did not let subsequent experience, or lack of it, nullify that insight.

As described in the Introduction, his first attempt to convey his vision met with no success. Without a title, with an allusive epigraph, it proved too enigmatic for its first readers. Some were honest in their struggle – the frankness of James Montgomery has a particular charm:

> I am sure the poetry of two men cannot differ much more widely than his does from mine. I hate his baldness and vulgarity of phrase, and I doubt not he equally detests the splendour and foppery of mine; but I feel the pulse of poetry beating through every vein of thought in all his compositions…[4]

Even so, noting the absence of a title, he declared that 'the reader is turned loose into a wilderness of sublimity, tenderness, bombast, and absurdity, to find out the subject as well as he can'.[5] Southey got a bit closer when he identified an aspect of the *Ode* writing to Walter Scott in 1807, 'The Ode upon pre-Existence is a dark subject darkly handled. Coleridge is the only man who could make such a subject luminous'. Unfortunately Coleridge had his blind spots – and upon two of those the poem depends: the idea of soul's pre-existence, and the child as 'best Philosopher'. Francis Jeffrey's incomprehension on reading the *Ode* – 'illegible and unintelligible' – is severely put and comes from an unsympathetic reader, but the poem's genuine difficulties are evident in the fact that, although there was much admiration for what came to be called 'the Great Ode', there are few positive or intelligible readings for many years following its publication.[6] Much of the criticism comes from his use of the idea of pre-existence, taken as verging on heresy,

---

[4.] *Woof* 205; the quotes following are serially pp. 213, 237, 199.
[5.] Coleridge defined '*mental* bombast' as 'a disproportion of the expressions to the thoughts' (*BL* II 136-38).
[6.] Thomas Noon Talfourd was probably the first reader of unreserved enthusiasm who, in 1820, described it as 'the noblest piece of lyric poetry in the world' (*Woof* 867-68).

particularly troubling to the Victorians. Wordsworth's defence, that it is a poetic idea, not an inculcation of belief, takes up about half the Fenwick note.

Coleridge had ambivalent attitudes to the idea of the soul's pre-existence. In 1796 he thought that it 'may be very wild philosophy; but it is very intelligible poetry' (*CL* I 278), a thought to which he never recurs, even in defence of the *Ode*. In 1801, he said that 'Plato, it is known, held the pre-existence of human Souls' (*CL* II 680), which runs counter to what he wrote in 1810 that a 'a few Phantasts only have troubled themselves with the questions of Pre-existence ... concerning Pre-existence men in general have neither care nor belief' (*CN* III 3701); and in 1815 he thought that those who read the *Ode* aright 'will be as little disposed to charge Mr. Wordsworth with believing the platonic pre-existence in the ordinary interpretation of the words, as I am to believe, that Plato himself ever meant or taught it' (*BL* II 147).

Coleridge's inconsistent attitudes to pre-existence probably contributed to his failure to understand its importance to Wordsworth – who compared the idea to the lever with which Archimedes believed he could move the world or, to use another metaphor, the lynchpin upon which the resolution of the *Ode* turns. Despite this oversight, and despite his scorn for the child as philosopher, Coleridge clearly admired at least parts of the *Ode*: he quotes two long passages in the *Biographia* and *The Friend*, one common to both. He may also have come to appreciate the poem more as he grew older: in 1822, misquoting the beginning of stanza VI, 'Our birth is but a sleep – Earth strews her lap', he calls it an 'incomparable Passage in W. Wordsworth's incomparable Ode' (*CN* IV 4910). His unusual reading of that stanza is considered in the next chapter. To none of the long extracts does he append any interpretive comment. His first notice of the *Ode* in the *Biographia* opens with the 1815 subtitle – so he should have had no doubt as to Wordsworth's intentions – to which he then adds, 'the poet might have prefixed the lines which Dante addresses to one of his own Canzoni' which he translates as 'O lyric song, there will be few, think I, / Who may thy import understand aright; / Thou art for *them* so arduous and so high!' He adds the same quotation to his extracts in the 1818 *Friend*.[7] Presumably Coleridge considers himself one of '*them*' (his emphasis), but asserting the difficulty or profundity of a poem goes little way to understanding it. Curiously, he is determined not to leave readers with these extracts as representative

---

[7] *BL* II 147; *F* I 509-11; *Convivio* II i 53-55, also quoted in *CN* II 3219 (1807/8) without reference to the *Ode*.

of Wordsworth's poetry – 'which though highly characteristic must yet from the nature of the thoughts and the subject be interesting, or perhaps intelligible, to but a limited number of readers' (*BL* II 154). The thoughts are 'intimations' and the subject 'immortality'. Of interest only to a few? And that from the man who presumed that his readers would be able to follow the erudite philosophical speculations of Chapter 12 of the *Biographia*. Wordsworth made the opposite decision – always to take leave of his readers with that poem.

Coleridge is prevaricating. Only a few pages earlier he had said that 'the ode was intended for such readers only as had been accustomed to watch the flux and reflux of their inmost nature ... For such readers the sense is sufficiently plain' (*BL* II 147). Surely such readers are not so rare, and if ever there was such a reader, it was Coleridge. Could he not make the ode 'luminous', the sense 'plain', if it was so plain to him? It appears he couldn't. He called it 'incomparable', but there are very few references to it in his works, and those mostly quotations, and it goes unmentioned in his letters even at moments when some comment would have been most likely – on its completion in 1804, or its first publication in 1807. He never quotes from the first four stanzas nor the last two, nor stanza VII, and only from VIII to damn it. That is, he doesn't see the poem in the round, the way it set out to answer the question proposed – how to reunite seeing and feeling – the question that lit the blaze of the Verse Letter. That even Coleridge couldn't offer an intelligible reading of the *Ode* suggests just how puzzling the poem is.

1815: 'The Child is Father of the Man'

So the first readers asked the first question of the poem – what is its subject? In 1843, talking to Isabella Fenwick about what the Victorians by then called 'the Great Ode', Wordsworth said, 'To the attentive and competent reader the whole sufficiently explains itself' (*FN*). Those are modest requirements compared to Coleridge's requisite, the ability to watch the flux and reflux of one's inmost nature. However, Wordsworth was being a little ingenuous. The conditions he required in 1815 were more demanding as the poem 'rests entirely on two recollections of childhood, one that of the splendour in the objects of sense that is passed away, and the other an indisposition to bend to the law of death as applying to our own particular case' (*MY* II 189). He also adds, mysteriously, the reader should share his views about 'some of those elements of the human soul whose importance is insisted on in the Ex^n.' That may be a guarded reference to the idea of pre-existence, openly admitted in 1843, but is perhaps best read in the light of his earlier remark in the same letter: 'The Soul, dear Mrs. C. may be re-given when it had been taken away, my own Solitary is an instance of this'. As discussed below, Wordsworth distinguished self and soul. Unlike the damaged soul, which he goes on to describe, the undamaged – 'as strong as mountain River' – can pour out 'praise to the Almighty Giver' (To a Skylark), which is essentially what Wordsworth feels he is doing in *The Excursion*, transfusing from 'the Bible of the Universe' 'the innumerable analogies and types of infinity' (a modest ambition). It is also consistent with the idea of pre-existence, of coming from God, 'who is our home'.

His words, both in 1815 and in 1843, are those of a man nettled by many of the reviews the poem received from its first appearance onwards. That, in 1807, the whole did not sufficiently explain itself, even to sympathetic readers, is probably why, in 1815, encouraged by Henry Crabb Robinson, Wordsworth added the subtitle, 'Intimations of Immortality from Recollections of Early Childhood', 'to guide the reader to a perception of its drift'.[8] Paul Magnuson notes that at the time of its writing Wordsworth and Dorothy had referred to the poem as an 'ode' without other title or indication of subject matter.[9] Wordsworth gave most of his poems titles, such as the Ode to Duty, and therefore identifiable topics, even if they proved complex on reading. Perhaps that initial absence, followed years later by a lengthy subtitle, suggests that Wordsworth himself wasn't easily able to formulate his subject. Yet the subtitle is definitive, and if the whole still isn't easy to understand, the subject matter is surely no longer in doubt. It is not about pre-existence itself, but what might constitute the nature of immortality, and Wordsworth 'plans to argue for it from some aspect of the recollected memories of early childhood'.[10] Note the precision with which Wordsworth guides readers to perceiving the poem's drift: 'intimations' – not a declaration – therefore hesitant, suggestive, undogmatic; 'recollections', distinguishable from 'memories' as having some added quality, realized through reflection or 'after-meditation' (*1805* III 648).[11]

As an unintended consequence, Wordsworth's clarification raised the second major question about the poem: what constitutes, or where

---

[8] Robinson, *Correspondence*, Vol. II, pp. 838-39.
[9] Paul Magnuson, *Coleridge and Wordsworth: A Lyrical Dialogue* (Princeton, NJ, 1988), pp. 178-79.
[10] Anya Taylor, 'Religious Readings of the Immortality Ode', *Studies in English Literature, 1500-1900*, Vol. 26 (1986), p. 633.
[11] See *Experiments* 49, on To a Cuckoo: 'it records one of those "spots of time" that take on meanings during the very process of recollection'.

in the poem is, the 'immortality' of the subtitle? How do we render the term 'immortality' intelligible? This question continues to create major difficulties in our reading. In 1991 John Hayden updated Russell Noyes's 1971 biography of Wordsworth and began his analysis of the ode by claiming, "Wordsworth's great "Ode on Immortality" is not easy to follow nor wholly clear. A basic difficulty of interpretation centers upon what the poet means by "immortality".'[12]

Wordsworth must have hoped that his 1815 subtitle left no room for doubt. He also removed the original and allusive epigraph, and replaced it with the last three lines of 'My heart leaps up'.[13] Those lines begin, 'The child is father of the Man' – thus hammering home his idea of the subject – that man will discover his immortality by remembering aspects of his childhood.[14] That poem is emphatic: the third line begins not with a peaceable, 'so it was when my life began', but with a vigorous, 'so *was* it when my life began' and goes on through the tenses, 'so *is* it now I am a man', 'so *be* it when I shall grow old' and concludes with the passionate and unexpected 'Or let me die!'[15] The first six lines are a determined statement, which the final three seem to summarize, but summarize what? The concluding 'Or' suggests a preceding, though implicit, 'either': *either* my heart leaps up, *or* I die. Alan Grob writes that 'retention of the childhood response to the rainbow emerges as a spiritual necessity of such magnitude that death looms as the sole alternative to failure'.[16] Life and death are thus opposed: life lies in the ability to respond simply, but profoundly, to the rainbow; and death is the absence of that response, the absence of 'natural piety' – which is not the piety of nature, if there is such a thing, but the natural piety of the human being.[17] Note 'behold',

---

[12] Russell Noyes and John Hayden, *William Wordsworth* (Boston, 1991), p. 110.

[13] This may be Wordsworth hitting back at Jeffrey. In his review, Jeffrey had used such words as 'babyish', 'silly' and 'trash' to describe the 1807 poems, and quoted the whole of 'My heart leaps up…' to illustrate his point.

[14] Paul Magnuson, 'The Genesis of Wordsworth's "Ode"', *TWC*, Vol. 12, no. 1 (1981), p. 23, reminds us how, in *EY* I 334, Wordsworth saw the imagination growing in children.

[15] Emphases added. Geoffrey Hartman, *The Unremarkable Wordsworth* (Minneapolis, MN, 1987), p. 157, calls this phrase 'a 'true fit of passion … one of those Wordsworthian moments where feeling seems to overflow and be in excess of its occasion'. Not 'in excess' if this is Wordsworth's way of 'looking through death'.

[16] Alan Grob, 'Wordsworth's *Immortality Ode* and the Search for Identity', *ELH*, Vol. 32 (1965), p. 35.

[17] See Florence G. Marsh, 'Wordsworth's Ode: Obstinate Questionings', *Studies in Romanticism*, Vol. 5 (1966), p. 225: 'This piety has little to do with external nature. It has to do with human nature, with the divine spark still alive in the heart, with the memory of the fugitive glory.'

a biblical injunction often introducing the revelatory: Wordsworth's beholding is more than just a seeing, and his heart leaping up more than just a sensation of excitement; he is beholding something akin to a revelation or a vision.[18] And that capacity for vision is what he is praying that he can maintain in old age. 'Or let me die' suggests that, if he does hold onto that power, he won't die: that the act of beholding is a mode of immortality – is to experience 'bright shoots of everlastingness' as Vaughan put it (The Retreat). Just as Wordsworth himself addresses the rainbow, the Wanderer addresses the spirit of Nature, declaring, 'Thy bounty caused to flourish deathless flowers, / From Paradise transplanted: wintry age / Impends: the frost will gather round my heart; / If the flowers wither, I am worse than dead!'[19] The immortal things of Paradise transplanted into this world can only live in a living heart; but the living heart can also render the flowers of this world, like the rainbow, deathless, so recreating a paradise. It's a reciprocal relationship.

Its three-line epigraph is thus the ode's first intimation of the nature of immortality and how this might be disclosed. Peter Manning regards the 1815 epigraph as 'an act of interpretation', in which, by replacing the Virgilian motto, 'Wordsworth under-represents the pathos of change and separation in the Ode itself'.[20] This view arises in part because Manning identifies the poem as a pastoral elegy, a poem of loss, not recovery, and his reading depends on a closer comparison with Virgil's Fourth Eclogue than I believe merited by Wordsworth's selection of just three, unattributed, words. Nonetheless, the 1815 epigraph walks a fine line between an act of interpretation and an act of clarification.

Mortality and 'the malice of the grave'

Despite Wordsworth waving all these semiotic flags, some Victorian readers were determined to go on being inattentive and incompetent. Ruskin thought Wordsworth 'content with intimations of immortality such as may be in skipping of lambs and laughter of children – incurious to see in the hands the print of the nails'.[21] This passing reference to

---

[18.] See *Experiments* 33: 'The frequent use of imperatives in the little poems ... and the consistent use of the formal "thee" and "thou", signal the weight the poet makes these poems bear'.
[19.] *The Excursion* IV 53-56.
[20.] Manning, 'Wordsworth's Intimations Ode and Its Epigraphs', 539-40.
[21.] John Ruskin, *Art and Life: A Ruskin Anthology*, ed. John Alden (New York, 1886), p. 509.

Doubting Thomas (John 20:24-29), reinforced by Ruskin's knowledge of resurrection art, articulates the most familiar, if least credible, understanding of immortality. Throughout his work, it is precisely that false hope of physical resurrection which Wordsworth tacitly distinguishes from his idea of immortality: if there was one way of 'looking through death' that he was *not* talking about, it was physical or personal restoration, a conjuring trick with bones.

Wordsworth is reluctantly absolute when it comes to death: it is the end. Even for those he loves most dearly, he doesn't fudge it. Like the rest of us, he yearned to see again those whom he had lost, but he knew, in his loss of Catherine for example, that 'my heart's best treasure was no more; / That neither present time, nor years unborn / Could to my sight that heavenly face restore' ('Surprised by Joy'). He returns to that loss and that conclusion in Maternal Grief: the dream of Catherine was 'A shadow, never, never to be displaced / By the returning Substance, seen or touched, / Seen by my eyes or clasped in my embrace'. In Book III of *The Excursion*, there is a long and searching meditation on all the implications of Catherine's death; she 'was conveyed / ... to inaccessible worlds, / To regions / Where height, or depth, admits not the approach of living man'; 'to the grave' he 'spake / Imploringly; – looked up, and asked the Heavens / If Angels traversed their cerulean floors'; but got no answer: 'life was put / To inquisition, long and profitless' (640-98). His poetry of this kind is elegiac because it is infused with the melancholy that arises from that longing set against the certain knowledge that never again will the person lost be seen or embraced. Or as the Pedlar advised the poet, 'We die, my Friend, / ... and very soon / Even of the good is no memorial left' (*RC* D 68-72). Thus Wordsworth could even say of his drowned brother: 'The meek, the brave, the good, was gone; / He who had been our living John / Was nothing but a name.' ('I only looked for pain and grief'). Of Matthew, fondly remembered, his name memorialized among a list of past schoolmasters, Wordsworth asks, 'can it be / That these two words of glittering gold / Are all that must remain of thee?' ('If Nature, for a favorite Child'). However gloomy and despondent it makes him, Wordsworth always recognizes the impossibility of anything like physical or personal resurrection, quite reasonably refusing that form of immortality, though the struggle with conflicting impulses educes some of his most beautiful and tender poetry. In that he can be compared and contrasted to Browning, a fierce sceptic vis-à-vis both of the transcendental and of mortal resurrection, who nonetheless, against the grain of his poetry, but deep in the throes of love, persuades himself that after the 'black minute' of death he shall see his wife once more, and 'O thou soul of my soul! I shall clasp thee again' (Prospice). I think Wordsworth more honest in refusing that hope, and his 'handful of silver' much less of a betrayal than Browning's kow-towing to the incredible.

As suggested by his 2006 title, '"The Sunless Land": Intimations of Immortality from Recollections of Virgil and Ossian', this unrealized longing is, for Richard Gravil, the only substantial intimation of immortality in Wordsworth's poetry:

> The closest he ever gets to affirming the notion of recognizable personal survival is in his numerous anxiety-laden versions of the failure of Virgilian and Ovidian heroes and heroines to 'clasp' their deceased spouses, versions which begin in childhood and climax in the remarkable 'Laodamia'.[22]

This suggests that Gravil still considered immortality a material condition, but whatever constitutes immortality, Wordsworth knew it was not to be found in an after-death embrace. As Gravil acknowledges, Laodamia is punished for her presumption that Protesilaus should 'elude the malice of the grave', which though the most human of hopes, is nonetheless seen by Wordsworth as out of the order of things – 'Jove frowned in heaven'. It is Protesilaus who offers correct counsel:

> This visage tells thee that my doom is past:
> Nor should the change be mourned, even if the joys
> Of sense were able to return as fast
> And surely as they vanish. Earth destroys
> Those raptures duly...
> Learn, by a mortal yearning, to ascend –
> Seeking a higher object. Love was given,
> Encouraged, sanctioned, chiefly for that end;
> For this the passion to excess was driven –
> That self might be annulled: her bondage prove
> The fetters of a dream opposed to love. –

'That self might be annulled' – personal survival, or the survival of 'the joys / Of sense', is 'a dream opposed to love', which seeks 'a higher object', beyond time and space. Immortality and resurrection are not

---

[22.] Richard Gravil, '"The Sunless Land"', *Charles Lamb Bulletin*, NS Vol. 136 (October 2006), p. 116.

co-ordinate terms in Wordsworth's lexicon; 'resurrection' a word he rarely if ever used; and if its implicit absence in the Ode is considered a failure, that is to criticize Wordsworth for not discussing an archaic idea he refuted, for not answering a question he wasn't asking.[23]

Self and Soul

So how does Wordsworth 'look through death'? What is his 'higher object'? If not the articulation of bones, what else? In the latter part of the Fenwick note Wordsworth, merely in passing, speaks of being 'impelled to write this Poem on the 'Immortality of the soul' (*FN*). In the seventeenth century, from which much of Wordsworth's intellectual energy seems to spring, the idea of a physical resurrection was already outmoded, if not openly dismissed, and the task ordinarily undertaken was to demonstrate the immortality of the soul. Seventeenth-century titles show how common this idea was: Richard Baxter, *Immateriality of the Soul*; John Smith, *A Discourse Demonstrating the Immortality of the Soul*; Henry More, *The Immortality of the Soul*; Sir John Davies, *Of the Soul of Man and the Immortalitie thereof* – a platonic poem, from which Coleridge quotes (*BL* II 17) substituting imagination for soul, in order to demonstrate its ideal function, turning 'bodies to spirit by sublimation strange'.

Wordsworth believes that it goes without saying that the *Ode*'s subtitle refers to the soul, which he consistently differentiates from 'self' – for instance, the phrase 'The Soul that rises with us' distinguishes 'soul' and 'us'. Or, as he observes in 'Lines Written in Early Spring', 'To her fair works did nature link / The human soul that through me ran'. It is the soul, some aspects of which will be discussed below, and not the self, that is the subject of immortality.[24] To suppose, therefore, that he was offering intimations of physical immortality, personal survival, bodily resurrection or anything like, is to misread the label he'd attached to his tin.[25]

---

[23] Or as Wordsworth put it in respect of style in The Preface to *The Lyrical Ballads* 1802, 'that I may not be censured for not having performed what I never attempted'.
[24] This difference between self and soul is implicit in many passages which make no deliberate distinction – e.g. 'Fair seed-time had my soul, and I grew up / Fostered alike by beauty and by fear' (*1805* I 305-6). In a letter of January 1815, he writes, 'The Soul, dear Mrs. C. may be re-given, when it has been taken away' (*MY* II 188).
[25] One article which resists the gradual shading of Victorian literalism into historical materialism is Thomas Raysor's 'The Themes of Immortality and Natural Piety in Wordsworth's Immortality Ode', in Shiv K. Kumar (ed.), *British Romantic Poets* (London, 1968), pp. 45-62.

As Coleridge remarked, not to read a book or poem in the spirit in which it is written is to risk reading a sundial by moonlight (*M* II 561). However, understanding the spirit in which the poem was written remains as difficult now as it did then because neither 'immortality' nor 'soul' are words that point to distinct ideas for us. So we tend to avoid giving a specific meaning to Wordsworth's subtitle – indeed the absence of the word 'soul' allows us to read it with what might be called a determined linguistic indeterminism, at best refusing to think in either material or spiritual terms, or in Richard Gravil's words, '*Intimations* ... avoids giving any particular characteristics to its ostensible subject' ('Sunless Land', p. 113); and as Daniel Robinson puts it, 'the emphasis [has] shifted from reading the poem as the ... 'Immortality Ode' to admitting its metaphysical ambiguities as ... the 'Intimations Ode' ('Wordsworth: Ode', 1).[26] Thus, wavering as to the subject matter, we end up in a no man's land of meaning, acknowledging it as one of Wordsworth's greatest poems, admiring the rhetorical grandeur, entranced by its music. Yet, untouched by the truths it would point to, we are finally puzzled by its impetus, and both intellectually and emotionally confused by apparent conflicts in its rhetoric. As a critical community, we risk returning to the kind of judgements visited upon the poem by its first readers. It is, I think, a common experience to feel that we understand the poem as we read it, but to find that when the music stops that confidence fades, and then we struggle to say what we have understood. Thus, depending on one's degree of scepticism, the poem remains either enigmatic or inscrutable or simply unintelligible. Towards the conclusion of his 2006 paper, asserting that we can no longer read the poem as he believes Coleridge read it, Richard Gravil reaches for the far end of that spectrum in a striking peroration:

> Without [Coleridge's] particular confidence in things unseen, the fugitive argument of the Ode, like that of the *Extempore Effusion*, rests upon clouds and waves careering towards a nothingness crowned with darkness, as the poetic brothers pass in that gloomiest of valedictions, 'from sunshine to the *sunless* land'. What Carlyle sardonically referred to as

---

[26.] Daniel Robinson, 'William Wordsworth: Ode. Intimations of Immortality from Recollections of Early Childhood'; http://www.litencyc.com/php/sworks.php?rec=true&UID=34202. This is article is both a succinct critical history of the Ode, and a brief but persuasive reading of it. Robinson's distinction between Wordsworth as a poet of immanence and a poet of transcendence is particularly valuable.

> 'transcendental life-preservers' have been decommissioned. Without them, for all its rhetoric of compensations, the only heaven *Intimations* can truly envisage ... is that of infancy. Compared with its argument for pre-existence – which is overt, emphatic and (we are told) no more than a poetic idea – its argument for immortality was never more than implied. Consequently, for a reader who lacks such instinctive pre-assurances, it is no longer there.
>
> But it seems not to matter. Nowadays, for most readers, the poem's consolation derives from nature and nature's continuities ... This poet, after all, never lyeth because he nothing affirmeth. As an expression of an ability to take *disinterested* pleasure in the sound of 'mighty waters rolling evermore' – ... the *Ode* somehow crosses the bar between comforting faith and stoical unbelief. Neither those mighty waters nor 'the clouds that gather round the setting sun' have any bearing on personal immortality. Least of all does the poem's terminal *memento mori*, 'the meanest flower that blows'.

I presume that Gravil believes that it is of immortality that Wordsworth 'nothing affirmeth'; for though full of doubt, Wordsworth's poetry is also 'diversified by faith', which he affirms under the 'banners militant' of extraordinary experience.[27] What he affirms, in such phrases as 'our home, / Is with infinitude and only there', is however never 'personal immortality', for as we have seen in 'Laodamia', the self must be annulled in the quest for 'a higher object'; and so to look for evidence of individual survival is to ask the wrong question of the poem. Surely those great affirmations are not disconnected from the idea of immortality, to the 'human soul that through me ran'; and 'the mighty waters' and 'the meanest flower that blows' have some bearing on that 'higher object'; they should not be taken just as a pleasurable synthesis of images by which the poem 'somehow crosses the bar between comforting faith and stoical unbelief'. That 'somehow' slips past any insight as to how comforting faith is transformed into stoical unbelief, or vice versa. As will become clear in the course of this chapter, I do not share Gravil's view that the only heaven affirmed is that of infancy; nor that the argument for immortality, 'only ever implied', is 'no longer there'. Though I have learnt much from his papers on the *Ode*, I see Gravil's conclusion as an

---

[27.] For 'diverisified by faith' see Robert Browning, Bishop Blougram's Apology.

example of where we may end up if we are unwilling or unable to read a work in the spirit in which it was written: the language is different, but the tone and the conclusion are reminiscent of Francis Jeffrey's 'illegible and unintelligible'.[28]

One thing more: 'it seems not to matter ... the poem's consolation derives from nature and nature's continuities'. I think this natural form of consolation has little to offer – for what are 'nature's continuities'? Michael O'Neill has suggested a distinction between 'Earth' and 'Nature' in Wordsworth's idiolect;[29] and perhaps the former only becomes the latter when contemplated by an empowered mind or heart. Otherwise Earth – that Earth which duly destroys all other raptures – remains the earth, rolling round, for example, Lucy's dust with 'rocks and stones and trees'.[30] Without force or motion, Lucy has become 'nothing but a name', and the poet uses that diurnal continuity as the symbol of his loss, not as a pantheistic form of immortality.[31] His heart or spirit was silent, sealed, disempowered and faced with Lucy's insuperable death; all he knows is loss, and the awful difference between death and life. Unvisioned Earth teaches us about mortality, not immortality, and it has no consolations, only lessons. Although Margaret, as another example, lived amidst nature and its continuities just as much as the Pedlar, to all intents nature didn't exist for her, and all her holds on life are relentlessly destroyed by the 'touch of earthly years'. Not until, in *The Excursion,* she is given a power of a kind with the Pedlar's power of meditation does she find any form of consolation. Wouldn't it be truer to say that Nature, in the sense that it was salvational or consolatory, was in fact very discontinuous for Wordsworth? It was around him all his

---

[28.] See also Richard Gravil, '"Intimations" in America', in Richard Gravil and Daniel Robinson (eds), *The Oxford Handbook of William Wordsworth* (Oxford, 2015), pp. 767-85.

[29.] O'Neill, '"The Tremble from it is Spreading"', *The Charles Lamb Bulletin,* Vol. 139 (2007), p. 77. See also *1805* III 78-188: 'O heavens, how awful is the might of souls, / And what they do within themselves while yet / The yoke of earth is new to them'. Earth, our 'homely Nurse', is a place of distraction, but envisioned as Nature it becomes a form of Paradise.

[30.] Coleridge has an interesting reading of the two kinds of earth in *CN* IV 4190: 'Rhea, the Earth as the transitory ever-flowing Nature – the sum of Phaenomena or Objects of the outward Senses', and the life of 'Satyrs the sports and desires of sensuous Nature', in contradistinction 'from Earth as Vesta / = the eternal Law'. But this is more his distinction than Wordsworth's.

[31.] Which reading, a form of immortality or an unmitigated loss, is a vexed question. John Beer tends to the former: 'If Wordsworth had wanted to induce a sense of utter desolation he would surely have ended the poem with the deadness of rocks' (*Against Finality,* p. 31). Perhaps, but Wordsworth didn't think of rocks as dead. Most likely the required rhyme dictates the order of the words.

life, he was 'beset with [its] images', but think how often, in various and very different poems, he complains that 'The things which I have seen I now can see no more'. There is no consolation where there is no vision – where the heart does not leap up. The aesthete's gaze is no substitute for visionary power. So it does matter. Wordsworth denied he was a worshipper of nature – 'A passionate expression, uttered incautiously in the poem on the Wye', led, he says, one of his early readers into that mistake, and we may add, many others since (*MY* II 188). The *Ode*'s intelligibility does not depend upon our belief, upon our sharing that confidence in things unseen; but unless we achieve some kind of insight into Wordsworth's understanding of the idea of the soul and of immortality, we will find ourselves reading a sundial by moonshine.

Reason and the Soul; the Abyss and the Infinite

Of the various seventeenth-century texts on the immortality of the soul, that of Sir John Davies is the one Wordsworth is most likely to have read. Although there are clear differences between each man's conception, both begin with the notion that the life of the soul is independent of that of the body. 'Yet she survives, although the body dies', says Sir John, or as the next section title asserts 'the soul is a thing subsisting by itselfe, without the body',[32] just as Wordsworth suggests that the soul lives free of sense when the child, 'deaf and silent, read'st the eternal deep'; or when haunted by a consciousness of immortality, the grave, 'without sense or sight', is no more threatening than 'A place of thought where we in waiting lie'. Sir John and Wordsworth share a sense of the soul's origins – 'she is a spirit, and heavenly influence, / Which from the fountaine of God's Spirit doth flow', says Sir John (p. 41), with Wordsworth agreeing that 'The Soul that rises with us' comes 'From God, who is our home';[33] and both see the world as a place of distraction:

> So while the virgin Soule on Earth doth stay,
> She woo'd and tempted is ten thousand wayes,
> By these great powers, which on Earth bear sway;
> The wisdom of the world. wealth, pleasure, praise:

[32.] *The Complete Poems of Sir John Davies*, ed. Alexander B. Grosart (London, 1876), p. 29.
[33.] The child's initial imperviousness to mortal pleasures, and consciousness of God or heaven, is a consistent part of Wordsworth's thought: addressing God in *The Excursion*, he writes, 'Thou, who didst wrap the cloud/ Of infancy around us, that thyself, / Therein, with our simplicity awhile/ Might'st hold, on earth, communion undisturbed.' (IV 83).

> With these sometime she doth her time beguile,
> These doe by fits her Fantasie possesse;
> But she distastes them all within a while,
> And in the sweetest finds a tediousnesse. (p. 89)

What is assertion in Sir John derives from experience in Wordsworth, originating in his childhood. If as an adult Wordsworth confronted mortality head on, as a child he resisted the notion of death, not only as all children naturally resist the notion, which Wordsworth illustrates by his reference to *We Are Seven*, but with a separate spiritual force that would mature into a concept of immortality:

> it was not so much from [the source] of animal vivacity that my difficulty came as from a sense of the indomitableness of the spirit within me. I used to brood over the stories of Enoch and Elijah & almost to persuade myself that whatever might become of others I should be translated in something of the same way to heaven.[34]

There are two telling phrases here: 'the indomitableness of the spirit within me' (another implicit distinction of self from soul) and 'whatever might become of others'. His sense of immortality comes not from 'animal vivacity', but from the indomitability of the spirit, a carefully made distinction, also evident in Tintern Abbey, when he is laid asleep in body and becomes a living soul. That spirit will survive and he will somehow or other be translated, like Enoch and Elijah (perhaps in the manner imagined by Sir John Davies, turning 'bodies to spirit by sublimation strange') to that heaven which is our home. In his brother's *Memoirs*, Wordsworth is recorded as saying that in the *Ode* he was not making generalizations about the moral being of children, but only recording 'my own feelings at the time – my absolute spirituality, my "all-soulness", if I may so speak' (*P2V* 429) That 'all-soulness' resolves the reality of the physical world into thought, or as he later put it, 'I was sure of my own mind; everything else fell away, and vanished into thought' (*P2V* 430).

He cannot see this indomitability, this 'all-soulness', in others; and the implication is that their existence, like that of Margaret, will end in the grave, becoming 'nothing but a name'. This distinction informs

---

[34] *FN*. Cf. *F* I 337. In his funeral sermon for John Smith (in *Select Discourses*), Simon Patrick makes an extended comparison between Smith and Elijah.

his elegies, as he imagines a state for himself he tacitly admits he cannot imagine for others. Paradoxically, though, one of the two 'vivid' recollections Wordsworth required of a reader to understand the *Ode* was that individual indisposition 'to bend to the law of death' (*MY* II 189). That is, in some way Wordsworth expected everyone to have this divided view of death – as applying to others but not to themselves. In 1810, in *The Friend*, he had offered a fuller description of what he means by that indisposition: not a denial of mortality, but 'an intimation or assurance within us, that some part of our nature is imperishable ... If we look back upon the days of childhood, we shall find that the time is not in remembrance when, with respect to our own individual Being, the mind was without this assurance' (*F* II 337). Neither that vague phrase, 'some part of our nature', nor Wordsworth's reliance on childhood as providing 'an intimation or assurance' of our immortality are, in themselves, very reassuring. Wisely ignoring Coleridge's scornful rhetoric, Wordsworth declared childhood recollections his *sine qua non*, the base upon which he stands not only the *Ode*, but his conception of the greatness of our humanity.[35] The phrase 'not in remembrance' is particularly significant, given the struggle Wordsworth has in finding adequate words to look behind his early memories; for it indicates that the feeling of imperishability, which fades into a continuity with the time before memory can exist, is connected to a quality which, for him and Coleridge, is itself the mark of our humanity – 'the faculty of reason which exists in Man alone', that faculty to which I think 'some part of our nature' is referring:

> if we had no direct external testimony that the minds of very young Children meditate feelingly upon Death and Immortality, these enquiries, which we all know they are perpetually making concerning the *whence*, do necessarily include correspondent habits of interrogation concerning the *whither*.[36] Origins and tendency are notions inseparably co-relative. Never did a child stand by the side of a running stream, ['sport upon the shore'?] pondering within himself what power was the feeder of the perpetual current, from what never-wearied sources the body of water was supplied, but he

---

[35.] See *1805* XII 328-31.

[36.] A personal recollection. In a fragment printed in the Norton Prelude, speaking of Nature's mysteries, Wordsworth writes of 'the river that flows on / Perpetually, (whence comes it? whither tends? – / Gone and never gone)'. ('We live by admiration', ll. 42-44, p. 501).

must have been inevitably propelled to follow this question by another: 'Towards what abyss is it in progress? what receptacle can contain the mighty influx?' And ... though the word might be Sea or Ocean ... the *spirit* of the answer must have been *as* inevitably, a receptacle without bounds or dimensions; – nothing less than infinity. We may, then, be justified in asserting, that the sense of immortality, if not co-existent and twin birth with Reason, is among the earliest of its Offspring.[37]

The connection between the letter or image, and the spirit or idea, so succinctly made here, informs our reading of those images in the Ode. In Wordsworth's analogy, 'the perpetual current' is something like the soul, or the power of Reason, and the watching child the individual self; the recognition or acknowledgement of that power is distinct from the observing self, and the implicit suggestion is that the power survives the self – which is consistent with what he says in 'Laodamia'.[38] But to observe is also to experience that power, for in the Ode, it is the adult's separation, 'though inland far we be', that indicates loss, and the ability 'in a moment [to] travel thither', that enables a recovery of power. This sense of observing in oneself what is not self is epitomized in Book II of *The Prelude*: 'I seem / Two consciousnesses – conscious of myself / And of some other Being' (*1805* II 31-33). A comparable distinction can be seen in Wordsworth's summary of the course of *The Prelude*, which begins 'we have traced the stream / From darkness, and the very place of birth / In its blind cavern, whence is faintly heard / The sound of waters' and concludes with 'from its progress we have drawn / The feeling of life endless, the one thought / By which we live, infinity and God' (*1805* XIII 172-84.) The detachment is evident – what is happening in the individual is not a creation but a discovery of power, and yet that discovery or recognition enables in the self the 'feeling of life endless', the idea of infinity, which is co-ordinate with the idea of immortality.[39] Contemplating his own death ten years before he died,

---

[37] *F* II 337-38. The title of Sir John's poem quoted above is 'The Soul compared to a River'. Throughout his poetry, Sir John considers 'Reason' a spiritual power, and distinguishes it from 'reason' as a rational power.

[38] See also *Letters, Conversations and Recollections of S.T. Coleridge*, ed. Thomas Allsop (London, 1864), p. 74: 'Philosophy ... began with Pythagoras. He saw that the mind ... was itself a fact, that there was something in the mind not individual; this was the pure reason, *something in which we are, not which is in us*'.

[39] Cf. 'But *eternity*, as distinguished from immortality, seems to have commanded his absolute belief.' Melvin Reader, *Wordsworth: A Philosophical Approach* (Oxford, 1967), p. 173.

Wordsworth remained true to his imagery: 'I am standing on the brink of that vast ocean I must sail so soon; I must speedily lose sight of the shore; and I could not once have conceived how little I now am troubled by the thought of how long or short a time they who remain on that shore may have sight of me.'[40] Like Eliot, he saw mortal life as a 'temporal reversion'.

Wordsworth was defensive about his use of the idea of the pre-existence of the soul, but the sense of its mysterious origins is part of his experience, as he tells us early in *The Prelude*: 'Hard task to analyse a soul, in which / Not only general habits and desires / But each most obvious and particular thought – / Not in a mystical and idle sense, / But in the words of reason deeply weighed – / Hath no beginning' (*1805* II 232-37). Individuals recognize birth as the origin of self, but Wordsworth identifies a power which precedes and succeeds the life of the individual, the power which is 'Reason'. According to Coleridge, Reason has its source and origins in God – the fire or *nous* of our humanity – the ground of his magnificent essay on Aeschylus.[41] Logically preceding sense experience, and therefore preceding memory, the close connection between reason, infinity and immortality is part of the constitution of Wordsworth's mind, appearing at critical moments in his poetry, as in his experience in the Alps – 'That awful Power', the imagination, 'reason in her most exalted mood', rising 'from the mind's abyss', and on Snowdon – 'a blue chasm ... / Through which the homeless voice of waters rose / That dark deep thoroughfare' which is 'the imagination of the whole' (*1850* VI 594; *1805* XIII 56-64). Reason, not having its source in us, yet integral to our humanity, is perceived as flowing through us from abyss to abyss, from the unknowable to the infinite, as if we were a point in the landscape through which the river passes, the 'strong brown god' which is part of us and yet more than us, its source and destination invisible. The 'whence' and the 'whither' are thus tied together. The connection between origin and tendency enables Wordsworth to presume that his childhood experience, his past, speaks for his future. Helen Vendler puts it aptly when she says, 'the faith that *looks through death* could only occur in a poem that

---

[40] *Memoirs* II 352. See too 'The Longest Day', his stern but touching poem to Dora: 'Now, even now, ere wrapped in slumber, / Fix thine eyes upon the sea / That absorbs time, space, and number; / Look thou to Eternity!'

[41] See Coleridge's: 'Reason is from God, and God *is* reason, *mens ipsissima*' (SWF II 1281).

had already looked back through birth'.⁴² John Smith has a beautiful passage on the relationship of mortality, the soul and eternity, which is in effect an explication of Wordsworth's thinking, and speaks of the soul flying:

> upwards from one heaven to another, till it be beyond all orbe of Finite Being, swallowed up in the boundless Abyss of Divinity ... Those dismall apprehensions which pinion the Souls of men to mortality, churlishly check and starve that noble life thereof ... when once the Soul hath shaken off these, when it is once able to look through a grave, and see beyond death, it finds a vast Immensity of Being opening it self more and more before it ... when it can rest and bear up itself upon an Immaterial centre of Immortality within.⁴³

If John Smith's implicit metaphor is a flight to the empyrean, Wordsworth's, here, is that of a river flowing to a limitless ocean;⁴⁴ given that difference, there is a remarkable similarity of idea, in that the soul is shaking off sense, by 'sensible impressions not enthralled' (*1805* XIII 103), is looking through a grave, or death, seeking the boundless 'Abyss of Divinity', in which there is 'an Immensity of Being' or 'endless occupation' (*1850* XIV 119); and those to whom this power is disclosed 'are caught / By its inevitable mastery, / Like angels stopped upon the wing by sound / Of harmony from Heaven's remotest spheres' (*1850* XIV 98-99). In both men, this power originates from 'an Immaterial centre of Immortality within'. In sum, Wordsworth's idea of immortality is not an external condition, but a consciousness of power, a consciousness which is elusive, enabling him only to 'see by glimpses' as he grows older (*1850* XII 281). Such ideas and feelings of immortality are the premises of the *Ode*, and its intelligibility depends upon readers both suspending their rejection of them and understanding how Wordsworth used the words 'soul', 'infinity' and 'immortality'.

---

⁴². 'Lionel Trilling and the *Immortality Ode*', *Salmagundi*, Vol. 41 (1978), p. 79.
⁴³. John Smith, *Select Discourses*, 124-25. In the Ode Wordsworth also uses a metaphor close to Smith's: 'that imperial palace when he came'. Helen Vendler (p. 72) thinks that 'imperial' suggests 'empyrial', an association sanctified by Wordsworth in the passage from *Home at Grasmere* that became the Prospectus to *The Excursion*: 'unalarmed' he passes 'the choir / Of shouting Angels and the empyreal thrones – '.
⁴⁴. Cf. To a Skylark: 'With a soul as strong as mountain River / Pouring out praise to the Almighty Giver', quoted by Coleridge in *BL* II 124.

In the Fenwick note Wordsworth described this inner life, his 'all-soulness', as an 'abyss of idealism', which at first appeared to undermine the sense of an outer world, and as a result he was, as a schoolboy, 'often unable to think of external things as having external existence', believing them to be not separate from him, 'but inherent in, my own immaterial nature' – indistinguishable from John Smith's 'Immaterial centre of Immortality within'.[45] However odd, this is the germ of Wordsworth's principal belief that the 'Mind of Man, / My haunt and the main region of my Song' will, 'wedded to this goodly universe', reveal Paradise as 'A simple produce of the common day' (*HG* D 793-802). When a child, or even an infant, he 'wedded' or invested the external world with that glory without conscious effort, a glory which faded as the external world began to assert its separate reality in the mind of the growing boy, a separation he had begun to realize in Tintern Abbey. His need to acknowledge its separateness came upon him looking back on his boyhood, a youth travelling daily 'farther from the East', not as a child.[46] Whatever the status of its reality, it is the 'dreamlike vividness and splendor' of the child's visible world that he regards 'as presumptive evidence of a prior state of existence' (*FN*), because those objects already seem to be invested with the 'communications with our internal Being ... anterior to all these experiences ... with which revelation coincides'. These are, presumably, the communications of Reason, coincident with revelation, which Wordsworth declared counteract 'the impression of Death' that we receive from 'the outward senses' (*F* II 338). In 1817, sensing that the hiding places of his power were largely closed, in one of his most beautiful poems, he asked, 'This glimpse of glory, why renewed?', as if 'this transcendent hour' was troubling his stoicism. He addresses his answer to 'Dread Power', three lines later personified as 'Thee', declaring, 'O, let thy grace remind me of the light, / Full early lost and fruitlessly deplored'.[47]

[45.] See Jared Curtis's comment on Wordsworth's conflation of internal and external: 'This trait, or power as Wordsworth saw it, was one of the intimations of immortality he sought to sustain when upon him, to recover when lost' (*Experiments* 77).

[46.] In *1805* II 367-71, he remembers such occasions without anxiety: 'Oft in those moments such a holy calm / Did overspread my soul that I forgot / That I had bodily eyes, and what I saw / Appeared like something in myself, a dream / A prospect in my mind'.

[47.] Ode: Composed upon an Evening of Extraordinary Splendor and Beauty, 65. Wordsworth's 'fruitlessly deplored' seems to echo Gray's 'I fruitless mourn to him that cannot hear', which, if so, is ironic as he took exception to much of that poem.

'Beauteous objects' and 'unimaginable things'

Paul Magnuson suggests that, if we translate the words of the original epigraph, 'Paulo majora canamus', as 'Let us sing a loftier song', the *Ode* is informed by lines from the 1798 *Prelude* in which, describing how Nature 'peopled first / My mind with beauteous objects', Wordsworth nevertheless declares that he will not:

> Forget what might demand a loftier song
> How oft the eternal spirit, he that has
> His life in unimaginable things
> And he who painting what he is in all
> The visible imagery of all the worlds
> Is yet apparent chiefly as the soul
> Of our first sympathies –[48]

There is very little cause to think that Reason and the eternal spirit are different entities, rather that one is the partial personification of the other, and 'first sympathies' are surely akin to both the 'first affections' and the 'primal sympathy' of the *Ode*. This passage is central to its intelligibility because it makes clear that, though nature may people the mind with beauteous objects, nonetheless there is another 'anterior' life, that life which Wordsworth can only describe here as located in 'unimaginable things'; a life which, if painting itself into 'visible imagery', and so making itself known through that imagery, nonetheless remains separate, and seeks to be acknowledged in a loftier song – possibly the song of 'Reason in her most exalted mood'. The 'unimagineable things' of the life of Reason may be comparable to those ideas, or informing powers, that are the educt of Coleridge's primary imagination. That life is a 'Presence which is not to be put by', deeper than all knowledge derived from sense, and partially disclosed by 'those obstinate questionings / Of sense and outward things'; a life which can call the grave 'A place of thought' because what Wordsworth is trying to describe has no need of 'sense or sight / Of day or the warm light'; a life 'not from terror free', the awful power of the numinous making its presence felt through 'unknown modes of being', a life peopled by huge and mighty forms that do not live like living men; a life of 'high instincts' inspiring guilt and fear in our mortal sense-burdened nature, a life which the adult experiences only through 'shadowy recollections', but which the child knows immediately, 'Haunted for ever by the eternal mind'; a life so puzzling that Wordsworth

---

[48.] Magnuson, *Coleridge and Wordsworth: A Lyrical Dialogue*, pp. 280-81, who quotes from *1798-9*, MS JJ 122-29.

is constantly battling to find ways of expressing it throughout the *Ode*, *The Prelude* and *The Excursion*. As we will see, Traherne also struggles to articulate a comparable kind of experience.

And it is a life, not just a memory. The inexactitudes, particularly of stanza IX, by which he recalls this life are a problem to us, as they were to Wordsworth, but here, and throughout his poetry, he refuses to replace visionary confusion with fraudulent precision:

> I deem not profitless those fleeting moods
> Of shadowy exultation: not for this,
> That they are kindred to our purer mind
> And intellectual life; but that the soul –
> Remembering how she felt, but what she felt
> Remembering not – retains an obscure sense
> Of possible sublimity, to which
> With growing faculties she doth aspire,
> With faculties still growing ...   (*1805* II 331-39)[49]

The fleeting moods of shadowy exultation, 'kindred to our purer mind / And intellectual life' – again, surely akin to Reason – visited Wordsworth less and less, the recollections diminished, and increasingly he remembers 'how', but not 'what' he felt – itself a careful distinction. The final declaration in this passage also helps render the *Ode* intelligible – the memory of that past life guides aspiration, an aspiration to be realized through the still-growing, if undefined, faculties. Wordsworth here acknowledges that the possible sublimity is to be achieved not by a return, but by the growth of faculties undeveloped in the visionary child. The *Ode* is not an elegy and, though much is lamented, there is a looking forward, a determination to discover new powers.[50] The lost celestial light of childhood is to be replaced by another light generated by the philosophic mind, that 'auxiliar light' which 'on the setting sun / Bestowed new splendour' (*1805* II 387-89).

[49.] Note the construction: 'not for this' followed by 'but that the soul', similar to the Ode's, 'Not for these' followed by the repeated 'But for those'.

[50.] See Geoffrey Hartman, *Wordsworth's Poetry 1787-1814* (New Haven, CT, 1971): 'His questionings, more explicit in the Intimations Ode and *The Prelude*, are as to whether the "marvellous Boy" in him can survive being changed into the "philosophic mind", whether poetry must die with maturation' (p. 203). However, Harold Bloom, *The Visionary Company* (London, 1962), seems to concede that the Ode is an elegy in saying, 'Wordsworth raises his "song of thanks" for the infant's doomed resistance to mortality' (p. 171).

Chapter 6

Recollections

Wordsworth's Originality?

Thus Wordsworth looked forward, but what he looked forward to he validated by looking back, or in his words, 'I look into past times as prophets look / Into futurity'.[1] This chapter takes a look at the quality of consciousness informing the *Ode*, principally derived from distinct experiences during childhood, which are continuous with Wordsworth's idea of immortality, and necessary to the process of recovery. One peculiar feature of this consciousness is that it appears unprecedented. Henry Vaughan's 'The Retreate' is comparable, and a link to the seventeenth century, but the association more or less stops there. In 1922, L.R. Merrill drew out most of such links as remained, and it is clear that Wordsworth drew more from his well-thumbed copy of Vaughan's poems than simply the idea of the child who 'saw heaven o'er his head, and knew from whence / He came'.[2] But none of the *Ode*'s early readers seemed able to place it as arising *from* any tradition, except a loose Platonism or Neoplatonism, which tells us little more than does Wordsworth himself, that he was aware of the idea of the soul's pre-existence. This apparent lack of predecessors is inherent in Keats's remark when he distinguished the nature of his genius from that of 'the wordsworthian or egotistical sublime; which is a thing per se and stands alone'.[3] This is not necessarily a comment on that trait he disliked in Wordsworth, but an acknowledgement of difference,

---

[1] DCMS 44.84, quoted from *Experiments* 42. The similar 'Mayst thou a store of thought lay by / For present time and long futurity' of The Barberry Tree and 'Such stores as silent thought can bring' of Simon Lee can be compared to his finding in the past a store of images – the 'ready wealth' of The Tables Turned, 'What wealth the show to me had brought' of 'I Wandered Lonely as a Cloud' and the 'life and food / For future years' of Tintern Abbey.
[2] L.R. Merrill, 'Vaughan's Influence upon Wordsworth's Poetry', *Modern Language Notes*, Vol. 37, no. 2 (February 1922), pp. 91-96. M.H. Abrams, *Natural Supernaturalism* (Oxford, 1971), p. 383, notes further parallels in seventeenth-century sources.
[3] 27 Oct 1818, to Richard Woodhouse.

comparable to Coleridge's distinction of Shakespeare's genius from that of Milton. Keats's perception has allowed those who are not sympathetic to Wordsworth's type of consciousness to use the phrase 'the egotistical sublime' as a form of dismissal, because, supposing it unique, they can safely do so without fear of dismissing anything else. Even those who are sympathetic to what they find in the *Ode*, and whom one might expect to be aware of any tradition from which it emerged, such as Gerard Manley Hopkins, still stress the originality of Wordsworth's insight, of that particular quality which seems almost to belong to him alone. However, apart from Vaughan, Wordsworth has at least one other substantial predecessor, Thomas Traherne, who was unafraid to claim the strange thought 'that an infant should be heir of the whole World', and that 'all Things seem'd to end in Me alone'.

Although none of his poetry and prose, except a couple of polemical works, were published until the twentieth century, and thus there is no question of direct influence, Traherne's intellectual and spiritual impetus is close to that of Wordsworth, and based on comparable forms of experience. The structure of this chapter will follow a course common to both: the association of childhood with glimpses of what they variously call eternity, Paradise or infinity – this last a word used judiciously by Wordsworth, but splattered through Traherne's works (over 500 times in the *Centuries* alone), usually meaning 'uncountable', but often in the sense intended by Wordsworth; this is followed by a recognition that the adult has suffered some kind of apostasy, or fall – regarded by both poets as the consequence of contamination by the demands of a social life; then the search for a method of recovery that requires retirement and a return to nature; and there, safely ensconced, the development of that faculty they both call reason, which looks forward to a recovery of the original vision, but also to the belief that love, or Love, is the pervading force of the universe.[4]

'Thou Child of Joy'[5]

The *Ode* centres around the vision Wordsworth ascribes to the young child: 'Heaven lies about us in our infancy' is the fulcrum of the poem. And where Wordsworth begins, Traherne begins, not only in the

---

[4.] For a thorough consideration of Traherne's ideas of infinity, see Rosalie L. Colie, 'Thomas Traherne and the Infinite: The Ethical Compromise', *Huntington Library Quarterly*, Vol. 21, no. 1 (November 1957), pp. 69-82.

[5.] Cf. 'I must become a child again'; Traherne, Innocence.

sense that it is his founding vision, but also because poems describing his childhood experiences are placed at the beginning of the carefully structured Dobell manuscript. The second poem in the volume is titled 'Wonder' and opens, reminiscent of Wordsworth's 'trailing clouds of glory':

> How like an Angel came I down!
> How bright are all things here!
> When first among his Works I did appear
> O how their GLORY did me crown?
> The World resembled his *Eternitie*,
> In which my Soul did Walk;
> And evry Thing that I did see,
> Did with me talk.   (*TPW* 5)

The idea of pre-existence hovers at the edge of Traherne's vision, more a question posed than a question answered. In the very first poem, Salutation, he asks of 'These rosie Cheeks wherewith my Life begins' (his passport 'Into this Eden so divine and fair') 'Behind / What Curtain were ye from me hid, so long! / Where was? in what Abyss, my speaking Tongue?' That certainly supposes that a 'me' existed prior to his gaining rosy cheeks. On the other hand, if Wordsworth has to assure his readers that 'we come / From God, who is our home', Traherne's single word 'down' is a confident assumption not requiring explanation; and confidence is a feature of all Traherne's insights: he presents us with few uncertainties, hesitations or unsettled intimations. Of course, like Traherne, Wordsworth remembered 'how bright' were 'all things here', with 'every common sight / ... Apparelled in celestial light, / The glory and the freshness of a dream'. The childhood vision is recalled by both poets as a 'glory': 'there hath past away a glory from the earth' and 'O how their GLORY did me crown' – that is, the glory of 'all things here' and 'every common sight'.[6] Wordsworth, part way through what proves to be the failed recovery of the first four stanzas, declares 'My head hath its coronal'. Both poets are or were crowned with glory; and possibly the word had particular significance for Wordsworth because a coronal, as well as being a nimbus or aureole, is also a nuptial crown, which would speak of his primary intention, of being wedded or rewedded to nature: 'Think not of any severing of our loves'.

[6.] Wordsworth uses 'glory' or 'glorious' eight times in the *Ode*. It is a word easily passed over in our reading.

'Thou best Philosopher'

In the third *Century*, Traherne remembers and puzzles over his curious state of mind:

> I was entertained like an Angel with the works of God in their splendour and glory, I saw all in the peace of Eden ... All Time was Eternity, and a perpetual Sabbath. Is it not strange, that an infant should be heir of the whole World, and see those mysteries which the books of the learned never unfold? (*Centuries* III 2)

Strange indeed, and too strange for some. Coleridge, taking Wordsworth to task, considered it more or less impossible that the child has a kind of wisdom lost to the adult.[7] He is particularly, perhaps professionally, irritated to find the child addressed in phrases Traherne would understand, such as 'Thou best philosopher', 'Mighty Prophet!', 'seer blest!' The passage from the *Biographia* (*BL* II 138-39) is a powerful piece of rhetoric, almost two pages of sustained derision, but Coleridge has momentarily forgotten his own principle, that a man is right in what he asserts, wrong in what he denies.[8] Wordsworth was very sensitive to Coleridge's criticism, and omitted the passage about the grave as a lonely bed, which was Coleridge's next target; but he stood by the divine visions of the child, and the language with which he is described, because he had experienced what Coleridge had not, and was confident enough not to doubt his own memories. As some manuscript lines declare, even though in the published poem he chose to speak of the child in the third person, this was a personal experience, as we know from other sources. He considered the title given to the child very carefully:

> I speak not in delusion – but from a feeling
> Of my past self, an insight, revealing
> And trusting to the same
> Child as Thou art I give thee highest name
> Thou best Philosopher   (*P2V* 397)

[7.] And yet Coleridge now and then says things that ought to make him sympathetic to Wordsworth's idea: 'N.b. the seeming Identity of Body and Mind in Infants, and thence the loveliness of the former – the commencing separation in Boyhood – the *struggle* of equilibrium in youth...' (*CN* III 4398).

[8.] See *CL* IV 567: 'But I always admired the following Aphorism of Leibnitz – J'ai trouvé, que la plupart des Sectes ont raison dans une bonne partie de ce qu'elles avancent, mais non pas tant en ce qu'elles nient.'

Soon after finishing the *Ode*, Wordsworth reasserted the centrality of childhood – 'Our childhood sits, / Our simple childhood, sits upon a throne / That hath more power than all the elements' – perhaps a throne in 'that imperial palace'.[9]

Coleridge's remarks, however mistaken, open the door to doubts about the validity of this sort of childhood vision, and briefly I would like to consider two other views.[10] Jerome McGann rejects Wordsworth's vision as one member of the 'body of illusions' that he believes constitutes Romantic ideology;[11] a tragic illusion, in which Wordsworth turns away from the real world of discharged soldiers, politically created poverty and the hopes accompanying the French Revolution; or as Marjorie Levinson rephrases McGann's thought, one of the chief illusions of the Romantic ideology is 'the triumph of the inner life over the outer world'.[12] For better or for worse, all agree: Wordsworth retires.[13] Haunted by 'thoughts of more deep seclusion' he sought a 'sublime retirement' (*HG* B 723), which is part of the process by which Traherne advocated the recovery of his lost vision. It is this that McGann cannot tolerate: 'Between 1793 and 1798 [he] lost the world merely to gain his immortal soul' (p. 88). Indeed, but in valuing 'world' above 'soul' McGann has inverted the spirit in which Wordsworth wrote – 'The world is too much with us' – asserting his ideology, or quality of consciousness, in preference to Wordsworth's, thus reading an immortal sundial by material moonshine.

'the mighty waters'

However, a thinker who does not reject childhood experience of this kind, even though alien to him, seems to provide a much more worrying critique of the basis of Traherne's and Wordsworth's poetry. The first chapter of Freud's *Civilization and its Discontents* is devoted to a

---

[9] *1805* V 531-33. For the dating of this passage see footnote in the Norton *Prelude*.

[10] Matthew Arnold held a view not dissimilar to Coleridge's, quoting Thucydides on the early achievements of the Greek race – 'It is impossible to speak with certainty of what is so remote; but from all that we can really investigate, I should say that they were no very great things' (*Selected Poems of William Wordsworth*, ed. H.R. Steeves, (NY, 1922), p. 16.

[11] *The Romantic Ideology* (Chicago, 1983), p. 12.

[12] *Wordsworth's Great Period Poems* (Cambridge, 1986), p. 82.

[13] Cf. 'the recovery from the crisis of despair after his commitment to the French Revolution comprises the insight that his destiny is not one of engagement with what is blazoned "with pompous names / Of power and action" in "the stir / And tumult of the world," but one of withdrawal from the world of action so that he may meditate in solitude: his role in life requires not involvement, but detachment.' (Abrams in *Norton Prelude* 590, and quoting from *1805* XII 44-76, 112-16; cf. *HG* 664-752).

discussion of what he calls the 'oceanic feeling', which Romain Rolland, a friend who experienced what Freud did not, 'would like to call a sensation of "eternity", a feeling of something limitless, unbounded'. Freud questions whether this experience is being correctly interpreted, as it fits so badly, he feels, 'with the fabric of our psychology'.[14] Romain Rolland is not a figure we remember now, but he won the Nobel Prize for Literature in 1915; differ though they did, Freud had a deep-seated respect for Rolland and their friendship was not disturbed by their differences.

What is particularly telling in Freud's reading is that, though his starting point is Rolland's immediate sense of eternity, he goes back to early childhood in order to explain it. Rolland himself does *not* suggest that it had anything to do with childhood. In Freud's reading, the oceanic feeling belongs to the time before the ego has distinguished itself from the world, before the reality principle has taken hold. Thus, for Freud, 'Our present ego-feeling is ... only a shrunken residue of a much more inclusive – indeed, an all-embracing – feeling'. He certainly doesn't deny the validity of that kind of consciousness, but thinks that it is something the adult ought to have grown out of. Unlike Coleridge, McGann and Levinson, he leaves the question open. He does not present it as pathological or illusory, but merely as a reversion to the primitive. These poets also saw their vision as requiring a reversion, and expressed their desire to rediscover that original condition in such poems as The Retreate and The Return. The question is whether it is a reversion to an illusion, or a reversion to a truth.

In Dumnesse, Traherne remembers a time before 'the accursed Breath' of language had poured into him society's 'infected Mind' – or, in the comparable words of D.H. Lawrence, 'I despised myself and the voices of my accursed human education' ('Snake'). What Traherne then describes seems an exact account of the oceanic feeling:

> Then did I dwell within a World of Light
> Retir'd and separat from all mens Sight, ...
> There I saw all the World enjoy'd by One;
> There all Things seem'd to end in Me alone.

[14.] *Civilization and its Discontents* (London, 2002), p. 253. Freud's, probably the finest of reductionist accounts of such experience, though sympathetic, still challenges what Vaughan, Traherne and Wordsworth had to say.

It would be easy to imagine Freud, to prove his point, latching onto that last line, which asserts the perfect union of the self and the objective world in the infant or child, what Wordsworth perhaps meant by 'the primal sympathy'. This is an idea, originating in his childhood, that can be seen in all parts of Traherne's work, and is often focussed through God's original placing of Adam alone in Eden, in which the world is seen as a gift to just one man. Thus he writes, 'Certainly Adam in Paradise had not more sweet and curious apprehensions of the world, than I when I was a child' (*Centuries* III 1).[15] Wordsworth, writing of a briefly recovered vision, is even more ecstatic: 'What Being ... since the birth of Man / Had ever more abundant cause to speak / Thanks'. This marks the singularity of his vision, but trumping Traherne, his gift is greater than the original Paradise:

> The boon is absolute; surpassing grace
> To me hath been vouchsafed; among the bowers
> Of blissful Eden this was neither given
> Nor could be given – possession of the good
> Which had been sighed for, ancient thought fulfilled,
> And dear Imaginations realized
> Up to their highest measure, yea and more.
> (*HG* B 122-28)

It is an extraordinary, extravagant realization – highest, yet higher still.[16] By the time he came to write the first four stanzas of the *Ode*, Wordsworth had lost the wonderful confidence with which he wrote *Home at Grasmere*. Yet the following passage, although the context is one of recovery, illustrates how closely Traherne's memory of what he had lost matches what Wordsworth had felt briefly his:

> This solitude is mine; the distant thought
> Is fetched out of the heaven in which it was.
> The unappropriated bliss hath found
> An owner, and that owner I am he.

[15.] Simon Jarvis, *Wordsworth's Philosophic Song* (Cambridge, 2006), p. 204, thinks that Wordsworth's insight into the nature of Paradise is 'singular'. As well as Vaughan and Traherne, he seems to have forgotten Marvell's The Garden: 'Two paradises 'twere in one / To live in paradise alone.'

[16.] And comparable some closing lines in *HG*, that he must 'breathe in worlds / To which the heaven of heavens is but a veil' (*HG* D 782-83).

> The Lord of this enjoyment is on Earth
> And in my breast. (*HG* B 79-96)

Prior to his appearance in Grasmere, 'With paradise before me', this bliss was 'unappropriated', that is, belonged to no one. He is now the owner, the sole owner, the 'Lord of his enjoyment', or as he put it in a lost fragment, speaking to himself, 'Thou, thou art king, and sole proprietor' (*P2V* 12). It is a solitude, not disrupted but enhanced by Dorothy's presence, celebrated in some of the most beautiful lines he ever wrote – for her or anyone: 'Her voice was like a hidden Bird that sang; / The thought of her was like a flash of light / Or an unseen companionship, a breath / Or fragrance independent of the wind'.[17] Finally, just as immortality is a power, so this is an internal condition – 'in my breast'.

As an internal power, paradoxically, this proprietorship can be a universal experience, not requiring any kind of material ownership – an example, in passing, of Coleridge's distinction between an absolute and a commanding genius, the latter requiring some visible power or possession.[18] At the very beginning of the *Centuries*, explaining his purpose, Traherne asks Susanna Hopton, for whom they were written, 'Is it not a great thing that you should be Heir of the World? It is my design therefore in such a plain manner to unfold it that my friendship may appear in making you possessor of the whole world' (*Centuries* I 3). A few entries later he expands this to explain the uniqueness of every individual in God's creation:

> He maketh every one the end of the World: and the supernumerary persons being enrichers of his inheritance. Adam and the World are both mine. ... So that I alone am the end of the World: Angels and men being all mine. ... So that Seneca philosophized rightly when he said ... God gave me alone to all the World, and all the World to me alone. (*Centuries* I 13)[19]

This same spirit – in which unique possession is a gift at first utterly hidden in the individual – is nonetheless a gift that Wordsworth believes is for all, and that he hopes he has the power to deliver:

[17.] *HG* B 110-13. In MS D, the lines are exactly the same, but '*unseen*' is thus emphasized for no reason I can discern.

[18.] Cf. *LS* 66.

[19.] Cf. what Hazlitt says of Wordsworth in relation to *The Excursion*: 'It is as if there were nothing but himself and the universe'. *The Complete Works of William Hazlitt* (London, 1930), Vol. XIX, p. 11; cited from *Woof* 371.

> Possessions have I, wholly, solely mine,
> Something within, which yet is shared by none –
> Not even the nearest to me and most dear –
> Something which power and effort would impart.
> I would impart it; I would spread it wide,
> Immortal in the world which is to come.
> (HG B 897-902)

It is a nice question whether it is the 'something within' himself that he wants to immortalize in the minds of his readers, or whether that power, 'spread wide', is the gateway to immortality, the entrance to 'the world which is to come'. Wordsworth wasn't averse to fame, once wishing 'to fill / The heroic trumpet with the muse's breath!' (*HG* B 954-55), and later carefully managing his poetic reputation.[20] But here his principal intention is to 'give utterance in numerous verse' to the 'sweet passions traversing my Soul', singing of 'hope – / Hope for this earth and hope beyond the grave' and of 'joy in widest commonalty spread' (*HG* B 961-69).

'Disowned by memory'

Traherne, like Freud, believed that the origin of the sense of unity belonged to the pre-verbal period of childhood – in Dumnesse he writes, 'I then my Blisse did, when my Silence, break'. Wordsworth, if not so precise, looks back to a time he cannot distinctly remember, and to describe which he has no adequate words:

> I began
> My story early, feeling, as I fear,
> The weakness of a human love for days
> Disowned by memory –   (*1805* I 640-43)

These are 'shadowy recollections', but they are 'the fountain light of all our day', 'the master-light of all our seeing', as they were for Traherne. They look through 'Our noisy years' to 'moments in the being / Of the eternal Silence', that is from a place where language, impossible except in time, obscures rather than clarifies the 'truths that wake, / To perish never', truths that spring from and return to an eternal, immortal condition outside time, and without words.

---

[20] See Peter J. Manning, 'Wordsworth Reshapes Himself and is Reshaped', *TWC*, Vol. 51, no. 1 (Winter 2020), pp. 35-53.

It is very difficult to understand how one can remember a world not invested in language, or conceive of a bliss dependent on silence – or even wanting to realize or return to such a world. How does that kind of experience come into our consciousness without language, how can days disowned by memory be known or loved? The whole of their vision depends upon these kinds of paradoxical experience. Several times in Book I of *The Prelude* Wordsworth, as if struggling to explain himself, insists on the significance of 'obscure feelings representative / Of joys that were forgotten' (*1805* I 634-35) of 'those first-born affinities that fit / Our new existence to existing things, / And in our dawn of being, constitute / The bond of union betwixt life and joy' (*1805* I 582-85), or to 'a dim and undetermined sense / Of unknown modes of being' (*1805* I 419-20). To criticize, with Lionel Trilling and others, the vagueness of phrases such as 'be they what they may' is surely not to recognize the difficulty Wordsworth and Traherne both have in describing either the variety of memories from 'our dawn of being' or experiences such as the spots of time, puzzling in their depth, variety and inarticulacy.

In sum, there is no substantial difference between Freud's understanding and the insights that belong to Traherne and Wordsworth. Freud does not describe or classify the oceanic feeling as pathological or illusory, as do Coleridge, McGann and Levinson, but developmental or phylogenetic. It is that condition in which a child's consciousness makes no distinction between itself and the world, or as Shelley put it:

> Let us recollect our sensations as children. What a distinct and intense apprehension had we of the world and of ourselves ... We less habitually distinguished all that we saw and felt from ourselves ... There are some persons who in this respect are always children ... [who] feel as if their nature were dissolved into the surrounding universe, or as if the surrounding universe were dissolved into their being.[21]

Freud described this as a 'limitless narcissism', but what he saw as a distinction necessary to establish a stable relationship between the ego and the external world, Wordsworth and Traherne, if not Shelley, saw as a fall, tragic but remediable.[22] Wordsworth defended the notion of

---

[21.] *Shelley's Poetry and Prose* (New York, 1977), p. 477. My thanks to Timothy Michael, of Lincoln College, Oxford, for bringing this passage to my attention.

[22.] Not a view shared by Peter Manning, who believes that 'Wordsworth ... survives to speak the elegy over his own youthful narcissism': 'Wordsworth's Intimations Ode and its Epigraphs', p. 532.

the soul's pre-existence at some length, not as a theologian reacting to accusations of heterodox opinions, but as a poet trying to explain his sense of remembered perfection. Of pre-existence he says, though 'not advanced in revelation, there is nothing there to contradict it, and the fall of Man presents an analogy in its favor' (*FN*).[23] That may be 'very wild philosophy', but it offered Wordsworth an entirely satisfactory explanation of his experience, of the quality of his consciousness.[24] Freud used a different idea to explain the same experience: you pays your money and you takes your choice.

The Apostacy

Traherne, who is always more forthright, if less subtle, than Wordsworth, describes exactly how he thinks this process happens. In a poem entitled The Apostacy, the very business of childhood, life among his peers, expunges 'the Shining Skies':

> ... and when I once with blemisht Eys
> Began their Pence and Toys to view,
> Drown'd in their Customs, I became
> A Stranger to the Shining Skies,
>   Lost as a dying Flame;
> And Hobby-horses brought to prize.   (*TPW* 121)

At the beginning of the Third Century he tells Susanna Hopton that 'The first Light which shined in me in my Infancy ... was totally eclipsed ... If you ask me how it was eclipsed? Truly by the customs and manners of men, which like contrary winds blew it out' (*Centuries* III 7). In the *Ode*, Wordsworth reflects his loss indirectly, or vicariously, by describing the key stages of the growing up of a small child. As an inmate here, of this world, his 'six years Darling of a pigmy size', is looked after by parents who are blind to his 'soul's immensity', and the whole vocation of his childhood becomes the endless imitation of

---

[23.] He also added that it 'is far too shadowy a notion ('shadowy recollections'?) to be recommended to faith as more than an element in our instincts of immortality'. Such words as 'instincts' and 'intimations' indicate Wordsworth's caution.

[24.] 'Now that the thinking part of Man, i.e. the Soul, existed previously to it's appearance in it's present body, may be very wild philosophy; but it is very intelligible poetry, inasmuch as Soul is an orthodox word in all our poets; they meaning by "soul" a being inhabiting our body, & playing upon it' (*CL* I 288). Coleridge is defending a sonnet written after the birth of Hartley (*PW* I 135). Lucy Newlyn, *Coleridge, Wordsworth, and the Language of Allusion* (Oxford, 2004), p. 148, suggests that possibly a memory of some conversation with Coleridge catalysed and validated Wordsworth's use of the idea.

these people and their society, at the expense of his divine insights. The charming picture of the little actor conning part after part is nothing but a drama of distraction. Traherne finds even the company of other children corruptive:

> Thoughts are the most present things to thoughts, and of the most powerful influence. My soul was only apt and disposed to great things; but souls to souls are like apples to apples, one being rotten rots another. ... So I began among my play-fellows to prize a drum, a fine coat, a penny, a gilded book, &c., who before never dreamed of any such wealth. Goodly objects to drown all the knowledge of Heaven and Earth! (*Centuries* III 10)

As Wordsworth laments that custom will come to lie as heavy as frost on his once-visionary child – perhaps that frost withering the flowers transplanted from paradise (*The Excursion* IV 55-56) – so Traherne frequently resorts to the word 'custom' when analysing his loss: 'our misery proceedeth ten thousand times more from the outward bondage of opinion and custom than from any inward corruption or depravation of Nature: And that it is not our parents' loins, so much as our parents' lives, that enthrals and blinds us' (*Centuries* III 8) thus agreeing precisely with Wordsworth. Though both poets take on an idea of apostasy or a fall, which Wordsworth connects to the idea of pre-existence, neither think original sin the cause: our apostasy is our willingness to conform to the dictates of the respectable world – which, in Freud's terms, may be nothing but the reality principle kicking in. Therefore that fall is not an irreversible condition: restitution comes within the ambit of the will. Traherne provides a radical solution to what he sees as a radical problem:

> For we must disrobe ourselves of all false colours, and unclothe our souls of evil habits; all our thoughts must be infant-like and clear; ... Ambitions, trades, luxuries, inordinate affections, casual and accidental riches invented since the fall, would be gone and only those things appear, which did to Adam in Paradise, in the same light and in the same colours. (*Centuries* III 5)

Or as he put it in the opening lines of 'Blisse', which also appear in 'The Apostacy': 'All blisse / Consists in this: / To do as Adam did' (*TPW* 69).

This retiring from the world and returning to Paradise is grounded on Christ's injunction that we should be as little children if we wish to enter the kingdom of heaven: 'I was corrupted, and made to learn the dirty devices of this world. Which now I unlearn, and become, as it were, a little child again! That I may enter the Kingdom of God' (*Centuries* III 3).[25] Wordsworth too was very careful not to be sullied by the dirty devices of this world. Remembering his 'mountain solitudes' where he received his 'earliest visitations', he earnestly declares:

> whatever falls my better mind,
> Revolving with the accidents of life,
> May have sustained – that, howsoe'er misled,
> I never in the quest of right and wrong,
> Did tamper with myself from private aims;
> Nor was in any of my hopes the dupe
> Of selfish passions; nor did wilfully
> Yield ever to mean cares or low pursuits;
> But rather did with jealousy shrink back
> From every combination that might aid
> The tendency, too potent in itself,
> Of habit to enslave the mind – I mean
> Oppress it by the laws of vulgar sense,
> And substitute a universe of death,
> The falsest of all worlds, in place of that
> Which is divine and true.   (*1805* XIII 128 ff.)[26]

He was determined to have as little as possible to do with 'false colours ... evil habits ... Ambitions, trades, luxuries, inordinate affections, casual and accidental riches invented since the fall', unwilling to endure 'this state of meagre vassalage', to reconcile 'our stinted powers', with the throne upon which our childhood sits, unwilling, 'Uneasy and unsettled', to 'confess' or 'submit' to the fact that these powers become 'yoke-fellows / To custom' (*1805* V 542-45). For both

---

[25.] A point Abrams also makes in *Natural Supernaturalism*, p. 382. Cf. *1805* VIII 553 ff.
[26.] *1805* XIII 128 ff. The *1850* version has some significant variants, replacing, for instance 'Of habit to enslave the mind' with 'Of use and custom to bow down the soul', omitting 'the falsest of all worlds', and adding a punch to the last two lines with 'For that which moves with light and life informed, / Actual, divine, and true'. By inserting 'custom' he is probably referring to the *Ode*, where custom is the heavy frost that may gather round his heart; if it does, he is 'worse than dead' (*The Excursion* IV 50-56). Custom 'deep almost as life' might mean penetrating to the roots of, and so extinguishing, life.

Wordsworth and Traherne the fall was the consequence of leaving Eden, rather than anything that happened in that garden.

A sublime and inviolate retirement

To return to or rediscover the lost paradise, the contaminating world has to be left behind – by removing oneself from it as far as possible.[27] Traherne did retire – from the honours, riches and beauties of courtly life, from what he called 'the cream of earthly delights', which he tells us 'have pursued me as much as they have fled from other men', all of which he categorizes as 'Solomon's Vanity: their frailty and Narrowness maketh them worthless' (*Inducements* 11). Wordsworth was more ambivalent about what he would leave behind:

> Yes, the Realities of Life – so cold,
> So cowardly, so ready to betray,
> So stinted in the measure of their grace
> As we report them, doing them much wrong –
> Have been to me more bountiful than hope,
> Less timid than desire. Oh bold indeed
> They have been!

How hard he found it to give up those realities follows a few lines later:

> And did it cost so much, and did it ask
> Such length of discipline, and could it seem
> An act of courage, and the thing itself
> A conquest? Shame that this was ever so   (*HG* B 54-67)

Traherne went back to Herefordshire, becoming, at least for a time, a local parish priest in the same spirit as George Herbert. In the Third Century, he speaks of coming into the country, and 'being seated among silent trees, and meads and hills', resolving to spend all his time 'in search of happiness, and to satiate that burning thirst which Nature had enkindled in me from my youth'.

That is much like Wordsworth returning to the Grasmere he first saw as a boy. Because he had already realized his desire for seclusion when the poem opens, there is no retirement as such in the *Ode*. Rather there is a return to the childhood vision, to the 'perpetual benediction'

[27.] The heading of this section is a combination of *HG* B 725 and 970.

of past years, to those things which appeared 'to Adam in Paradise, in the same light and in the same colours'. That return begins the process of recovery. Thoughts 'of more deep seclusion' had haunted Wordsworth ever since he had begun to feel a distinction between what he was as a child and as a man, first evident in Tintern Abbey – 'that time is past'. Therefore retirement as a condition for recovering his vision was as deeply embedded in Wordsworth as it was in Traherne. By the time the first part of the *Ode* was written, it was a condition achieved, not a condition sought. *Home at Grasmere* records his wrestlings with the hopes and problems of retirement some years earlier. As a schoolboy, Wordsworth had stood on Loughrigg Terrace looking down into Grasmere, and thought

> 'What happy fortune were it here to live!
> And if I thought of dying, if a thought
> Of mortal separation could come in
> With paradise before me, here to die.'   (*HG* B 9-12)

In 1798, he and Dorothy had deliberately made their way back to this paradise – and a cold coming they'd had of it – 'Bleak season was it, turbulent and bleak, / When hitherward we journeyed, and on foot, / Through bursts of sunshine and through flying snows' (*HG* B 218-20). 'Paradise' is no casual metaphor, but an idea and a hope that pervades the poem in all its strange seriousness. His retirement is accompanied by a vivid, even occasionally bizarre, thankfulness for having overcome the temptations of the world:

> But I am safe; yes, one at least is safe;
> What once was deemed so difficult is now
> Smooth, easy, without obstacle; what once
> Did to my blindness seem a sacrifice,
> The same is now a choice of the whole heart.
>   (*HG* B 74-78)

Wordsworth had more of a struggle to give up things of this world, particularly in respect of the writing of poetry. More than once he bade 'farewell to the Warrior's deeds, farewell / All hope, which once was mine, to fill / The heroic trumpet with the muse's breath!' (*HG* B 953-55).

It was a choice of the whole heart. Nevertheless, a particular sensation makes this place of retirement distinctive. Having described Grasmere's local features, some in common with other places, he then asserts:

>   'tis here,
> Here as it found its way into my heart
> In childhood, here as it abides by day,
> By night, here only; or in chosen minds
> That take it with them hence, where'er they go.
> 'Tis (but I cannot name it), 'tis the sense
> Of majesty and beauty and repose,
> A blended holiness of earth and sky,
> Something that makes this individual Spot,
> This small abiding place of many men,
> A termination and a last retreat,
> A Centre, come from wheresoe'er you will,
> A Whole without dependence or defect,
> Made for itself and happy in itself,
> Perfect Contentment, Unity entire.   (*HG* B 154-69)

The qualities that make this paradise are both at one with what he knew as a child, and yet not easily described. Having said of 'the one sensation', 'I cannot name it', his attempted definition is replete with significant capitalization — Centre, Whole, Contentment, Unity. The overall impression is that he has found refuge from the world's peripheral and distracting activities, and here he knows the One Life, the experience of his childhood. Wordsworth went back to Grasmere in the very spirit that Traherne went back to Herefordshire.

Having long harboured 'thoughts of more deep seclusion', in *Home at Grasmere* Wordsworth decides that his task, in lines that became the Prospectus to *The Excursion*, is to sing 'Of the individual Mind that keeps her own / Inviolate retirement'. Both Wordsworth and Traherne felt that the mankind-ordered world was an apostasy from a more perfect God-given state, and a violation of the condition known to the child. How profoundly Wordsworth took on that vale as another Eden is evident in other lines from *Home at Grasmere*:

> In this majestic, self-sufficing world,
> This all in all of Nature ... In the daily walks
> Of business 'twill be harmony and grace
> For the perpetual pleasure of the sense,
> And for the Soul – I do not say too much,
> Though much be said – an image for the Soul,
> A habit of Eternity and God.   (*HG* B 204-15)

The *Ode* was written in the light of this belief, that the majestic, self-sufficing world all around him in Grasmere was, in that curious but telling phrase, 'A habit of Eternity' – for the soul, not for the body – which however would die happily in such a place. This world, 'This all in all of Nature', self-presented in its simplicity, bears the stamp of Paradise: the immediate is the eternal; or, in the words of Traherne, 'the World is a place of Eternal Joys, a Region of Heavenly light, a Paradice of Glory, and all Kingdoms every mans Possessions, that to retire to them is to enter into Heaven' (*Inducements* 27). It is a thought to which he frequently recurs:

> The world is a mirror of infinite beauty, yet no man sees it. It is a Temple of Majesty, yet no man regards it. It is a region of Light and Peace, did not men disquiet it. It is the Paradise of God. It is more to man since he is fallen than it was before. It is the place of Angels and the Gate of Heaven. (*Centuries* I 30)

All Wordsworth needed was the power to see that paradise he knew was around him, so that he could enter into it; recording first that loss of power and then its tentative recovery is the purpose, the progress and the envisioned immortality of the *Ode*. Or as Raymond Carver wrote, when he went for an early-morning walk, he was 'determined not to return / until I took in what Nature had to offer'. Distracted by other thoughts, that offering did not come easily: 'I had to will / myself to see what I was seeing / and nothing else.' (*This Morning*).

Three Final Things: Reason, Infinity and Love

It is not just a question of looking, nor even of ridding one's mind of distracting thoughts. Nature will not speak without being spoken to, and one must have a language in which to speak. The will has to do more than silence distracting thoughts.

Of his childhood, Traherne remarks, 'I knew by intuition those things which since my Apostasy, I collected again by the highest reason.' (*Centuries* III 2). Wordsworth sets himself the same task, though finding it more arduous, when he remarks of the child, 'On whom those truths do rest / Which we are toiling all our lives to find.' Traherne's turning to reason sets the tone for everything that he has to say on recovering his vision, remarking bluntly, 'To walk abroad is, not with Eys, / But Thoughts the Fields to see and prize' (*TPW* 189), because 'Thoughts are the highest things / The very offspring of the King of Kings' (*TPW* 74) – not of course the kinds of thought that disturbed Raymond Carver on his morning walk.[28] Traherne's sense of loss, grounded on the same cause and as deep as Wordsworth's, is countered by a confidence that 'highest reason' (Wordsworth's 'grand / And simple reason') is a power that can revive his childhood vision.[29]

Wordsworth believed that 'genius' – which is less elitist that it sounds, referring to a power potential in everyone and comparable to Eliot's 'All touched by a common genius' (*BN* III) – finds in Nature 'His best and purest friend – from her receives / That energy by which he seeks the truth, / Is roused, aspires, grasps, struggles, wishes, craves / From her that happy stillness of the mind / Which fits him to receive it when unsought'.[30] The list of vigorous, violent verbs indicates the levels of energy required to seek the truth. Yet 'the forms / Of Nature have a passion in themselves' (*1805* XII 289-90), and are a preparation for the reception of reason. For by Nature:

> I had been taught to reverence a Power
> That is the visible quality and shape
> And image of right reason … / /…
> Holds up before the mind, intoxicate
> With present objects and the busy dance
> Of things that pass away, a temperate shew
> Of objects that endure –   (*1850* XIII 20-32).

Those objects are not things, but the thoughts or ideas, the king of kings, what Coleridge calls the ideas of reason. Finding infinity within the bounds of the finite, Traherne describes these 'liquid, clear satisfactions' as 'the emanations of the highest reason, but not achieved till a long time afterwards. In the meantime I was sometimes, though seldom, visited and inspired with new and more vigorous desires after that bliss which Nature whispered and suggested to me' (*Centuries* III 22). Wordsworth asserts the close connection between the work of nature and the work of

---

[28] Thoughts as the offspring of the King of Kings is close to Coleridge's assertion that 'to suppose God without ideas … would destroy the very conception of God' (*OM* 223).

[29] *1805* XI 123-24. Traherne regularly uses the phrase 'highest reason', and connects it with God: e.g. 'For we naturally expect infinite things of God: and can be satisfied only with the highest reason' (*Centuries* III 63). See also *Centuries* IV 8 and 81. Cf. Coleridge: 'We name God the Supreme Reason' (*F* I 156). Wordsworth also uses the phrase when speaking of 'all the adamantine holds of truth, / By reason built, or passion (which itself / Is highest reason in a soul sublime)' (*1805* V 38-40).

[30] The paradoxes of this passage may be read through the distinction between vernal impulses and the wise passiveness of Expostulation and Reply and The Tables Turned.

reason, both towards the beginning and the end of *Home at Grasmere:* 'On Nature's invitation do I come / By Reason sanctioned' and 'That which in stealth by nature was performed / Hath Reason sanctioned.' (*HG* D 71-72; 941-42). In both poets, Reason and Nature work in comparable ways to the same end, the recovery of a lost vision: 'I remember the time when the dust of the streets were as precious as Gold to my infant eyes, and now they are more precious to the eye of reason' (*Centuries* I 25).

'In this faith all things counterfeit infinity'[31]

We are familiar with some of the instances of Wordsworth's use of 'infinity' and its cognates: the haunting lines 'Suffering is permanent, obscure and dark, / And shares the nature of infinity' from *The Borderers*; 'Our destiny, our being's heart and home, / Is with infinitude and only there' (*1850* VI 604-5); 'It appeared to me / The perfect image of a mighty mind, / Of one that feeds upon infinity' (*1805* XIII 69-70); and the Pedlar's experience in the mountains where he felt his faith:

> All things there
> Breath'd immortality, revolving life,
> And greatness still revolving; infinite.
> There littleness was not; the least of things
> Seemed infinite;   (*RC* E 216-20)

The infinite is often, but not always, linked to the idea of God. The Pedlar's insight originates in that 'high hour / Of visitation from the living God' (*RC* E 202-3); the mighty mind 'is exalted by an under-presence, / The sense of God, or whatso'er is dim / Or vast in in its own being' (*1805* XIII 71-73); infinity and God is 'the one thought / By which we live' (*1805* XIII 183-84); and of course, along with infinitude, 'we come / From God, who is our home'. God is probably not an experience for most readers – visitations are rare, he does not look into our minds (*1805* III 144) and so infinity is read in much the same spirit: something of a hyperbole neither alive nor meaningful.

Not so for Wordsworth or Traherne. Whatever it means, it means closely comparable things to both. Consider this from Traherne:

> How rich and admirable then is the Kingdom of God, where the smallest is greater than an infinite treasure! Is not this

---

[31] *CL* I 349.

> incredible? Certainly to the placits and doctrines of our schools: Till we all consider, That infinite worth shut up in the limits of a material being, is the only way to a real infinity. (*Centuries* III 20).

and this from Wordsworth:

> The commerce between Man and his Maker cannot be carried on but by a process where much is represented in little, and the infinite Being accommodates himself to a finite capacity. In all this may be perceived the affinities between religion and poetry; ... between religion – whose element is infinitude, and whose ultimate trust is the supreme of things, submitting herself to circumscription and reconciled to substitutions; and poetry; – etherial and transcendent, yet incapable to sustain her existence without sensuous incarnation. (Essay, Supplementary to the Preface 1815; *MW* 643-44)

Sensuous incarnation and a material being housing the infinite are but two ways of saying the same thing – much like Blake believing that 'To see a World in a Grain of Sand / And a Heaven in a Wild Flower' is to 'Hold Infinity in the palm of your hand' (*Auguries of Innocence* 1-3). Like Wordsworth, Traherne saw infinity as the power that both gives life to and is represented by material beings, for it 'excludeth nothing, and containeth all things, being a power that permitteth all objects to be, and is able to enjoy them' (*Centuries* II 24). Infinity as the power that permits being is precisely the conclusion that Paul Davies comes to in *The Mind of God*.[32]

Henry Crabb Robinson recorded what, without a context, seems one of Wordsworth's strangest remarks when he spoke of 'that infinity without which there is no poetry'. *No* poetry? What he meant makes some sense in the light of the Supplementary Essay, but he is clearer still in the letter he wrote to Catherine Clarkson about the *Ode*. He is taking Miss Patty Smith to task both for her tin ear and attributing to the 'Author of the Excursion' a '*Spinosistic*' conflation of God and Nature, which he refutes. She is also 'blind to the innumerable analogies and types of infinity ... which I have transfused into that Poem from the Bible of the Universe', which he later calls 'those images of sense ... holding that relation to immortality and infinity which I have before

---
[32.] See Chapter 1.

alluded to'.[33] These features of nature are, as he put it elsewhere, 'workings of one mind ... /.../ The types and symbols of eternity' (*1805* VI 571), a mind he addresses early in *The Prelude* as 'Wisdom and spirit of the universe! / Thou soul that art the eternity of thought / That giv'st to forms and images a breath / And everlasting motion' (*1805* I 428-31). Infinity or eternity is the power 'that permitteth all objects to be'.

A remark by Traherne also justifies lines in the *Ode* which Coleridge unfortunately persuaded Wordsworth to remove:

> Suppose a man were born deaf and blind. By the very feeling of his soul, he apprehends infinite[y] about him, infinite space, infinite darkness. He thinks not of wall and limits till he feels them and is stopped by them. That things are finite therefore we learn by our senses. But infinity we know and feel by our souls: and feel it so naturally, as if it were the very essence and being of the soul. (*Centuries* II 81)

The child, 'Haunted for ever by the eternal mind', still mastered by his immortality, who even 'deaf and silent, read'st the eternal deep', therefore finds the grave no more than 'a lonely bed without the sense or sight / Of day or the warm light, / A place of thought where we in waiting lie'. Uncomfortable the image may be; but it is entirely consistent with both Wordsworth's and Traherne's insights into the relations of the immortal or infinite mind to that of sense. Wordsworth believes that the soul is brought hither by and belongs to 'an immortal sea'; Traherne puts it slightly differently when he describes the soul as 'a miraculous abyss of infinite abysses, an undrainable ocean, an unexhausted fountain of endless oceans, when it will exert itself to fill and fathom them' (*Centuries* II 83), but they are speaking the same language.

'With the drawing of this Love'[34]

Towards the end of *The Prelude* Wordsworth makes this definitive statement:

> From love, for here
> Do we begin and end, all grandeur comes,

---

[33] *MY* II 188. Wordsworth is saying something not unlike John Smith: 'When *Reason* once is raised by the mighty force of the Divine Spirit into a converse with God, it is turn'd into *Sense*'. *Select Discourses*, p. 16.
[34] *EC* V.

> All truth and beauty – from pervading love –
> That gone, we are as dust   (*1805* XIII 149-152).

What love we might ask, and his answer is a rising scale: love of nature – 'the fields / In balmy springtime, full of rising flowers / And happy creatures'; love of another person – 'in some green bower / Rest, and be not alone, but have thou there / The one who is thy choice of all the world', both of which are ordinarily called love; and so they are, but 'how pitiable! / Unless this love by a still higher love be hallowed', a love that 'proceeds / More from the brooding soul, and is divine'.[35] In *The Five-Book Prelude* Wordsworth calls the narrative to this point 'A history of love, from stage to stage / Advancing hand in hand with power and joy' (*5BP* V 143-45).[36] That sense of the continuity of love with the profoundest intentions of all forms of *The Prelude* follows immediately:

> This love more intellectual cannot be
> Without imagination, which in truth
> Is but another name for absolute strength
> And clearest insight, amplitude of mind,
> And reason in her most exalted mood.

Love, imagination and reason are thus united in a narrative which concludes with 'the one thought / By which we live, infinity and God' (*1805* XIII 166-84). The next section begins, 'Imagination having been our theme, / So also hath that intellectual love, / For they are each in each, and cannot stand / Dividually' (*1805* XIII 185-88).

The *Centuries* were written for Susannah Hopton, in an empty book which, Traherne tells her, 'Love made you put … into my hands'; and he intends to 'fill it with those Truths … which, if it be possible, shall shew my Love' (*Centuries* I 1). With Wordsworth, Traherne believes in the gradations of love, acknowledging, for instance, that in 'a curious and fair woman' some men 'have seen the beauties of Heaven' – though more often it is 'sparkling eyes and curled hair, lily breasts and ruddy cheeks' that have attracted their attention (*Centuries* II 68). For Traherne as for Wordsworth 'Love is the root and foundation of nature … There are

---

[35.] This reading is a combination of the 1805 and 1850 versions, easily compared in the Norton edition of *The Prelude*.

[36.] Wordsworth's belief that the power to love originates in Nature is fully expressed in *The Pedlar*: 'But he had felt the power / Of Nature, and already was prepar'd, / … to receive/ Deeply the lesson deep of love' (*RC* E 180-83); and 'The clouds were touch'd, / And in their silent faces did he read / Unutterable love' (*RC* E 194-96).

many glorious excellencies of the material World, but without Love they are all abortive ... a silent wilderness, without some living thing more sweet and blessed ... Love in the fountain and Love in the end is the glory of the world and the Soul of Joy' (*Centuries* II 62).

Or as he put it three entries later, 'For he that delights not in Love makes vain the universe'.

Part III

A Crisis: The Poetry of 1802

Chapter 7

Several Kinds of Poem

Writer's Block: 1801-1802

AFTER THE PUBLICATION of *Lyrical Ballads* (1800) at the end of January 1801, Wordsworth appears to have faced some kind of creative impasse. His known compositions that year are few and far between. From March to December, Mark Reed records almost no composition at all. Much of December is spent reading and 'translating' Chaucer, including a good chunk of *The Manciple's Tale*.[1] But he finds a definitive focus at the end of December, returning to the history of the Pedlar, the narrator of Margaret's story – which formed much of the first, 1797, version of *The Ruined Cottage*. In 1798, Wordsworth expanded the story to include some of the intellectual or spiritual history of the Pedlar, then divided the two parts in 1799, coming back to develop his intellectual history in 1801. From 21 December 1801 to 10 March 1802, Dorothy's journal records some 20 entries concerning *The Pedlar*. That period of composition was clearly taxing, as many of the entries speak of Wordsworth making himself tired and ill with the effort. James Butler summarizes the work of these months as Wordsworth's 'growing fascination with his own past experience' (*RC* 17), the poet recognizing that 'the character I have represented in [the Pedlar's] person is chiefly an idea of what I fancied my own character might have become in his circumstances' (*Reed* 17).

---

[1] *Reed* 132. There are differing views of what Wordsworth was doing in these months. See Paul Magnuson, 'The Genesis of Wordsworth's "Ode"', p. 28; Jonathan Wordsworth and Stephen Gill in *The Prelude* (Norton), p. 524; *Reed* 63. James Butler notes four passages from the 1798 work on The Pedlar used to complete part of Book III of *The Prelude* – see *RC* 181, 365-66.

Poems short and small

The conclusion of *The Ruined Cottage* sometime in March 1801 begins what Jared Curtis calls 'The Poetry of Crisis', some of which, through Wordsworth's unremitting interest in his early years, was continuous with his work on The Pedlar. Before considering the poetry of early 1802, it is worth remembering that Wordsworth did not see the poems of those months as we now see them, as struggling with the problems that may have thwarted his work on The Recluse, and thus, paradoxically, entering one of his most intense periods of creativity, producing some of his finest verse, which ran on with little intermission until the Poem to Coleridge was completed in 1805.² In an unpublished Preface to *Poems in Two Volumes* of 1807, in which the poems of 1802 are diffused through the collection, Wordsworth views his poetry as attempts to cheer himself up when he felt he was not in a position to do anything else – that is, he presents them as poems of distraction:

> The short Poems, of which these Volumes consist, were chiefly composed to refresh my mind during the progress of a work of length and labour, in which I have for sometime been engaged; and to furnish me with employment when I had no resolution to apply myself to that work, or hope that I should proceed with it successfully ... They were composed with much pleasure to my own mind, and I build upon that remembrance a hope that they may afford profitable pleasure to my readers.   (P2V 527)

The seeds of doubt evident in the 'Advertisement' may have been sown by Coleridge. From 1798 onwards, Wordsworth was dogged by Coleridge's insistence that he should get on with The Recluse, that 'work of length and labour' whose progress had been suspended. Perhaps neither of them then knew that *The Pedlar*, completed by early March 1802, would form the first book of *The Excursion*, itself planned as the first book of The Recluse. Coleridge mentions the poem existing as 1,200 lines to Joseph Cottle in March 1798, 'superior, I hesitate not to

---

[2.] Gregory Leadbetter notes that 'Wordsworth found something of what he was looking for in the very act of turning from his task'; and 'it does not seem to have fully dawned on Wordsworth that the lyric verse of *Poems, in Two Volumes* might itself embody, in another form, that "philosophic Song / Of Truth that cherishes our daily life"' (*1805* XIII 230-31; Leadbetter, 'The Lyric Impulse of *Poems, in Two Volumes*', in Richard Gravil and Daniel Robinson (eds), *The Oxford Handbook of William Wordsworth* (Oxford, 2015), p. 224).

aver, to anything in our language which in any way resembles it' (*CL* I 391); then in September 1799, he urges Wordsworth to keep at it, protesting against the publication of 'small poems' (*CL* I 527); mentioning it again in October that year, aware by then that it was going to be addressed to him (*CL* I 538); saying only a few months later, February 1800, 'I grieve that "The Recluse" sleeps' (*CL* I 575). In October 1803, he looked back, asserting that 'The habit too of writing such a multitude of small Poems was in this instance hurtful to him – such Things as that Sonnet of his in Monday's Morning Post, about Simonides & the Ghost'. By then, however, Wordsworth was back on track, despite the Simonides poem, working on *The Recluse* and Coleridge rejoices:

> With a deep & true Joy, that he has at length yielded to my urgent & repeated – almost unremitting – requests & remonstrances ... A Great Work, in which he will sail; on an open Ocean, & a steady wind; unfretted by short tacks, reefing, & hawling & disentangling the ropes ... It is what Food is to Famine. I have seen enough, positively to give me feelings of hostility towards the plan of several of the Poems in the L. Ballads: & I really consider it as a misfortune, that Wordsworth ever deserted his former mountain Track to wander in Lanes & allies; tho' in the event it may prove to have been a great Benefit to him.[3]

The comment on the *Lyrical Ballads* is surprising, and Coleridge never unpacked his reservation, although some ten years later he said much the same more discreetly: 'Mr Wordsworth added two or three poems written in his own character, in the impassioned, lofty, and sustained diction, which is characteristic of his genius.' (*BL* II 8). The implicit comment is that many of Wordsworth's poems in that collection were out of character, not following the bent of his genius. The most obviously *in* character is Tintern Abbey, so unlike many of the ballads, but clearly of a kind with the *Ode* and The Poem to Coleridge.[4] That Wordsworth's desertion of 'his former mountain Track' could prove of benefit to him

---

[3.] *CL* II 1013, 14 October 1803. In the *Biographia*, Coleridge uses a different metaphor to the same end: 'his only disease is the being out of his element: like the swan, that having amused himself, for a while, with crushing the weeds on the river's bank, soon returns to his own majestic movements on its reflecting and sustaining surface' (*BL* II 119-20).

[4.] The editors of the *Biographia* suggest that Coleridge may have also included 'one or two of the following ... Lines Written at a Small Distance from my House, Lines Written in Early Spring, Expostulation and Reply, and The Tables Turned' (*BL* II 8).

was probably because Coleridge had described the planned Recluse as 'a poem non unius populi', not one for the people, whereas the small poems might prove more popular, as they did (*CL* I 538).

Wordsworth colludes with this view in the 'Advertisement': 'Having already, in the Volumes entitled Lyrical Ballads, offered to the World a considerable collection of short poems, I did not wish to add these to the number, till after the completion and publication of my larger work'. The irony of that statement is that he had already completed what would be his major work, *The Prelude,* even if he then still saw The Recluse as capable of completion So instead he offers the 'short poems' of the two volumes as a stop-gap. This sounds in tune with Coleridge's strictures on small poems, his differentiation from poems 'characteristic of his genius', and tells us that Wordsworth thinks of these poems as of a kind with *Lyrical Ballads*.

However, that is not quite the end of this story. If in 1803, as he had in earlier years, Coleridge protested that Wordsworth's writing of small poems had been 'hurtful to him' – note the past tense – in 1802, his judgement was more moderate. In May, he transcribed '2 little pleasing poems' (nicely balanced adjectives) for Tom Poole: To a Butterfly and The Sparrow's Nest (*CL* I 800). On reflection, his choice is odd. The two poems are memories from Wordsworth's childhood shared with Dorothy – and they are short and small. At the end of the letter he tells Poole, precise about the date as always, 'I ought to say for my own sake that on the 4th of April last I wrote you a letter in verse; but I thought it dull & doleful – & did not send it'. Of course it wasn't for Poole at all, but he wanted Poole to know about it. The date, 4 April, was when he heard the first four verses of the *Ode,* to which the Verse Letter was an astonishing response and, as he always claimed, completed that evening. We now see those four verses as *the* poem of crisis. Because his verse letter responded to Wordsworth's desperate questions, surely his verses would have been uppermost in Coleridge's mind, but it goes unmentioned in his letter to Poole. Later in the year he told Southey: 'He has written lately a number of Poems (32 in all) some of them of considerable Length / (the longest 160 Lines) the greater number of these to my feelings very excellent Compositions'.[5] The poem of 160 lines must be Resolution and Independence, Wordsworth's response to the Verse Letter, clearly in Coleridge's consciousness as it is the only one he distinguishes. Coleridge

---

[5.] *CL* II 830, 29 July 1802. Coleridge's unusually precise numeration closely matches the number that Jared Curtis has collected. 'The Poetry of Crisis' is his introductory chapter to *Experiments*.

was aware that something had come upon Wordsworth that made most of these poems 'very excellent Compositions', different from his many other small poems. Coleridge takes us no further than that, and there is no suggestion that he saw these poems as in any way helping either to present or to resolve issues that might enable Wordsworth to do what Coleridge wanted him to do – return to The Recluse.

The beginnings of the *Ode* sits amongst these poems as one of many, as what might have been a temporary mood of his own mind – for the previous day he had composed the much more optimistic 'My heart leaps up …'.[6] If Wordsworth had not returned to the poem two years later, one could imagine those four stanzas complete, ending with the acknowledgement that his questions could not be answered, and leaving it that. What the surrounding poems show is that Wordsworth was troubled by the problems he raised throughout the earlier months of 1802, particularly the relation of celestial vision to terrestrial life. He did not relinquish the struggle to understand his loss, with which Coleridge's Verse Letter gave him no help whatsoever. But because they got to Coleridge in a way none of these other poems did, epitomizing the problems he confronted, including an attempted reconciliation, and because they will lead to a reading of the completed poem, those four stanzas, together with further comments on 'My heart leaps up…', are considered at the beginning of Chapter 9.

'Disentangling the ropes'

There are two or three distinct ropes or strands discernible among those 32 poems, each arising from crises entangled with each other, though not all the crises manifested themselves in poetry. Curtis identifies the first crisis as Lord Lonsdale's failure to pay his debt to the Wordsworths; their correspondence and Dorothy's journal suggest it had no apparent bearing on the production of his poetry. Curtis next suggests that his forthcoming marriage was a crisis that required him to resolve his relationship with Annette and Caroline – a 'painful and complicated issue … too often glossed over' (*Experiments* 3). This in itself did not produce the poetic crisis of the first four stanzas of the *Ode*, though his and Dorothy's journey to France produced some fine poems – 'It is a beauteous evening…', 'Milton! thou should'st be living at this hour' and Westminster Bridge among them.

[6.] Jared Curtis prints the *Ode* as complete in his 1802 collection. This anachronistic decision risks blurring the difficulties that Wordsworth was facing in those months.

The length of time that they spent in France, about a month, raised questions of which Coleridge was aware and Mary must have pondered. Were they resolving legal matters, or were they so much enjoying the company of Wordsworth's former mistress and her daughter that they were reluctant to return? The real crisis, from Wordsworth's point of view, was not a reconsideration or a resolution of his relationship with Annette, however much he might have enjoyed her company (once in love, always in love?), or even a decision whether or not to marry Mary Hutchinson – towards which he nevertheless moved so slowly that Coleridge noted that he 'continued talking with Wordsworth the whole night till the Dawn of the Day, urging him to conclude on marrying Mary Hutchinson' (*CN* III 3304). There is evidence that the decision to marry had been made formally for months, informally for much longer. Therefore the phrase 'to conclude on' suggests that not the marriage itself but that something else caused him to hesitate.[7] In the same note, Coleridge commented on Wordsworth's 'calculating Foresight' and his 'pride in not being hurried away by present Emotions', which indicates there must have been some emotions needing control.

Poems for Dorothy

Some of the poetry of the early months of 1802 points to his relationship with Dorothy, with whom he had lived continuously since 1795, as the cause of his hesitation. They had formed a bond upon which Wordsworth's creativity largely depended, preventing his genial spirits from decaying. Of the 30 or so poems that Curtis believes embodied the poetry of crisis the easiest strand to identify is the nine or ten addressed to or involving Dorothy, all written during the spring and summer as his marriage approached in October.[8] Wordsworth's worries are obliquely expressed, or can only be inferred – but their shared anxieties are explicit in Dorothy's journal. That crisis is not the principal subject of this chapter – the realization of and attempts to recover a lost joy. Wordsworth did not feel that such a recovery had anything to do with marriage, even though Coleridge blindly insisted that a happy marriage was as necessary to Wordsworth's recovery as it was to his own. It is inversely connected, though, as it seems likely that, however

---

[7] Kathleen Coburn says that the date for this conversation (3 April 1802) is 'well substantiated', but gives no evidence.

[8] The following list contains probables as well as definites: I travelled among Unknown Men, Louisa, 'Stay near me', The Glow-worm, 'I've watched you now', Travelling, Farewell, 'There is a trickling water', 'Dear fellow-Traveller' and the least probable, Foresight.

desirable, Wordsworth saw marriage as a threat to the stability he had achieved with Dorothy, risking separation from a uniquely focused love, powerful in its celibacy, through which she 'in the midst of all, preserved me still / A poet'.[9] Intimations of the depth of their relationship can be found throughout his verse, but one poem, 'Among all lovely things my Love had been', The Glow-worm, written on 12 April, epitomizes what he and Dorothy feared they might lose through his marriage. In a letter to Coleridge, Wordsworth acknowledged that 'the incident of this Poem took place about seven years ago between Dorothy and me' (*EY* 348), and speaks openly of lover and beloved, an openness rare if not unique in his poems for Dorothy.[10] Their relationship was of a kind with that of Charles and Mary Lamb, which Sara Coleridge described 'as a fraternal marriage'.[11] An unpublished fragment reveals what lay beneath the surface:

> Witness thou
> The dear companion of my lonely walk,
> My hope, my joy, my sister, and my friend,
> Or something dearer still, if reason knows
> A dearer thought, or in the heart of love
> There be a dearer name.   (*WPW* V 347)

It is curious that Wordsworth recalled 'the incident' seven years earlier when approaching his marriage in 1802. Nevertheless, it fits in with what Dorothy tells us, that it was written while he was riding *away* from Mary and *towards* the home he shared with Dorothy: that is, it is a poem of homecoming, describing the delight he and Dorothy found in the gift he brought her: 'Oh! joy it was for her, and joy for me!' It as if one marriage was under threat from another, and it was the maintenance not the recovery of joy – Coleridge's solution to his creative impasse – that Wordsworth required. In this poem he is not imagining the joyful home that he and Mary might make together, but the home, or the spirit of the home, that he and Dorothy had shared for so many years, and which both knew might be disrupted. Four days later, as Wordsworth composed 'Written in March...', Dorothy walked along repeating The Glow-worm; a few days afterwards they sat in the orchard, reading the poem together. Written on this particular occasion, during months of anxiety, there can be no doubt that it is a poem reassuring them both

---

[9.] *1805* X 918-19.

[10.] The unpublished *Home at Grasmere* is the obvious exception.

[11.] *Biographia Literaria*, ed. Sara Coleridge, 2 vols (London: Pickering, 1847), Vol. II, p. 333.

of their love for each other. If some ten poems were written for Dorothy in this period, probably not a single one was written for Mary. True, she later became the addressee of this and other poems not originally for her, including 'She was a phantom of delight' – kind and tactful decisions which however obscured their curious origins.[12] And if we can see Wordsworth's anxieties reflected in his verse, Dorothy's disturbance at his approaching marriage is openly recorded in her journal, notably in the entry for his wedding day. She had passed the previous night with the ring he was to give to Mary on her finger, and when she took it off to return it, Wordsworth put it back on and blessed her 'fervently'. Dorothy could not bring herself to witness the marriage, and it seems to have been a tense day for all. Oddly, and happily, Dorothy's equanimity was restored on their wedding journey back to Grasmere, all three together, where they quickly settled down to become a very happy and harmonious family – an outcome that must have been largely due to the good will of the two friends, and Mary's sensitive insight into what William and Dorothy were to each other – 'a blessed marriage', as Coleridge enviously called it some four years later.

As a consequence of this crisis, that spring Wordsworth wrote some of his most delicate and delightful verse. Through the great dignity of all involved, including Annette and Caroline, the crisis was fully resolved soon after Wordsworth and Mary were married. With that resolution, the impetus of his and Dorothy's shared need for reassurance faded away, and few if any such poems were written subsequently. In her journal, Dorothy wrote 'Let that pass I shall be beloved – I want no more' (31 May 1802). It did pass, and she was beloved by both William and Mary.

Poems of Solitude

A corollary, or a subcrisis, of his approaching marriage, which gave rise to another short strand of poetry, might have been Wordsworth's fear as to what effect a new allegiance and the rigours and incidentals of family life would have on his desire and respect for retirement, his willingness to stand alone, a solitary. He often claims solitude when it is evident that Dorothy was with him, as in the paradoxical 'The dear companion of my lonely walk'. That indicates how much they shared a vision, and how much the presence of a third might disrupt that

---

[12.] Wordsworth himself says that this poem is linked to 'A Highland Girl' (*P2V* 404; *FN*).

union.[13] His need for and admiration of an unfettered freedom appears in The Tinker, Personal Talk, Resolution and Independence, 'These chairs they have no words to utter' – 'And I am alone / Happy and alone' – as well of course in the later 'I wandered lonely as a cloud'. Even in poems that seem principally to celebrate the coming of spring, such as The Green Linnet, which begins 'The May is come again: – how sweet / To sit upon my Orchard-seat!', his thoughts do not lightly turn to love, but solitude or singularity:

> Presiding spirit here to-day,
> Dost lead the revels of the May...
> Thou, ranging up and down thy bowers,
>   Art sole in thy employment;
> A Life, a Presence like the Air,
> Scattering thy gladness without care,
> Too bless'd with anyone to pair,
> Thyself thy own enjoyment.

He might almost have been remembering Marvell's 'delicious Solitude' in the garden at Appleton House, where 'Two paradises 'twere in one / To live in paradise alone', but it is an odd sentiment coming from a man soon to be married. Wordsworth did not always enjoy the freedom springing from this sole employment: as he recognized in *Home at Grasmere* – 'Something must be done'; in the Prefatory Sonnet to *Poems in Two Volumes* he feels 'the weight of too much liberty'; and in the Ode to Duty declares, 'Me this uncharter'd freedom tires'.

Ballads and Poems of Sublimity

There are two other potential groupings of the poetry of early 1802, the first of which is the narrative poems he wrote in the spirit of the *Lyrical Ballads*. Into such a category fall The Sailor's Mother, Alice Fell, Beggars, The Emigrant Mother and perhaps The Affliction of Mary. These poems are, *pace* Coleridge, who considered them lanes and alleys, a distinct strand of Wordsworth's genius, through which he manifests real empathy with unusual states of mind not his, as he had earlier in such remarkable poems as The Idiot Boy – all poems of the varied music of humanity.

[13.] In Book III of *The Prelude* he declares that 'Points have we all of us within our souls / Where all stand single'; this is associated with his dedication to poetry, for later he invokes Milton, 'our blind Poet, who in his later day, / Stood almost single, uttering odious truth, / Darkness before, and danger's voice behind' (*1805* III 186-88; 284-87).

The first three of these were all composed over three or four days, 11-14 March. Wordsworth's insights into the human condition often precede a vision 'of aspect more sublime', as in Tintern Abbey, Book VIII of *The Prelude* and in the resolution of *The Ruined Cottage* – 'enough to sorrow we have given'. Unless a prelude to what is to come, they cannot however really be described as the poetry of crisis.

Nonetheless, having written those poems, it is as if he now feels free to deal with aspects of sublimity, embodied in the group of poems that may be loosely categorized both as concerned with the lack of, and as evidence for, the visionary, and include love of the immediate and reflections on childhood – some of which overlap with poems for Dorothy. In terms of his creative difficulties, this is the most significant group, for his underlying intention, as always, is to find his vision in the present, to marry heaven and earth, and many bear upon the concerns of the *Ode*. His memories of childhood and his early life, hardly present in the *Lyrical Ballads*, become increasingly important as he discovers a power previously hidden, the strand of his 1802 poetry that is continuous with work on The Pedlar. The irony or tragedy is that his discovery of the power inherent in childhood ('Children are powerful' – Personal Talk) is more or less simultaneous with his experience of its loss, possibly reflected in a paradoxical phrase in *The Prelude*, which speaks of 'that dubious hour / That twilight when we first begin to see / This dawning earth' (*1805* V 536-38). This group might include To a Skylark, To a Butterfly, To the Cuckoo, My Heart Leaps Up, the first four stanzas of the *Ode*, To H.C. Six Years Old, Written in March, The Green Linnet, aspects of all three poems To the Daisy, The Barberry Tree, Personal Talk, the first two of the Small Celandine poems and 'It is no Spirit who from Heaven hath Flown'.[14]

In Tintern Abbey, Wordsworth couldn't see into the life of things until the images of present sense became memories and so were enabled to pass into his purer mind. The immediate recalls the memory, and the lack of vision in the immediate does not seem to overly worry him. Many of the 1802 poems seem to be struggling to bring together the immediate and the vision, but the dominant experience is of separation, epitomized in the opening stanzas of the *Ode*. Nor is he content that in such moments 'there is life and food / For future years'. Beginning, in Tintern Abbey, to look back to that unity of vision, when the 'sounding cataract / ... the tall rock, / The mountain, and the deep and gloomy

---

[14.] To a Skylark, To a Butterfly and To the Cuckoo are also considered in Part IV 'Reading the Ode'.

wood, / ... / ... had no need of a remoter charm / By thought supplied, or any interest / Unborrowed from the eye', childhood as the time of immediate vision makes a tentative presence in the 1802 poems, but is not yet the certain source – 'There was a time ...' does not specify when that time was, and it is not until Wordsworth finds a way forward in 1804 that he puts all his eggs in that one basket.

Chapter 8

Heaven and Earth

Our destiny, our nature, and our home,
Is with infinitude – and only there

> *the very world which is the world*
> *Of all of us, the place in which, in the end*
> *We find our happiness, or not at all.*[1]

THIS CHAPTER MINES a vein running through the poems thus categorized above, but does not discuss their various qualities as poetry, their verse structure, their rhythms, rhymes, their debts to earlier poetry or even their success as poems. Wordsworth's mind went to and fro over distinct and not so distinct ideas, hopes, thoughts; driven by the various kinds of impetus of which he himself may not have been fully aware, writing poems, not working out a philosophy. He believed he was taking a rest, giving himself 'refreshment' from 'a long labour', and this took him away from what Coleridge called his 'lofty diction' and back into the local and immediate, which called forth a much lighter-hearted verse, despite an underlying seriousness. As mentioned above, because for the time being he could not carry on with the great task set in part for him by Coleridge, he brought back into these poems some of the struggles of that thwarted enterprise. The beginnings of the *Ode* were written quite early in this burst of creativity, and the problems it raised continued to haunt Wordsworth in the following months.

A feature of these 'short Poems, chiefly composed to refresh my mind' is often a modesty of subject matter – two to the butterfly, three to the daisy, two to the celandine and three to birds.[2] In other poems the verse has a simplicity almost collapsing into simpleness, as discussed later in relation

---

[1] *1805* VI 538-39; X 725-27.

[2] He thought it remarkable that the celandine 'should not have been noticed earlier in English verse' (*FN*). Dorothy's journal of 15 April 1802 describes pile-wort (celandine) exactly as does Wordsworth.

to 'Written in March...'. Such poems may have provoked Coleridge's remark that 'here & there is a daring Humbleness of Language and Versification' (*CL* II 830) quite different from his 'impassioned, lofty, and sustained diction' (*BL* II 8) to which, in 1802, he wished Wordsworth would return. Both verse and subject matter are mostly in evident contrast with what might have been – the magnificent spectacles that often held Wordsworth's attention: there are no cataracts (bar the *Ode*), no Alpine or apocalyptic landscapes, no moons rising above misty mountain tops, no sunsets of extraordinary splendour, none of the greater glories of nature incarnate in a body of verse rich, mysterious and evocative. Wordsworth's choices of subject matter and manner of versification are calculated decisions.[3]

The Butterfly Poems

The first of these two poems was written on 14 March, and opens the section titled 'Moods of my own Mind' in *Poems in Two Volumes*. The first lines suggest a fleetingness that he connects with his childhood. He begs the butterfly to 'Stay near me' because it is the 'Historian of my infancy', and 'much converse do I find in Thee'. Should the butterfly take flight, that conversation is ended, and though the second verse is only the story of his and Dorothy's different childhood attitudes to butterflies, and so no great matter, that fear of the butterfly disappearing suggests the difficulty of both accessing and sustaining the presence of early memories. The very direct, decisive 'Dead times revive in Thee' speaks of the resurrection of a long-buried life where Wordsworth will find his power lying hidden. These two verses are no more than a hint of what he will realize, though the gaiety of the butterfly paradoxically betokens the seriousness of his quest, for it brings 'A solemn image to my heart, / My Father's Family!' Whether or not Wordsworth connects that 'solemn image' with his father's death, and so with the second of the two original spots of time (already composed), there is a renovating virtue catalysed by the cheerful presence of the butterfly: from the dead times the workings of his spirit, if not fully brought forth, begin to appear.

The second butterfly poem – 'I've watched you now a full half hour' – was composed just over a month later, on 20 April. Like the first, it begins with the stillness of a butterfly, but a deep stillness, 'not frozen seas / More motionless!' (an unusual metaphor to associate with a butterfly) and unworried that flight must follow the waiting. Wordsworth advocated that kind of deliberate inactivity, happy, as he says, to sit by the fire in

---

[3.] Cf. Curtis's title *Wordsworth's Experiments with Tradition*.

'Long, barren silence ... / ... without emotion, hope, or aim', (Personal Talk), waiting, one presumes, for a 'mild, creative breeze' to come upon him. So the butterfly waits until the breeze 'calls you forth again' when 'What joy awaits you'. The stages of this process are significant – the waiting – the breeze – the joy. A patient waiting is followed by inspiration and that draws out a power, felt as joy – a word never to be passed over in Wordsworth's or Coleridge's lexicon.

The structures of the two butterfly poems are very similar, two verses, the first of which develops the principal idea, the second returning to the presence of Dorothy, of home, either their first home, or the orchard at Dove Cottage, and both reviving warm and happy memories of their childhood – 'We'll talk of sunshine and of song; / And summer days when we were young, / Sweet childish days'. If not clothed with celestial light, here the days of childhood are unclouded by the pain and sorrows of adult life. Whether earth or heaven, home is where one starts from – and returns to.

In passing, it is worth noting that breeze and joy are also closely linked in *The Barberry Tree,* which Wordsworth never published but is one of his most delightful poems.[4] The barberry's blossoms 'laugh'd and danc'd upon the gale; / They seem'd as though they could never fade': the poem continues

> In very joy their colours gleam'd:
>   But whether it be thus or no;
> That while they danc'd upon the wind
> They felt a joy like humankind:...
> The piping breeze and dancing tree
> Are all alive and glad as we: ...
>   And when my trance was ended
>   And on my way I tended,
> Still, so it was, I know not how ...
>   It seem'd part of myself to be:
> That in my inner self I had
> Those whispering sounds which made me glad.

[4.] The authorship of this poem has been questioned, notably by Jim Mays, 'The Authorship of the "Barberry Tree"', who thinks it a parody. If either the naivety or the jolliness seem unlike Wordsworth, then remember Written in March and The Tinker respectively. On 24 April 1802 Wordsworth took Dorothy out to see 'a waterfall behind the Barberry tree'. The definite article suggests it was a tree they both knew.

We should not let the light-heartedness of the verse obscure the fullness of his vision – by which, as Nature's priest, he is on his way attended – for 'that most happy mood of mind / ... / ... pass'd it not away' after his trance had ended. The joy (a word he uses three times in the poem) he attributes both to the natural world and humanity: 'They felt a joy like humankind'. Of nature he also says the 'piping breeze and dancing tree / Are all alive and glad as we' and of himself that 'in my inner self I had / Those whispering sounds that made me glad'. The immediate joy in nature and the immediate life in man are one and the same, a rare union in Wordsworth's poetry. As in Tintern Abbey, here too 'Mayst thou a store of thought lay by / For present time and long futurity'.

The Flower Poems

The three poems to the daisy – 'In youth from rock to rock I went', 'With little here to do or see' and 'Bright Flower' may have all been written between 16 April and 8 July, although the last was possibly developed between March 1804 and March 1805 (*P2V* 240). Wordsworth chose 'In youth ...' as the first poem of his 1807 collection. Whether by accident or design the energy and discontent of the opening lines echo some in Tintern Abbey, the last poem of the first volume of *Lyrical Ballads* (1802), 'when like a roe / I bounded o'er the mountains ... //... more like a man / Flying from something that he dreads, than one / Who sought the thing he loved'. Is Wordsworth pointing to some continuity between the two collections? If so, he is also pointing to the contrast between his condition then and now. The pleasure in his discontent then was 'high and turbulent', but what he asks of nature now is very much more modest – 'My thirst at every rill can slake', and participates in 'Nature's love' through the presence 'Of thee, sweet Daisy!' The daisy is a flower for all seasons and all places, often ignored, always present if looked for, 'a Friend at hand, to scare / His [the poet's] melancholy'. Given the cheerfulness of the poem so far that is a surprising irruption, comparable to the contrast between gladness and despondency of Resolution and Independence, beginning in one and ending in the other.

But the 'sweet power' of the daisy runs deeper, and hints at the indefinable and inarticulate qualities that underpin vision, 'Some apprehension; / Some steady love; some brief delight; / Some memory that had taken flight' – that last phrase reminiscent both of his fear of the butterfly leaving him, of days disowned by memory, and suggestive of his only seeing by glimpses as the hiding places of his power open briefly, closing as he approaches (*1805* XI 335-37). The repeated 'some' marks Wordsworth's refusal to try and define these indistinct powers – a brave decision – for the mind always seeks to define what it cannot fully comprehend. By not doing so, Wordsworth leaves open the precise source of that power, the kind of intelligent reservation implicit in Eliot's remark that words are always a new beginning, an exploration of the unknown, 'a raid on the inarticulate' (*EC* V). Wordsworth repeats this refusal a couple of verses later, firmer still that it should 'blow where it listeth', by confessing to the daisy that he owes it 'another debt' – 'An instinct call it, a blind sense; / A happy, genial influence, / Coming one knows not how nor whence, / Nor whither going.' If one considers just how important the word 'genial' is to both Wordsworth and Coleridge in relation to their sense of power – the presence of Dorothy as they wander by the Wye will prevent his 'genial spirits' from decaying, matched by Coleridge's confession that 'My genial spirits fail', declaring that the impressions of nature cannot restore his power – then the word used here has implications of which Wordsworth would have been fully aware. He is talking, as he often does, about the breeze, the winds, the breath of poetic and spiritual power.

He realizes that he is not always attuned to the daisy's meekness: 'If stately passions in me burn…' may refer to the kind of power he needed to return to The Recluse, or may suggest those passions that lift him from the earth to higher worlds. If so, catching a glimpse of the grounded daisy he returns to the earth, and drinks 'out of an humbler urn / A lower pleasure' – the cup of common life and homely sympathy. Where he really lives – in his stately, soaring passions, or in his admiration of what is universal and bedded in the earth – remains unresolved.

Wordsworth tells us that the other two daisy poems were written one after the other, 'With little here to do or see', followed by 'Bright Flower, whose home is everywhere!' Because all three daisy poems may have been written more or less simultaneously, we might expect to find thematic links: the undefined locality, the universality, of 'In youth from rock to rock…' is explicit in the opening line of 'Bright Flower, whose home is everywhere'; if the first of the three inspired 'a lowlier pleasure', the opening lines of 'With little here…' consider the daisy's ordinariness, 'Thou unassuming Common-place / Of Nature, with that homely face'; but the two lines that follow – 'And yet with something of a grace / Which Love makes for thee' – raise the flower from mere ordinariness, to a symbol of universal Love irradiating nature.

Love is a power imbuing the daisy with grace, but a grace already potential in the plant. To understand that love as a power, and not merely an aesthetic pleasure – 'I love daisies' – it is best considered as closely related to joy, the power Coleridge believed would reunite seeing and feeling. The beginning of the last stanza of the *Ode* asks the 'Fountains, Meadows, Hills and Groves' to 'Think not of any severing of our loves' – that is the poet ascribes to them the power, as he ascribes grace to the daisy, to maintain a union upon which his vision depends. That such a union appears to have been disrupted in this poem inspires the petition of the final lines, 'Do thou, as thou art wont, repair / My heart with gladness'. His severed heart is in need of repair, and it is gladness or joy or love – all synonyms of the same power – that can effect that reunion. His final assertion that he wants to share in the daisy's 'meek nature' may be an antithesis to the 'web of similies' he weaves for his 'Sweet Flower', the epitome of which is his seeing it as 'a pretty Star' when 'glittering from afar'. The daisy has been elevated into the heavens – 'Self-pois'd in air thou seem's to rest' – not dissimilar to the sky-canoe of Peter Bell – an elevation in contrast with its humble, ground-level life; between the two the poet seeks a reconciliation: 'May peace come never to his nest / Who shall reprove thee!' Reprove thee for what? For being a star, it seems, for being of the air, separate from the earth. The mortal should not reprove the immortal, for the lofty sanctifies the low. Peace will only come to the mortal nest, when whoever nestles there realizes the realms above.

The final daisy poem, 'Bright Flower', is much shorter than the first two, just three stanzas as against their ten and six respectively. The qualities emphasized are of a kind with the other two, but are more explicit. The first, universality, as we have seen is stated in the first line, 'Bright Flower, whose home is everywhere'; the second, tied to the first, is the image of a wandering pilgrim, 'the heir to joy and sorrow', a small phrase but comparable to that division between gladness and despondency frequent in many of these poems; the third, linked to the second, is an active relationship with the consequences of being human – 'there abides in thee / Some concord with humanity / Given to no other Flower'. That concord is not some kind of parallel experience, but the ability to teach, to resolve. What it is that requires resolution he then describes, and one of the clearest expressions of the debate Wordsworth was having with himself in the spring of 1802, of the sense of loss he was trying to overcome:

> Is it that Man is soon deprest?
> A thoughtless Thing! who, once unblest,
> Does little on his memory rest,
>   Or on his reason

What causes Man to find himself 'unblest' – or lacking joy – is not explained, but the premise of what follows. From that condition, there are only two possible routes out, memory or reason. The one or the other (or, as it will prove, the one followed by the other) is a key distinction in the method Wordsworth chooses for his recovery. It is through his memories of childhood that he knows that the world was once clothed in celestial light, that seeing and feeling were at one, and that that seeing was enabled by a light divine. The memory of that vision is vital, for it confers a belief in the possibility of recovering from its loss, which in one form or another he is becoming increasingly conscious of in these months.

That the other route should be 'reason' is a little more surprising, but fully in accord with the importance he attached to the word. As the completed *Ode* makes clear, only the 'years that bring the philosophic mind', of which reason is the foundation, can offer any kind of restoration. Though not certain, it seems likely that that phrase was a step towards his decision to invest reason with the highest of human powers, and that in earlier years he had been moving towards this decisive formulation.[5] In 'Bright Flower' the daisy seems to fulfil the functions of reason by teaching Man 'how to find / A shelter under every wind, / A hope for times that are unkind'. As joy and sorrow, gladness and despondency, are often in deliberate antithesis – if not one, then the other – here hope and times unkind are set in similar opposition. The modesty of the daisy, 'uncheck'd by pride or scrupulous doubt', is set deliberately at odds with the task imposed upon it as the poem concludes. Wandering 'the wide world about', fitting its purpose to 'the occasion's call, / And suffering all things from all' the daisy thus performs its 'function apostolical / In peace fulfilling'. The humble daisy can achieve the consummate reconciliation so long sought for. What can hardly be an accidental comparison with the wandering and the sufferings of the apostles is an extraordinary mission for such a modest flower – but therein lies the point: no grand visions are required.

There are three celandine poems, To the Small Celandine, To the Same Flower and The Small Celandine – the latter written in 1803-4, the first two on the same or following days, 30 April and 1 May 1802. The last is a stoic poem, in which there is much less hope, and was perhaps the darkness before the dawn in his search for the lever that would move his world.

[5.] Whether the use of 'reason' in 'Bright Flower' preceded or followed either the philosophic mind of the *Ode* and the paean to reason in *The Prelude* is uncertain as it may have been part of the possible revision of the poem between 1805 and 1806 (*P2V* 240).

To the Small Celandine shares the unusual distribution of attributes found in the daisy: on the one hand, an earth-bound modesty,

> On the moor, and in the wood,
> In the lane – there's not a place,
> Howsoever mean it be,
> But 'tis good enough for thee

and on the other inspiring in the poet with a deep enthusiastic joy, a rapturous hallelujah:

> Prophet of delight and mirth,
> Scorn'd and slighted upon earth!
> Herald of a mighty band,
> Of a joyous train ensuing,
> Singing at my heart's command,
> In the lanes my thoughts pursuing,
> I will sing, as doth behove,
> Hymns in praise of what I love!

This apposition of the humbleness of Wordsworth's chosen objects and the soaring ambitions with which he clothes them is characteristic of many of his poems, not only of his flower poems, where perhaps it is most marked. It is a habit of his mind, evident in the function that the spear-grass plays in reconciling the Pedlar to Margaret's fate. However, in the second of the celandine poems this distinction is less evident. It opens with 'Pleasures newly found are sweet / When they lie about our feet', so looking earthward – as 'The Pansy at my feet' looks earthward, hopeless of heaven. If the next verse points very delightfully upwards praising the man,

> Who first with pointed rays,
> (Workman worthy to be sainted)
> Set the Sign-board in a blaze
> When the risen sun he painted,
> Took the fancy from a glance
> At they glittering countenance

the poem concludes with a return to earth: 'Thou art not beyond the moon, / But a thing "beneath our shoon"', for which all he wants is 'three or four / Who will love my little Flower'. If there is a choice in this poem, it is earth not heaven.

Three Birds: To a Skylark and Two Cuckoos

The first written of this group reflects the division between the terrestrial and the celestial that is so much part of the *Ode*. He petitions the skylark to draw him up from where he is to where he has yet to be:

> With all the heavens about thee ringing,
>   Lift me, guide me, till I find
> That spot which seems so to thy mind!
>
> I have walked through wildernesses dreary,
>   And today my heart is weary
>   Had I the soul of a Faery,
>   Up to thee would I fly.

The distinction between the ringing heavens and 'wildernesses dreary' is that between heaven and earth – the earth that 'fills her lap with pleasures of her own' just as the skylark 'has a nest, for thy love and thy rest'; but the 'joy divine' that Wordsworth finds in 'that song of thine' – as 'Joyous as Morning' – is sung 'laughing and scorning' the terrestrial and celebrating the celestial.[6] He is petitioning the skylark to lead him back to '[t]hat spot', 'thy banqueting-place in the sky' (that 'imperial palace') to which his soul would fly were it that of a faery, free of its material nature. 'Joy and jollity be with us both!' he declares, determined to share 'the gladness of the May!' But as in the *Ode*, he falls back to earth, acknowledging the difference of their conditions when, addressing the skylark as a 'Happy, happy Liver', he says 'thou woulds't be loth / To be such a traveller as I', clarifying his meaning in the last two lines, 'I on earth will go plodding on, / By myself, chearfully, till the day is done.' The division between heaven and earth has yet to be healed. That kind of stoicism, here the knowledge that he does not know what the skylark knows, who can pour out 'praise to the Almighty Giver', will be revisited in the *Ode*, when asking 'What though the radiance which was once so bright / Be now for ever taken from my sight', he is determined to 'grieve not, rather find / Strength in what remains behind' – just as he will take comfort from the stoicism of the solitary Leech-gatherer.

Wordsworth wrote two cuckoo poems, To the Cuckoo, just before the first four stanzas of the *Ode*, and 'Yes! full surely 'twas the echo', in

---

[6.] Wordsworth distinguishes 'joy divine' from 'vulgar joy' (*1805* I 609, 625) together with 'the mean and vulgar works of man' (*1805* I 435) and 'vulgar hope' (*1805* I 493), all suggesting another kind of heaven and earth distinction.

1806, two years after its completion. The first dematerializes the earth, thus still leaving a division between one world and the other. Whether, as a result of completing the *Ode*, Wordsworth brings the two worlds together in the second poem is considered in Chapter 9. He builds both poems upon the fact that the cuckoo is heard not seen. The first stanza of To the Cuckoo closes with, 'shall I call thee Bird / Or but a wandering Voice?'[7] Like Shelley's skylark – 'Bird thou never wert' – the cuckoo's song is an intimation of another mode of being – 'thou art to me / No bird; but an invisible Thing, / A voice, a mystery', and 'that Cry' 'in the vale / Of visionary hours', takes him back to his childhood, and now he 'can lie upon the plain / And listen, till I do beget / That golden time again'.[8] He is discovering childhood as the source of his vision. Jared Curtis points out that the tense changes across the first two lines, 'O blithe new-comer I have heard / I hear thee and rejoice', 'contains in it the kernel of the poet's effort to conquer time' (*Experiments* 47). Yes, because the begetting is successful: the hiatus between the glories of time past and the vacuities of time present, the hiatus first seen in Tintern Abbey and at the core of the *Ode*, has been resolved – at least momentarily. It is worth reflecting on 'beget': associated principally with the making of children, and of the Son in relation to the Father – 'begotten, not made' – the word here suggests the fundamental nature of the creativity associated with this revival of childhood's 'visionary hours'; and it is a revival in the poet – 'I do beget' – internal even if catalysed by the cuckoo's 'wandering Voice'; not a revival wholly dependent on the impulses of nature. The begetting is transformative, remaking the dull substance of the world, so that 'the earth we pace / Again appears to be / An unsubstantial, faery place; / That is fit home for Thee!' The deliberate repetition of 'again' from the previous verse refers to the 'golden time', the remaking of childhood experience, and in that 'fit home', 'an unsubstantial, faery place', we hear echoes of Wordsworth's other imagined homes – the 'Paradise, and groves Elysian' of *Home at Grasmere*, the 'imperial palace' of the *Ode* – forms of

---

[7] Wordsworth quotes this couplet in his Preface to Poems (1815), with a considerable commentary: 'This concise interrogation characterises the seeming ubiquity of the voice of the Cuckoo, and dispossesses the creature almost of a corporeal existence; the imagination being tempted to this exertion of her power by a consciousness ... that the Cuckoo is ... heard throughout ... Spring, but seldom becomes an object of sight.' The imagination is 'tempted' to present an idea of disembodied, and thus immortal life, which suggests that the imagination is here at the edge of her legitimate powers.

[8] Cf. 'youth's golden gleam' (*1805* VI 245) and 'the visionary gleam' of the *Ode*. The 'visionary hours' are experienced in separation from the source of the sound, just as in *The Prelude* 'Visionary Power / Attends the motions of the viewless winds' (*1850* V 596).

the heaven that are our home. Meanwhile the earth itself is left behind, unsubstantial and unreal. It is not the world clothed with celestial light, but a 'faery place', the world no longer the world.

'To H.C., Six Years Old'[9]

Hartley has many of the qualities ascribed to the child in the *Ode*. The first line, 'O Thou! whose fancies from afar are brought', is echoed twice in the *Ode* in the lines 'The Soul that rises with us / ... cometh from afar' and 'Though inland far we be, / Our souls have sight of that immortal sea'. All three phrases are irradiated by De Quincey's comment on how the word 'far', carrying 'the voice / Of mountain torrents' into the Boy of Winander's heart, was the means 'by which space and its infinities are attributed to the human heart'.[10] Hartley has the capacity to bring those qualities into the temporal world. With that ability, however, comes the concomitant problem of articulation: words he has, but in attempting to fit them 'to unutterable thought' he makes of them 'a mock apparel' – that is, they are inadequate to the task of realizing those thoughts. This is a constant Wordsworthian theme.[11]

As a 'Faery Voyager', sailing in a boat above the earth, Hartley is, like the poet in the Prologue to Peter Bell, floating through the clouds in his 'Sky Canoe' (*VL* 44).[12] The business of the world is left behind – 'what care we / For treasons, tumult and for wars?' and 'you quite forget / What in the world is doing'. They drive 'deep into the heavens' (24) travelling 'Through many a breathless field of light', arriving at 'the world of fairy', a word that echoes through this poem as 'the land of fairy' and 'Fairyland'.[13] Hartley and the poet are in the same boat, 'Faery Voyager[s]', a boat that seems more to 'brood on air than an earthly stream'; that idea, the heavenly brooding over the earthly, is revived in the *Ode*, where the child's 'Immortality' 'Broods like the Day, a Master

---

[9]. This poem is omitted from Curtis's *Experiments*, probably because he thought it composed in 1804 (*P2V* 100). Stephen Gill believes that it was composed between March and May 1802, which Curtis accepts as a possibility. If in 1802, it occupies a critical place in Wordsworth's growing awareness of the powers of childhood (*MW* 702).

[10]. *1805* V 409 and note, from De Quincey, *Recollections of the Lakes and the Lake Poets* (Edinburgh, 1862), p. 161.

[11]. He offers the title 'Imagination' to that power only as a consequence of the 'sad incompetence of human speech' (*1850* VI 593).

[12]. Cf. Coleridge's description of his son: 'a fairy elf – all life, all motion – indefatigable in joy – a spirit of Joy dancing on an Aspen Leaf' (*CL* I 668).

[13]. Perhaps Wordsworth changed the spelling to 'Faery' in To H.C. to distance the notion of 'fairies', which would have trivialized his intention. 'Faery' also bears the same significance in The Skylark and To the Cuckoo.

o'er a Slave', the relation of power exactly that Wordsworth would have between heaven and earth. If not in the poet, there is in Hartley, as in the child in the *Ode*, a union of worlds 'Where heaven and earth do make one imagery'. However, the survival of this union is threatened by Hartley's having to accommodate himself to the world, by his growing up. The light-hearted recognition of this division in the Prologue to Peter Bell:

> There was a time, a time indeed,
> When poets lived in clover.
> What boots it now to keep the key
> Of Fairyland? for, woe is me!
> Those blessed days are over

finds a calm, even sombre, articulation in the opening of the *Ode*, 'There was a time …', later expressed with greater force in Resolution and Independence, as the decline from youth and gladness to despondency and madness. However, in Peter Bell, Wordsworth was still optimistic and descends to earth to tell a not quite successful story of the reconciliation of the two worlds, the natural supernaturalized, a reconciliation he fails to find for most of the characters of his longer narratives – Michael or Ruth or Margaret. If those people, suffering the consequences and conditions of mortality, are given no redeeming vision, then Hartley, living in a faery and mystical world, were he encumbered with the mundane, would cease to be what he is. Not 'doomed … / … to be trailed along the soiling earth', nor to be the guest of pain, sorrow or 'the injuries of tomorrow', he must either remain a visionary child, with a 'young Lamb's heart among the full-grown flocks' or 'Nature will end … thee quite' and Hartley will 'Slip in a moment out of life'.[14] Nature potentially at odds with Hartley's childlike life is comparable to the earth as the 'homely Nurse' intending 'To make her Foster-child, her Inmate Man / Forget the glories he hath known'. What Wordsworth has not achieved in To H.C., a resolution between two worlds not much like each other, he will tentatively envisage, twice over, in the *Ode*.

If the course of nature and the sorrows of mortality are a threat to Hartley, society and its habits are an equal threat to the quality of life he represents. Imitating the ways of adults, conning part after part,

---

[14.] It is this unresolved division which makes the composition in 1802 more likely than in 1804.

imitating the ways of business, love or strife, children thus strive blindly against the blessedness Wordsworth saw in Hartley, their souls borne down by the weight of custom. In Personal Talk (*P2V* 253) an unnamed speaker defends gossip and chatter. Wordsworth then weighs in with a condemnation hardly proportionate to the offence:

> 'Sound sense, and love itself, and mirth and glee,
> Are foster'd by the comment and the gibe.'
> Even be it so: yet still among your tribe,
> Our daily world's true Worldlings, rank not me!
> Children are blest, and powerful: their world lies
> More justly balanced; partly at their feet,
> And part far from them: – sweetest melodies
> Are those that are by distance made more sweet;
> Whose mind is but the mind of his own eyes
> He is a Slave; the meanest we can meet!'[15]

His contempt for those he elsewhere called 'the vacant and the vain' is marked in the derision behind 'your tribe' – the 'true Worldlings' who are too much with us. Children have a sense of another world – 'part far from them' – which acts as a balance to this world, at their feet. The next line and a half hardly seem to follow: what are the sweetest melodies that distance makes more sweet? Perhaps the clue is in 'far from them'. They hear something they recognize but it seems far off, and in seeming far off is all the sweeter. Yet this is not a music they hear through their senses.[16] In the *Ode*, Wordsworth celebrates as a 'perpetual benediction' the determined obstinate questioning 'Of sense and outward things', the embers of childhood still alive in us. Although the metaphor of the last two lines changes from hearing to sight, the two are closely related – a 'voice to light gave being' (On the Power of Sound). The sweetest melodies, near or far, as sound or celestial light, cannot be heard or seen by a worldling enslaved to sense. If now as an adult Wordsworth is shut out from the world children know, better than participating in idle chat is a 'long, barren silence', sitting 'without emotion, hope, or aim' by his half-kitchen, half-parlour fire. Better be 'still, and wait

---

[15] For 'worldlings' see also *To the small Celandine* (*P2V* 79, 54). Keats could have read Wordsworth's lines; his are a pithier variant – 'Heard melodies are sweet, but those unheard / Are sweeter' (*Ode to a Grecian Urn*).

[16] Cf. 'The mind of Man is fram'd even like the breath / And harmony of music' (*1805* I 351-52).

without hope / For hope would be hope for the wrong thing', wait without thought because we are not ready for thought (*EC* III), and so endure a hopeless patience exemplified in the stoicism of the Leech-gatherer.

Towards the end of 1802, Wordsworth wrote a sonnet, 'It is no spirit who from Heaven hath flown' (*P2V* 216) in which he speaks of himself, instead of finding his conflicts and ambitions in the birds, butterflies and flowers around him. Sara Hutchinson had called him to the window of Dove Cottage to look at the evening star shining alone in the sky. The classical idea of a star is that it is an earthly hero translated to heaven. Wordsworth's first line deliberately counters that, for whether or not a spirit, Hesperus is not from heaven. Nor is he like Peter Bell, 'gone from Earth the Heavens to espy'. Both his solitude and his sole possession of the sky appeal to Wordsworth – 'the sky, / He hath it to himself – 'tis all his own'.[17] Hesperus has achieved something Wordsworth would achieve – 'O most ambitious Star!' – initiating an 'inquest' into his own ambitions, which constitute the final six lines of the poem:

> And, while I gazed, there came to me a thought
> That I might step beyond my natural race
> As thou seem'st now to do; might one day trace
> Some ground not mine; and, strong her strength above,
> My Soul, an Apparition in the place,
> Tread there, with steps that no one shall reprove!

He wants to step beyond his 'natural race' – off the earth, perhaps, as does Hesperus, and look for some 'ground not mine'. What ground is the difficulty: not exactly heaven, but perhaps aided by the power of heaven – 'strong her strength above' – he will be able to step onto a ground not principally material, for it will be where his soul goes, an apparition; and yet his soul will be material enough to 'Tread there' with steps unreproved. Some balance is sought, difficult to discern. Yet those two worlds unresolved are also features of 'With little here to do or see', the second of the daisy poems. The daisy is an 'unassuming Common-place / Of Nature, with that homely face' and also a star

---

[17.] Cf. 'Possessions have I, wholly, solely mine' (*HG* B 897) and 'I had a world about me – 'twas my own, / I made it; for it only lived to me, / And to the God who looked into my mind' (*1805* III 142-44).

'glittering from afar'. Like Hesperus in the sky, the daisy 'Self-poised in air thou seem'st to rest'. As we have seen, that in-betweenness, as here, meets the poet's approval: 'May peace come never to his nest, / Who shall reprove thee!' It seems to be this balance between the mortal and immortal, between earth and heaven, 'A blended holiness of earth and sky' (*HG* B 159-61), that will bring peace to Wordsworth's nest.

Part IV

Reading the Ode

'Wordsworth's words always *mean* the whole of their possible Meaning'   (*CL* II 977)

Chapter 9

Origins

Wordsworth's Questions

IN HER JOURNAL ENTRY for Saturday 27 March 1802 Dorothy wrote 'A divine morning', casually adding that 'Wm wrote part of an *Ode*' at what must have been a very interrupted breakfast. The next day they went to Keswick to stay with Coleridge. On 4 April, Dorothy records that she 'walked down to Coleridge's. Mrs C. came to Greta Bank to Tea. Wm. walked down with Mrs C. I repeated his verses to them. We sate pleasantly enough after supper.'

The two poets sharing their verses was common enough, particularly that spring. Unique to this occasion is the shock that reverberated through Coleridge when he heard those stanzas, evident in his immediate and remarkable response. He always claimed, however difficult to believe, that the 340 lines of the Verse Letter were written that same evening, up to and probably beyond midnight, when he had small thoughts of sleep. Jim Mays notes that 'MS 2 [of the Verse Letter] is unambiguously headed "April 4, 1802. – Sunday Evening.", a date repeated in all subsequent reworkings of the lines' (*PW* II 2 861). When transcribing parts of the poem in his letters, Coleridge often mentions the date and time – but to whom would that date be significant? If not only, then primarily to the Wordsworths and Mrs Clarkson, if she is the 'Mrs C.' Dorothy mentions. Sara Hutchinson might also have known indirectly, but otherwise very few and probably only those who knew both of Coleridge's desperate state, and the date of his hearing Wordsworth's stanzas. So it was an extremely pointed and persistent ascription.

But what was it that so got to him, separating these verses from the rest of the 32 poems 'some of them of considerable Length ... the greater number ... very excellent Compositions' that Wordsworth had written by the time of this letter, not even hinting at the existence of the unfinished *Ode*? (*CL* II 830, 29 July 1802). It is a peculiar and probably unanswerable paradox that its apparent importance to him is not reflected in any of his other works: there is no mention of the *Ode* in his letters, a couple of minor references in his notebooks, and quotations but no commentary in *The Friend*, and none in the *Biographia* bar the exceptions he took to the child as philosopher and lying awake in the grave. Coleridge frequently quotes from his own ode in his letters, but never mentions Wordsworth's. Yet no one doubts that the Verse Letter was catalysed into life by the first four stanzas of the unfinished *Ode*.

The last line of each of the first two verses ends in different versions of the same question: has the power gone from me, or has it gone from the earth? The two questions are summed up at the conclusion of the final verse – 'Whither is fled the visionary gleam / Where is it now, the glory and the dream?' Two years elapsed before these questions were successfully addressed. That the stanzas were only 'part of an *Ode*' suggests he might have been expecting an answer, though it would be possible to read them as merely describing a condition, but it does indicate he knew it was unfinished.[1]

How seriously Wordsworth took them at the time, how much they reflected the essence of the debate he was having with himself that spring, is difficult to determine. It is perfectly possible that in Coleridge's reaction Wordsworth saw their importance. Two much more optimistic poems, To The Cuckoo – 'I do beget / That golden time again' – and 'My heart leaps up' were written on 23 and 26 March respectively, the latter the evening before that interrupted breakfast the next morning. It is easy to forget that these stanzas were at first just one of the many poems that Wordsworth wrote that spring, only finally distinguished by the addition of seven stanzas answering the questions, and the importance Wordsworth would attach to the completed *Ode*.

Did Wordsworth have any inkling of what he would eventually make of them? Did he realize that in those questions lay the crux of the problem, the hiatus between seeing and feeling? If the questions that the *Ode* asks are visible through the veil of his lighter verse, here they are set down with a resolute clarity. The Wordsworths were with Coleridge at Greta Hall for a week before Dorothy read the verses to him. This might be taken as either regarding them of no immediate importance; or that they were anxious about telling Coleridge something he would not want to hear.

[1.] Stephen Gill thinks of the first four verses as complete and 'a poignant lament, an elegy for inevitable loss' (*A Life*, p. 253).

Were those unfinished verses an announcement – 'I can't do it' – and Wordsworth reluctant to admit defeat? If so, perhaps Dorothy decided it was important for Coleridge to hear the questions, tacitly asking him to come up with an answer, and so she not William read the verses.[2] They might both have been hoping that his response would enable William to resolve the problem, finish the poem and then go on 'swimmingly' with his 'Great Work', as she later said of *The Excursion* (*MY* I 64).

Coleridge's Answer

In the Verse Letter (*PW* I 289), which he read to William and Dorothy three weeks later, on 21 April, Coleridge, as might be expected, got to the nub of the matter, and provided an answer. He first declared a loss in himself of the same kind as Wordsworth's, by listing in finer detail some of the lovely sights around him, and then succinctly summarizing their common experience with 'I see, not feel / How beautiful they are'. They were, Coleridge told Wordsworth, both capable of an aesthetic response, both suffering some kind of grief, and both divorced from that power which renders mind and nature one. His answer was as confident as it was clear:

> JOY, Sara! is the Spirit & the Power,
> That wedding Nature to us gives in Dower
>   A new Earth & a new Heaven
> Undreamt of by the Sensual & the Proud

and for those who can rejoice, 'all Things live from Pole to Pole', the one life celebrated by both poets. That Wordsworth would have believed all this as fervently as Coleridge is not in doubt, given that such a belief permeates his poetry – for instance, in Tintern Abbey he had declared that through 'the deep power of joy, / We see into the life of things'; in *The Prelude* that 'I saw one life, and felt that it was joy' (*1805* II 430), which a few lines later he calls the 'never-failing principle of joy' (465).

Behind this lie two problems – one for us and one for Wordsworth. Our problem in advancing the Verse Letter as providing a solution to their common difficulty is that it is addressed to Sara Hutchinson, and not to Wordsworth. However, because it picks up Wordsworth's themes,

---

[2.] Dorothy is prepared to take Coleridge to task on William's behalf. Thus in her journal of 15 February 1802, Dorothy is glad to get a letter from Coleridge, 'this was satisfactory but his letter was not an *answer* to William's which I expected...'

deliberately echoing lines and phrases from these stanzas, Tintern Abbey and Peter Bell, and that as far as we know its first reading was to Dorothy and William, it was almost certainly *for* Wordsworth, even if *to* Sara. Its metamorphosis into *Dejection* substantiates this. Wordsworth became the addressee, remaining so for twelve years, and it included further echoes of his stanzas. If Sara's name had to be removed to make it a publishable poem, Wordsworth was not his only choice; he might have, and finally did, make that person a nameless 'Lady'. Alternatively, it could have remained a private poem, a *cri de cœur* for his closest friends; but he chose to publish it, and on Wordsworth's wedding day, the seventh anniversary of his own disastrous marriage.[3] That should not be taken as an ironic comment on marriage: quite the opposite, because marriage, in one form or another, is Coleridge's route back to joy, delineated here and throughout his letters: 'Domestic Happiness is the greatest of things sublunary – and of things celestial it is perhaps impossible for unassisted Man to believe any thing greater' (*CL* I 158).

Therein lies Wordsworth's problem. He and Dorothy had to listen to Coleridge weaving one great web of domestic misery, stifled powers and hopeless love, unveiling a picture of his life that until then they had probably only seen in part. Dorothy was dismayed by this desperate and lengthy confessional, 'a Scream / Of agony by Torture lengthen'd out'.[4] But Wordsworth, much less sympathetic to Coleridge's suffering, must have wondered, if he recognized that Coleridge had identified the problem, what the resolution of such misery – finding joy through marriage – had to do with him; for although he had not yet married Mary, he and Dorothy shared a deep domestic joy. Coleridge could not even apply his remedy to himself ('Past cure, & past Complaint'), and in the Verse Letter, it is conditional upon Sara Hutchinson becoming 'married' to the Wordsworth household, 'nested with the Darlings of thy Love'.

So why might Coleridge himself have thought his cure at all relevant to Wordsworth? He knew how stable his and Dorothy's domestic life was, how close to a kind of marriage. He also knew that Wordsworth was not in a rush to marry Mary Hutchinson, that he was hesitating, quite

---

[3.] For other events associated with 4 October, significant to both Wordsworth and Coleridge, see *EFL* 6.

[4.] *VL* 187-88. Dorothy does not record William's reaction but her journal contains several references to Coleridge's unhappiness in December 1801 and the early months of 1802. Thus, 29 January 1802, 'A heart rending letter from Coleridge – we were as sad as we could be. Wm. wrote to him.' On 6 February, Dorothy was 'made ill' by 'two very affecting letters from Coleridge'.

possibly for fear of disrupting his domestic stability. Coincidentally or not, the night before Dorothy read the four unfinished stanzas, Coleridge remembered, some six years later, that ill in bed he had 'continued talking with Wordsworth the whole night till the Dawn of the Day, urging him to conclude on marrying Mary Hutchinson'.[5] If Coburn's dating is correct, that is some conversation for an ill man, and Coleridge's insistence must have been matched by Wordsworth's reluctance. The next day Coleridge heard the *Ode*, and that very evening he wrote the Verse Letter – a knackering 24 hours. One thing is certain: Coleridge would have had Wordsworth in mind when writing about any kind of marriage. Another thing is very likely: when Wordsworth heard the Verse Letter three weeks later he remembered that night-long conversation whenever it had taken place. The pros and cons of marriage were in both their minds.

When the poem was published in *The Morning Post* as *Dejection: an Ode* all references to marriage had disappeared. This is possibly because from that day onwards the realization of joy was no longer conditional upon marriage. Some small variations in the *Morning Post* version corroborate this:

> Joy lifts thy spirit, joy attunes thy voice,
> To thee do all things live from pole to pole,
> Their life the eddying of thy living soul!

Joy has arrived in the present tense. Through his marriage – 'rais'd from anxious dread and busy care' – Wordsworth has rediscovered 'the Spirit & the Power, / That wedding Nature to us gives in Dower / A new Earth & a new Heaven'. Coleridge imagines Wordsworth getting up next morning with a light heart and cheerful eyes to 'sing his lofty song', that is, return to The Recluse, by doing which Coleridge hopes that Wordsworth will also 'teach me to rejoice'. He has outlined the programme by which he would have Wordsworth return to 'his former mountain Track'.

Wordsworth's Response

Wordsworth replied to the Verse Letter almost as swiftly as Coleridge had to the unfinished *Ode*. Some two and a half weeks later, on 4 May, Coleridge almost certainly heard much if not most of The Leech-gatherer,

---

[5.] *CN* III 3304. As noted in the previous chapter, Coburn supplies no evidence for this date, and John Worthen throws some doubt on it (*Life*, p. 250).

the first version of which was finished on 7 May.[6] It can be considered a response or reaction to the Verse Letter for its partial recreation of the spring morning evoked in the first stanzas of the *Ode*, followed by the onset of gloom, of poets beginning in youth and gladness and descending into despondency and madness, a progress comparable to the depressing division between seeing and feeling in both the *Ode* and the Letter. Wordsworth finds his answer, here if not elsewhere, in the patient stoicism of the Leech-gatherer, an answer quite opposed to the ecstatic resurgence of joy that closes the Letter.

Nothing proposed in the Letter fits Wordsworth's hope of resolving his understanding of Coleridge's conception of their common problem – it is an outright rejection of his method. The title chosen for publication, Resolution and Independence, indicates Wordsworth's determination to be strong – a key word in the *Ode* and elsewhere in his poetry – in the face of grief, not to give in – which may also have been tacit advice to Coleridge, who regularly succumbed to his grief; and with that resolution comes the willingness to be independent, to stand alone, as the Leech-gatherer, all his family gone, stands alone but stands firm.[7] Wordsworth might also have been inverting Coleridge's negative words in order to point him to a more positive end – that his wisest plan was to be still and patient all he could – advice Coleridge had given himself when he saw no resolution to his own hiatus between seeing and feeling.

So Wordsworth declares his determination to follow the old man's example – and if he dissolves into the landscape, as the Leech-gatherer appears to do, or is rolled round with rocks and stones and trees with Lucy, so be it. That stoicism enabled Wordsworth to be patient, to wait for the answer; and it came some two years later, when discovering the embers of a celestial fire still alive in him, he felt the return of a modest joy, able to believe that reflection on our past years 'doth breed / Perpetual benediction'. His solution, when it came, had absolutely nothing to do with a happy marriage, or even, it seems, with an 'abiding Home'. So neither of them produced an answer satisfactory to the other, and one may speculate whether Wordsworth's wasn't the resolute patience of an essentially happy man (who lived in a 'happy Castle') willing to face a

---

[6.] On the morning of 4 May, Wordsworth 'read & repeated the Leech gatherer' to Dorothy, and around 4 o'clock 'Wm and C repeated and read verses'. It is most unlikely that a just-completed poem was not read to Coleridge, especially if it was a response to his 'doleful' verses.

[7.] Wordsworth pointed to 'the fortitude, independence, persevering spirit, and the general moral dignity of this old man's character' (*EY* I 367, 14 June 1802).

long, barren silence, impatient with someone very unhappy, who had been driven to find at least a vicarious solution to his suffering.[8]

Coleridge has the Last Laugh?

Jim Mays reminds us that The Leech-gatherer always follows the Verse Letter in the extant manuscripts. Whoever decided on that collocation, Coleridge could hardly have missed the import of Wordsworth's response. In the six months between the writing of the Verse Letter and the publication of *Dejection*, he had time enough to realize that Wordsworth did not connect marriage with the revival of joy. Yet it seems that he was determined to insist on his answer in the face of Wordsworth's willingness to 'go plodding on, / By myself, chearfully, till the day is done' (To a Skylark). By 19 July, he had cut and reorganized the sprawling 340 lines of the Letter to just 140 of the Ode. Sent to Sotheby that day, it was already addressed to Wordsworth, and although not finally ordered, it had gained those significant present tenses of the final verse. So by the middle of July it had in essence become the poem he would publish on 4 October, apparently challenging Wordsworth to deny that joy had revived in him or that marriage would not instigate that joy.

Nothing Wordsworth ever wrote corroborated Coleridge's opinion, always insisting that his recovery of joy came from a quite different source. Yet, within a year of his marriage, Coleridge was able to rejoice that Wordsworth had returned to his 'Great Work, in which he will sail; on an open Ocean, & a steady wind' (*CL* II 1013, 14 October 1803). From 1803 to 1805, as well as completing the *Ode*, Wordsworth produced much of and completed the thirteen books of *The Prelude*, as well as many other poems. Any ordinary mind must boggle at such an achievement.

So was Coleridge right? Had what he called a 'blessed Marriage' enabled Wordsworth to rediscover joy, even if marriage wasn't the direct source? (*CN* III 3304). The jury is out, and will remain out. All we know is that the two events – his marriage and his return to his 'mountain Track' – follow closely one upon the other.

[8.] 'Within our happy Castle there dwelt one'. The idea of a castle also points to separation from the outside world, and perhaps Wordsworth feared that marriage might breach those walls.

Chapter 10

Verse, Grammar and Imagery

IF BY PLACING IT AT THE end of all his collections, Wordsworth saw the *Ode* as the core and culmination of his work, it is neither a retrospective nor a summary.[1] It is a poem in which the reader is asked 'to follow the fluxes and refluxes of the mind' (*BL* II 147) and despite being two years or more in the making, what one might call the 'present-tenseness' or dramatic quality of the *Ode* is a key if little mentioned feature – for even when the past is looked to, it is alive with present feeling. Every time we sit down to it, it is something that we must, in Keats's words, 'burn through', discovering or recovering again and again various aspects of Wordsworth's experience. It is not a poem that orders and organizes past thought and feeling into a rational and coherent whole, not a poem in which emotion is recollected in tranquillity, but alive with a raw and sometimes puzzling spontaneity.[2] Or apparently so – for that spontaneity must in part be subjective (DF) and depend on the reader's mood – one can tire of a poem, and then the verse begins to feel inevitable rather than spontaneous. Yet sometimes familiarity breeds only increasing admiration. Stephen Gill, who must have read the poem more times than most, said in an email that the poem meant more and more to him the older he gets. So, subjective, yes, but if one continues to feel the spontaneity after repeated readings, and other readers agree, then perhaps there are objective qualities substantiating that feeling. One may also ask whether a poem 'so long deliberated' can possibly retain its spontaneity through several periods of composition? It seems unlikely, but 'true art is to conceal the art' (DF). The seeming

---

[1.] He said the same of On the Power of Sound, although this only came at the end of the poems on imagination: the *Ode* sits outside all Wordsworth's classifications – except that immortality follows death. See *MW* 725.

[2.] After reading this chapter, David Fairer sent me several informative and salutary comments, here acknowledged as DF.

spontaneity may not be spontaneous, but if not, then it is true art at its best. I believe that Eliot said that a poem can originate in a sense of rhythm; it might be possible to carry that sense of rhythm through several periods of composition.

Verse and Form

That feeling of spontaneity may in part derive from the irregularity of the length and structure of every stanza of the poem. This is in contrast to Wordsworth's habitual practice, in shorter poems, of maintaining a regular verse form and stanza length. The spontaneity is also evident in Dorothy's recording of the poem's origins.

Although he would have been familiar with versions of the Pindaric ode such as Dryden's Alexander's Feast, Gray's The Bard..., or Collins's The Passions, the *Ode* is often linked to the English original of this form, Cowley's Pindarics, partly because of a visible similarity of structure, and partly because, according to Duncan Wu, 1801 is the *terminus ad quem* for Wordsworth's reading of Cowley.[3] His only recorded comment on his poetry is brief: 'Read all Cowley; he is very valuable to a collector of English sound sense' – the subtext of which seems to be 'but not valuable in any other way'.[4] Apart from any we might recognize in his poetry, Wordsworth left no examples of such a collection, nor any other comments on Cowley. Nevertheless, together with his knowledge of the Pindaric tradition, Cowley's irregular rhyming and the variety of his line and stanza lengths may have given Wordsworth a sense of freedom not often present in his previous verse. In respect of these remarks David Fairer provided the following caveat:

> The classical Pindaric ode was strictly regular. Congreve's very influential 1706 preface attacked the Cowleyan irregular

---

[3.] See the following for more detailed and informed opinions: Curtis, *Experiments*, p. 95, who recommends J.D. Rea, 'Coleridge's Intimations of Immortality from Proclus', *Modern Philology*, Vol. 26, no. 2 (1928), pp. 203-4; and Herbert Hartman, 'The Intimations of Wordsworth's *Ode*', *RES*, Vol. 6 (1930), p. 136; both compare the *Ode* with '*Ode* on the Immortal Memory and Friendship of that Noble Fair ...' by Ben Jonson. See also, Simon Jarvis, 'Hyper-Pindaric: The Greater Irregular Lyric from Cowley to Keston Sutherland', in Julie Carr and Jeffrey C. Robinson (eds), *Active Romanticism*. (Alabama, 2015), pp. 127-44.

[4.] *Memoirs* II 477, quoted from Duncan Wu, *Wordsworth's Reading 1800-15* (Cambridge, 1996), p. 65. I cannot agree with Jarvis (p. 127) that 'those irregular grand lyrics ... appear to come almost from nowhere ... Coleridge's "Dejection" and Wordsworth's *Ode* ("There was a time").'

ode as not being Pindaric: 'a bundle of rambling incoherent thoughts express'd in a like parcel of irregular stanzas, which also consist of such another complication of disproportion'd, uncertain, and perplex'd verse and rhymes'.[5] Both Gray and Collins understood the two traditions – using the strictly regular classical Pindaric for their poems on poetry (Gray's The Progress of Poesy and Collins's Ode on the Poetical Character) but the irregular for others (e.g. The Bard and The Passions). Pindar, the master-craftsman of Greek metre, employed a different stanza for each of his 45 surviving odes. So Wordsworth's choice of an irregular ode was clearly deliberate. He would know the fierce debate about the Pindaric throughout the 18th Century.

At first glance, Wordsworth's debt to Cowley seems limited to a linguistic and metrical freedom, as the tenor and substance of Wordsworth's poetry is very different.[6] For instance, Resurrection, Cowley's immortality ode, promotes the very idea that Wordsworth rejects: drowning all life's lesser noises, the Last Trumpet:

> This mightier sound shall make
> When Dead t'arise,
> And open Tombs, and open Eyes
> To the long Sluggards of five thousand years.
> This mightier Sound shall make its Hearers Ears.
> Then shall the scatter'ed Atomes crowding come
>   Back to their Ancient Home...   (32-38)

So why did Wordsworth decide to read 'all Cowley'? – hardly necessary if he was just in search of 'sound sense' or metrical freedom: perhaps because now and then an idea or attitude crops up to which he would have been sympathetic. In 'Life', Cowley sees the burden of 'Custom' much as Wordsworth does:

---

[5] Samuel Johnson shared Congreve's disdain for the irregular, but seems to have associated the Pindaric with the irregular. 'This lax and lawless versification so much concealed the deficiencies of the barren, and flattered the laziness of the idle, that it immediately overspread our books of poetry; all the boys and girls caught the pleasing fashion, and they that could do nothing else could write like Pindar. ... Pindarism prevailed about half a century; but, at last, died gradually away, and other imitations supply its place.' *Lives of the English Poets* (Glasgow, 1825), p. 15.

[6] For Cowley's poems online, see http://cowley.lib.virginia.edu/worksol.html.

> My Eyes are opened, and I see
> Through the Transparent Fallacie:
> Because we seem wisely to talk
> Like men of business; and for business walk
> From place to place,

which is, in other words, fitting ourselves to dialogues of business, love or strife; and so

> We grow at last by *Custom* to believe,
> That really we *Live*.
> Whilst all these *Shadows* that for *Things* we take,
> Are but the empty *Dreams* which in *Deaths sleep*
> we make.[7]

The earthly freight of custom comes to weigh upon us almost as heavily as that life which is not life. If he read them, these are lines Wordsworth would have endorsed, illustrating as they do some of the metaphysics of a poet whom Samuel Johnson declared 'almost the last of that race, and undoubtedly the best' – taking on what Milton gave up – trying 'the metaphysick style only in his lines upon Hobson, the carrier. Cowley adopted it, and excelled his predecessors, having as much sentiment, and more music' (*Lives* 11, 7).

Cowley's metaphysics may have had a particular source. He was at Cambridge with Henry More, and perhaps his influence made Cowley sympathetic to the broad aims of the Cambridge Platonists; for Cowley advocated the use of reason in the study of nature, or Experimental Philosophy, as well as seeing no conflict between Reason and the mysteries of the Godhead. Samuel Johnson approved: 'His two metrical disquisitions for and against Reason, are no mean specimens of metaphysical poetry' (*Lives of the English Poets*, p. 12).

> Reason, which (God be prais'd!) still walks, for all
> It's old original fall.
> And since itself the boundless Godhead join'd
> With a reasonable mind,
> It plainly shows that mysteries divine
> May with our Reason join.[8]

[7.] The emphases are Cowley's.
[8.] Reason, the Use of it in Divine Matters.

That fundamental Cambridge Platonist belief is embedded in Wordsworth's poetry, and it is possible that Wordsworth recognized Cowley as having an intellectual background comparable to his own, finding in him a progenitor, few of whom he found elsewhere.

If he did read all Cowley out of a potential sympathy, in the end it was 'sound sense' that he remembered. David Fairer suggested there may be more to the phrase, especially in respect of feminine rhyme.[9] Quoting Pope's line from the *Essay on Criticism* – 'And make the sound an echo to the sense' – he noted that on occasion Wordsworth not only finds a good rhyme, sometimes also onomatopoeic or alliterative, as in 'sound sense' itself, but that the sense is integrated with the sound. His example is how the feminine rhyme 'remembers'/'in our embers' underscores the gladness Wordsworth feels, and that, as 'rem*embers*' contains '*embers*' within it, the sense is echoed in the sound. I cannot better such a perceptive reading, adding only that perhaps Helen Vendler's connection between 'imperial' and 'empyrial' is another example (Vendler, 'Lionel Trilling', p. 72).

Whether Wordsworth saw the Pindaric ode as regular or irregular, it was Cowley's version and that of his successors that he adopted. Daniel Robinson notes that, 'As he explained to Isabella Fenwick, Wordsworth wrote the first four stanzas in 1802 "as an attempt at a Pindaric ode, in which the first two stanzas function as the strophe and antistrophe and the longer final two as the epode".' The first two stanzas are of the same length, nine lines, but the next are seventeen and twenty-two respectively; all are differently structured. It is as if Wordsworth had the idea of a formal and regular ode in mind, but abandoned it as the poetic impulse overtook him.

The hints of this formal beginning are then superseded by a real sense of spontaneity – though as no *vers* is ever wholly *libre*, so no poem is ever wholly spontaneous. Wordsworth worked carefully on his *Ode*, preventing himself from regularizing the original irregularities – which to Johnson were no more than signs of incompetence. The longest line is fourteen syllables, and the shortest three in its printed form ('Land and sea'), though the Longman manuscript has a very heavily inked correction that changes 'But He beholds the light, and whence it flows' to two lines, the first of which is just the two syllables, 'But He'. Another manuscript version, and all printed versions authorized by Wordsworth, make it a single line, but that leaves 'Heaven lies about us in our infancy' without a rhyme – one of only three such lines in

---

[9.] The effect of feminine rhymes is considered below.

the poem. It seems likely that, in reviewing the poem after it had been copied out by Sara Hutchinson, Wordsworth noticed that that line had no rhyme, saw that 'But He' would work, and temporarily modified the manuscript as a move towards regularity. He reverted to the original probably because that change made no structural sense and he felt that the orphaned line stood perfectly well by itself, even having the hint of a distant internal rhyme.

The process indicates a determination to maintain the sense of spontaneity, and having the art to achieve it. The rhymes and line lengths may have first occurred adventitiously, without much conscious effort. The poet reviewed his verse, noticed what might be termed a flaw, corrected that flaw, and then saw that the correction served no purpose. An internal rhyme would serve as well as an end-rhyme, or no rhyme, that no one would really notice that there was no rhyme, so irregular the verse; and when it came to proof Wordsworth had the good sense to reverse his own correction. That only the lineation was changed, leaving words and verse unchanged, says much about Wordsworth's confidence: he did not expand the line in order to fulfil a nominal metrical requirement. The *post-facto* decision-making reflects Wordsworth's method of composition. The rhymes occur where and when they will, not dissimilar to children speaking in rhyme – Johnson's boys and girls – and Wordsworth the critic permits the genius of Wordsworth the poet.[10]

Most of the rhymes in the poem are either couplets or quatrains (*abab*), but there are several triplets and split quatrains (*abba*), or quintains split by triplets (*abbba*), at least one sextain ending in a triplet (*abbaaa*), as well the two other unrhymed lines – 'I hear, I hear, with joy I hear!' and 'In the faith that looks through death'. Some are so widely separated as to be effectively unrhymed – for example 'life' (91) with 'strife' (98) – freely irregular perhaps, and something that, though writing largely in couplets, Collins does once or twice – 'fair' (29) with 'Hair' (38) – in The Passions. Rhymes occur between lines of very different length, and one can find examples of all kinds of rhyming – full rhymes, half-rhymes, internal rhymes, assonance and a large number of feminine rhymes and half-rhymes. The feminine rhymes have a particular effect

---

[10.] Having heard Wordsworth's first four verses, was Coleridge infected with the same spirit? He always asserted that the Verse Letter was written in an evening, up to and beyond midnight, and on very day he heard the first four stanzas of the *Ode*. Coleridge's rhymes, sometimes approaching doggerel, have that same sense of random spontaneity as those of Wordsworth. Neither poet wrote with quite the same freedom ever again.

upon the poem. Most often occurring in light-hearted or comic poetry, they add a cheerfulness and sense of zest to the poem – for example:

> Oh evil day! if I were sullen
> While earth is herself adorning,
>   This sweet May-morning,
> And the children are culling ...

'Adorning' and 'morning' are full feminine rhymes, and the first and last lines might be termed feminine assonance. There are also many feminine half-rhymes: for example, 'Land and sea / Give themselves up to jollity, / And with the heart of May/ Doth every beast keep holiday'.[11] Those rhymes substantiate the mood Wordsworth is seeking to evoke; but even at a critical moment in the poem where Wordsworth is describing the little that is left from all that is lost, the potential recovery from the 'earthly freight' of custom, they serve to underscore the emotion he is insisting on: 'O joy! that in our embers / Is something that doth live, / That nature yet remembers / What was so fugitive!' The fire is almost out, but the gladness that the poet finds in the embers still glowing is embodied in one full and one feminine half-rhyme. By contrast, it is worth noting that there are only three feminine-type rhymes in the last two stanzas – and all half-rhymes: 'primal sympathy' / 'must ever be'; 'thoughts that spring' / 'human suffering'; and 'an eye' / 'man's 'mortality'. All three principal words work against any kind of levity, reflecting the more sombre mood in which the poem closes.

Grammar

Coupled with this sense that the poet is in conversation with the reader, there is also, with a few exceptions, a beguiling simplicity of grammar, or what Coleridge identified as 'an austere purity of language both grammatically and logically; in short a perfect appropriateness of the words to the meaning' (*BL* II 142). The sentences are largely without convolution, plain declarations that require little effort to follow, even if their meaning proves elusive.[12] For example, 'The Winds come to me

---

[11.] I originally used these lines as an example as of a feminine rhyme. DF put me right: 'A feminine rhyme has to involve both lines. So that "sea-jollity" isn't a feminine rhyme, but "jollity-polity" would be. Similarly "May-holiday" isn't, but "holiday-jolly day" is.' Because such rhymes create a similar if less marked impression, I think they deserve the title of feminine half-rhymes.

[12.] See *Experiments* 117: 'In the manner of the short lyrics being written at the same time ... these stanzas ... build into units by accretion. The most frequent link is "and"

from the fields of sleep' is syntactically a simple statement, although the import is not self-evident. Such lines, scattered throughout the poem, Coleridge called 'curiosa felicitas', phrases that cannot be paraphrased, their *'untranslatableness*' 'the infallible test of a blameless style'.[13] Such phrases are simultaneously mysterious yet seemingly understood, because readers do not have to struggle with grammatical complexity, nor are brought to a pause in their reading. This varied, irregular, but uninterrupted movement onward is a component in the 'music' of the poem, the mystery of certain lines scattered through the verse adding to the music, the ebb and flow of a tide of thought which, as we read, we do not want to stop and question.[14] Think how much more of a struggle it is to follow the unfolding thought in much of Shakespeare's verse or Milton's: one frequently has to work hard first to grasp the grammar, and then the significance of the sentence. The *Ode* simply flows over these questions, almost preventing us asking them, and we have to make a deliberate effort to halt and interrogate the poem – to ask, for instance, what 'soothing thoughts' can possibly 'spring / Out of human suffering'? If we don't, or if our interrogation is unsuccessful, then as our reading ends, and the music fades, little or no meaning survives. We need both to find and, as best we can, answer, the questions the poem raises, but then forget that we asked them. Some of those questions will be considered in the chapters on Loss, Analysis and Recovery.

Imagery – Simpleness or Simplicity?

'For Simple Sence / Is Lord of all Created Excellence'[15]

Coupled to the uncomplicated sentence structure is a simplicity of imagery, which makes equally little demand on the reader, who is barely required to evoke what the poet describes.[16] Thus the universality of the poet's childhood vision is initially suggested by three very general pastoral terms – 'meadow, grove and stream' – which are further

---

(eleven times), the next ... "but" (four times). The links involving more complex structures are noticeably scarce ... Apart from simple counting, however ... each stanza is a subtle blend of the most basic, often paratactic, structures, and an occasional complex one.'

[13.] *BL II* 148, 142; 'a phrase first applied to the poet Horace by Petronius (*Satyricon*, 118) – noting the poet's ability to find an unexpected yet perfectly "right" word' (DF).

[14.] Though mysterious, Coleridge was sure that the sense of such lines was underpinned by Wordsworth's 'depth of feeling and imaginative power', without which 'his *mysticism* would become *sickly* – mere fog, and dimness!' (*BL II* 142).

[15.] Thomas Traherne, The Preparative.

[16.] Coleridge refuted 'the strange mistake so slightly grounded ... of Mr. Wordsworth's turn for SIMPLICITY!' (*BL II* 158).

generalized in the next line, 'The earth, and every common sight'.[17] It really doesn't matter what image the poet chooses, because the loss he laments is universal – and so perhaps it is important that the terms are general and not particular.[18] It is not the objects themselves that matter, but the 'affections' and 'apprehensions' with which they are beheld. What is lost is not the visible but the 'celestial light' in which things visible were 'apparell'd'. This suggests a power lost, but in the early stages of the poem the sources or origin of this power – in the mind of man or in the being of nature – is confused or undecided. It will be resolved before the poem closes.

Simple or general images are present in all parts of the poem – 'ye blessed Creatures', 'a thousand vallies far and wide', 'Earth fills her lap with pleasures of her own', 'A wedding or a festival / A mourning or a funeral; 'Thou little Child, yet glorious in the might / Of untam'd pleasures', 'on whom those truthes do light', 'blank misgivings', 'shadowy recollections', 'ye Fountains, Meadows, Hills, and Groves' – much is adduced, almost nothing particularized or dwelt on in detail. Even when a distinct object is selected, 'a Tree, of many one, / A single Field… / The Pansy at my feet', they are objects nominated, not objects described. Wordsworth, in the course of this poem is not searching for precision in his description of the appearances of nature. It doesn't matter, for instance, whether it is a pansy, a crocus, or a daisy at his feet. All would have done equally well.[19]

The simplicity of some of Wordsworth's poetry – its imagery, its structure and its sentiments – was mocked by early reviewers, and is still occasionally questioned. At the Coleridge Summer Conference

---

[17.] My wife suggested that these lines and some from *Home at Grasmere* may echo Satan's jealous description of Eden – following emphases mine: '*With what delight could I have walk'd thee round,* / If I could joy in aught; sweet interchange / *Of hill, and valley, rivers, woods,* and plains; / *Now land, now sea,* and shores with forest crown'd (*PL* IX 114-17). Wordsworth, though no Satan, has lost his delight and joy in what he sees, and so feels that he cannot inhabit the Paradise before him. However, in *Home at Grasmere* he was still in Paradise, but wondering what to do: ''tis not to enjoy, for this alone / That we exist; no something must be done. / *I must not walk in unreproved delight* / These narrow *bounds* and think of nothing more' (*HG* B 875-78) which may be a faint echo of Satan's words – whose views though are not confined to 'narrow bounds'.

[18.] 'Sublimity is produced by aggregation, and littleness by dispersion. Great thoughts are always general, and consist in positions not limited by exceptions, and in descriptions not descending to minuteness' (Johnson, *Lives*, p. 7).

[19.] But the selection of imagery matters in one general sense – in respect of genus: suppose a cabbage, a carrot, a strawberry – or 'The purple sprouting at my feet….'? It doesn't work because attention is being drawn to a genus unsuited to a pastoral poem.

in 1998, Raimonda Modiano remarked that in the second stanza, Wordsworth uses

> a collection of stock images in rather uninspiring lines such as 'The Rainbow comes and goes / And lovely is the rose', and 'The sunshine is a glorious birth.' This sounds almost as bad as 'roses are red and violets are blue.' The only way to salvage such lines is by assuming that Wordsworth initially might have actually intended to write a parody of the genre...

Perhaps not the only way. Delegates were troubled by Modiano's assertion that this was really very feeble poetry. Their discomfort tended to a dismissal of her argument. Yet we can all probably call up some lines of Wordsworth's poetry that lend themselves to this kind of criticism. This is the whole of 'Written in March', which Byron called 'not simple, but puerile', and of which he asked, 'what will any reader or auditor, out of the nursery, say to such namby-pamby':[20]

> The cock is crowing,
> The stream is flowing,
> The small birds twitter,
> The lake doth glitter,
> The green field sleeps in the sun;
> The oldest and youngest
> Are at work with the strongest;
> The cattle are grazing,
> Their heads never raising;
> There are forty feeding like one!
>
> Like an army defeated
> The Snow hath retreated
> And now doth fare ill
> On the top of the bare hill;
> The Plough-boy is whooping – anon – anon:
> There's joy in the mountains;
> There's life in the fountains;
> Small clouds are sailing,
> Blue sky prevailing;
> The rain is over and gone!

[20.] *Woof* 170.

The mood, if not the verse, is akin to that of the third stanza of the *Ode* – celebrating the freshness of a spring morning – and there are echoes of the *Ode* in the twittering birds, the whooping plough-boy (though which plough-boy ever shouted, 'anon, anon'?),[21] and perhaps the joy in the mountains comparable to the cataracts of the *Ode* or the voice of mountain torrents carried far into the boy of Winander's heart. The landscape of this short poem is summarized in a single, vocative line from the *Ode* – 'And oh ye Fountains, Meadows, Hills and Groves'. Nonetheless that association cannot prevent us wondering whether this poem was worth preserving. Has simplicity here become mere simpleness or naïvety: except in parish magazines and primary school creative writing classes, could anyone, then or now, write like this and be considered a respectable poet? It's one of those prac crit games that might be worth playing on under-read under-grads. I suspect they would dismiss this poem with derision. Who would be right? A name and reputation should be no defence against bad poetry.[22] Even if we are reiterating the judgement of earlier and confounded critics, are we necessarily wrong? If it isn't bad, why not, and why is it perhaps even good?

Dorothy's journal indicates that she and William spent a good deal of time seemingly doing little more than wandering around Grasmere and its environs. As R.G. Collingwood might have put it, what question was all that wandering answering? Waking up at an inn on Good Friday, 16 April 1802, Dorothy sets the context for Written in March:

> When I undrew my curtains in the morning, I was much affected by the beauty of the prospect, and the change. The sun shone, the wind had passed away, the hills looked cheerful, the river was very bright as it flowed into the lake. ... The valley is at first broken by little woody knolls that make retiring places, fairy valleys in the vale, the river winds along under these hills, travelling not in a bustle but not slowly, to the lake. We saw a fisherman in the flat meadow on the

---

[21.] But cf. 'I in my walks have often heard, / Sent from the mountains or the sheltered fields, / Shout after shout – whoop after whoop' (*HG* B 408-10).

[22.] 'Had Mr. Wordsworth's poems been the silly, the childish things, which they were for a long time described as being; had they been really distinguished from the compositions of other poets merely by meanness of language and inanity of thought; had they indeed contained nothing more than what is found in the parodies and pretended imitations of them; they must have sunk at once, a dead weight, into the slough of oblivion ... But year after year increased the number of Mr. Wordsworth's admirers. They were found too not in the lower classes of the reading public, but chiefly among young men of strong sensibility and meditative minds...' (*BL* II 9).

other side of the water... As we go on the vale opens out more into one vale, with somewhat of a cradle bed. Cottages, with groups of trees, on the side of the hills. We passed a pair of twin children, two years old. Sate on the next bridge which we crossed – a single arch. We rested again on the turf, and looked at the same bridge. We observed arches in the water, occasioned by the large stones sending it down in two streams... Primroses by the road-side, pile wort that shone like stars of gold in the sun, violets, strawberries, retired and half-buried among the grass. When we came to the foot of Brothers Water, I left William sitting on the bridge, and went along the path on the right side of the lake through the wood. I was delighted with what I saw. The water under the boughs of the bare old trees, the simplicity of the mountains, and the exquisite beauty of the path. There was one grey cottage... I hung over the gate, and thought I could have stayed for ever. When I returned, I found William writing a poem descriptive of the sights and sounds we saw and heard. There was the gentle flowing of the stream, the glittering, lively lake, green fields without a creature to be seen on them; behind us, a flat pasture with forty-two cattle feeding; to our left, the road leading to the hamlet. No smoke there, the sun shone on the bare roofs. The people were at work ploughing, harrowing, and sowing... a dog barking now and then, cocks crowing, birds twittering, the snow in patches at the top of the highest hills, yellow palms, purple and green twigs on the birches, ashes with their glittering spikes quite bare. The hawthorn a bright green, with black stems under the oak. The moss of the oak glossy. We went on.[23]

They went on, surrounded by the wonders of every day. The manner in which she and William are present in this landscape can be best understood by noting what they are not doing. They had some 9 or 10 miles to get home to Grasmere, but that considerable distance is not the object or the focus of their consciousness. They are not on a constitutional, deliberately taking exercise, marching across the countryside as did Miss Nancy Ellicot who – oblivious of 'Matthew and Waldo, guardians of the faith' – 'Strode across the hills and broke

---

[23.] The relationship between William's poem and Dorothy's journal entry is also discussed by Lucy Newlyn in *All in Each Other*, pp. 155-56.

them', blind to 'Emerson's eye'.[24] Miss Nancy imposed herself on and dominated the world she strode across. By contrast, William and Dorothy have decided to go out into the world and simply see it. They are wandering, wondering, observing, delighting in what simply *is*, glad to see the beauty of life reviving. There is a sense of patience – of allowing the landscape to be, to let it speak to them, rather than let their looking impose upon it. Also, it is a landscape not just of meadows, hills, streams and groves, but cottages, fishermen, children, dogs, cocks, birds, cattle (counted precisely) and labourers working variously in the fields. It is also a landscape from which Dorothy makes no attempt to draw the form or feeling of the sublime – or if she does, it is from one of its most modest features, 'the exquisite beauty of the path'. Time and the timeless intersect: the river travelling steadily to the lake, Dorothy thinking, as she hung over a cottage gate, that she could have hung there forever – a moment in and out of time.

Not only does she take in the immediately visible, but notices smaller features – 'Primroses by the road-side, pile-wort that shone like stars of gold in the sun' – a description Wordsworth probably remembered when writing 'Pleasures newly found are sweet' and 'With little here to do or see' – and 'violets, strawberries, retired and half-buried among the grass'. If there is intention here, it is to find and feel the 'is-ness' of the landscape, what Hopkins called the 'inscape', the intention of realizing an unmediated paradise all around them. As Jared Curtis notes, Wordsworth is 'not used to make / A present joy the matter of my song', but it is always the end to which he looks.[25] In other words, what Dorothy and William are trying to do is make 'simple Sence' the 'Lord of all created Excellence'.[26]

It is difficult to talk about this without rubbing off the bloom. It reflects, among other things, the mood of the opening of Resolution and Independence, the sense of a world waking to a new freshness – 'All things that love the sun are out of doors'. It is no coincidence that the *Ode*, begun earlier in the same month, is a poem of springtime, when Wordsworth's creativity often bloomed. How Dorothy is present in this world, her relation to it, is reflected in the almost unbroken continuity

---

[24.] T. S. Eliot, Cousin Nancy, *AP* I 24. Emerson introduced the concept of the 'transparent eye-ball' in *Nature*, an essay first published in 1836. It allowed 'all mean egotism to vanish' so that the appearances of nature and the existence of human thoughts become one. He had visited Wordsworth in 1833. Nancy Ellicott, on the other hand, is brim full of egotism.

[25.] *1805* I 56; *Experiments* 43.

[26.] Thomas Traherne, The Preparative.

between her getting up and going out; in the absence of any transition between drawing back the curtains and being out there. What Dorothy – and Wordsworth – want to see is the existence of things in the purity of their own being, or to put it in not quite appropriate Kantian terms, things in themselves. Therefore to modify that being by description, adjectivally or adverbially, is to render it impure, as does, say, anyone who sees a crocus and wonders whether they could make a profit out of saffron, or any other action that seeks to make some use of it, does not allow the thing to be in itself. They want nothing of the world than for it to be in them what it is in itself – one might say they are purifying their motive on the grounds of their beseeching.

But does Wordsworth achieve in his poem what Dorothy achieves in her journal? The apparent simplicity or naïvety of Written in March is remarkable. It reads like one of Blake's poems of innocence, which is probably the right way to think of it. Just as Dorothy records what she sees, so Wordsworth sets down the same vision in simple, declarative sentences. The reader's difficulty is that the verbs of the short rhymed couplets dominate the things seen – and the poem risks appearing not so much simple as childish. What rescues the first verse is the then unrhymed longer line, 'The green fields sleep in the sun', interrupting the short couplets, an unexpected change of rhythm, and surprising the reader with a metaphor of fields sleeping while the rest of the world is active and awake. It is just enough to arrest one's attention, not to dismiss the poem as a primary school exercise and to read it as a celebration of 'The innocent brightness of a new-born day'. Nonetheless, the attempt to achieve a simplicity or clarity of vision through a simplicity of language and syntax fails because we become too conscious of the verbs and rhymes, which, banal rather than simple, dominate the intended vision.[27] This is in contrast to what we feel of Dorothy's prose description – which subsumes itself to the things seen.[28]

On 27 March, three weeks before jotting down Written in March (written in April), Wordsworth had composed the first four verses of

---

[27] A problem various schools of poetry tried to solve, including the Symbolists and the Concrete poets. George Oppen was an Objectivist, and 'concerned himself with the question of "How can the poet communicate a realization of the concrete object *as object* without drawing the reader's attention to *the way* in which he communicates?"' https://www.poetryfoundation.org/poems-and-poets/poets/detail/george-oppen.

[28] Jared Curtis would not agree: 'The effect of paratactic simplicity in the shorter lyrics, in contrast with the more elaborate syntactic patterns in the long poems, is to support their straightforward appeal to common sights and sounds, to give them the limpid clarity they need to convey their beauty and singularity, finally their importance, to men' (*Experiments* 64).

the *Ode* – the lament for the loss he felt in himself or nature, ending in a two-fold question, which it will take the rest of the *Ode* and another two years to answer.[29] But in Written in March one can see the kind of answer Wordsworth was trying to find: if he sets down in verse the landscape as it appears to him, briefly and simply, without explanation or adornment, won't that be sufficient? The simplicity of the words will reflect the immediacy of the landscape. He wants no metaphorical medium, no 'as', but only 'is'. He is still trying to rediscover the lost visionary landscape of his childhood, but he is struggling with the method by which that revisioning might be achieved, and which is finally realized only in stanza IX of the *Ode*. The verse of Written in March doesn't work, and so, in part, the vision doesn't work, because visionary power is embodied in the mystery of words (*1805* V 619-21).

The subtext of criticism that suggests that Wordsworth may be parodying himself, or the genre he uses, is that he is a nature poet: so why does he write so imprecisely or naïvely about nature, when other poets (Hopkins for example) have done so much better a job? There are two kinds of answer to that. First, Wordsworth isn't principally a nature poet. Just as the 1802 poems are a debate about the sources of power, not a meditation on flowers, birds or butterflies, so in the *Ode* the subject is the loss of a childhood vision and the rediscovery of a comparable power, 'the philosophic mind', that can 'look through death'. Following the progress of that loss and partial recovery is the substance of the poem, of which the images are illustrative – they are not the thing or power itself – and therefore a more precise delineation of these objects would be a distraction, a burden of passive perception. The success of the poem in part depends on the onward flow of the argument or story, the music, and just as there are many sentences, which though mysterious in meaning are simple in structure, not inhibiting the progress of the poem, so most of the images work in a similar way, not self-consciously arresting the reader's attention, but subordinated to the progress of the poem. Nonetheless, as discussed in the following chapters, some of these images reverberate through his poetry, accumulating significance as they do so and, for whatever reason, they are embodied in the mystery of verse in a way that those of Written in March are not.

[29.] Dorothy's journal records that the poem 'Written in March' was composed on 16 April 1802, (*JDW* 87). Richard Gravil (email, 3 July 2018) points out that the Wordsworths' manuscript title is '"Written while resting on the Bridge near the foot of Brother's Water, between one and two o'clock at Noon, April 16th" (16th corrected from 15th).' Why Wordsworth decided to use the earlier month in the title is anyone's guess.

That argument has its own difficulties, in that Wordsworth perceives Nature as a power, something that can act, and not just be acted on, that he partly ascribes the loss to Nature itself, out there, and not just in his mind. The question, then, concerns the source of power and how that power enables or affects a quality of seeing. The habitually visible isn't sufficient – not the rainbow, not the rose, not waters on a starry night – but in what spirit they are to be seen, what irradiates them, is the question. Nonetheless, in waiting for that light, the objects and spectacles may themselves be the catalyst; and when it does shine, Wordsworth does not doubt the immaterial source, so finely described in the Ode, Composed Upon an Evening of Extraordinary Splendor and Beauty:

> But as long as god-like wish, or hope divine,
> Informs my spirit, ne'er can I believe
> That this magnificence is wholly thine!
> – From worlds not quickened by the sun
> A portion of the gift is won.

His wish is god-like, his hope derives from the divine; his mind is comparable to the mind of God, and it is that mind, independent of the sun – the source of all natural life – infused through this wonderful spectacle that gives it the power to be more than just an illusory collocation of natural phenomena. As both Coleridge and Benjamin Whichcote put it, we give in order to receive. The sad thing about this poem is that Wordsworth has lost the confidence that such power is still alive in him; so he pleads with the 'Dread Power', the divine,

> O, let thy grace remind me of the light,
> Fully early lost and fruitlessly deplored;
> Which at this moment on my waking sight
> Appears to shine, by miracle restored!
> My soul, though yet confined to earth,
> Rejoices in a second birth;

Momentarily he feels again an intimation of immortality, a rising from earth to heaven – a resurrection, to use a word he wouldn't have. But the light in which he was once confident now only 'Appears to shine', and this very beautiful poem ends with the melancholy ' – 'Tis past, the visionary splendour fades, / And night approaches with her shades.'

That was in 1817, years away from the remarkable asseverations of *Home at Grasmere*. The answer he provides in 1804 is still confident however, and is exemplified in many passages of *The Prelude*: for instance, the introduction to the spots of time: the 'efficacious spirit' by which our minds 'Are nourished and invisibly repaired' 'chiefly lurks / Among those passages of life in which / We have had the deepest feeling that the mind / Is lord and master, and that outward sense / Is but the obedient servant of her will'.[30] It is the mind that will provide the 'auxiliar light' to irradiate the forms of outward sense after the extinction of childhood's celestial light, and the work of the *Ode* is the realization of that light, in the presence of which, 'frail Mortality may see, / What is? – ah no, but what *can* be!' – Paradise regained.

[30.] *1805* XI 268 ff. Although Wordsworth asserts that it is so, and invested with a peculiar energy though they are, it is not easy to see how the mind is lord and master in these passages; nor is it easy to grasp how these two scenes, both linked to different kinds of traumatic death, can be 'spectacles and sounds to which / I often would repair, and thence would drink / As at a fountain' (*1805* XI 382-85).

Chapter 11

Competing Forces

THE ODE IS A PROGRESSIVE and structured poem, a story that has a beginning, 'There was a time…', a long and complex middle developed from a simple statement, 'Our birth is but a sleep and a forgetting' (an extraordinary statement considered by itself) and an end in which the beginning is revisited and revised, a double take also part of the structure of Tintern Abbey. From the outset Wordsworth knows what he wants to know, or rather feel, implicit in the 1815 epigraph, that is, to see all the visible and natural world in the same mode and manner as he had seen and hoped to go on seeing the rainbow – no more than what *is*, but imbued with power. One form of that power he remembers – the earth apparelled in the celestial light of his childhood; another he is in search of – the auxiliar light of the philosophic mind. With either form of power upon him, what is otherwise only illuminated by the light of common day will then be glorified by a heavenly or celestial light. There is no difference in the things seen, only in how they are seen.[1] And in that divine light, the visible world is transformed into Eden or Paradise – and this not just metaphorically, but so near the actual union of these different spheres of being that there is no ordinary word that can suggest both how far the condition exceeds metaphor and yet remains symbolic, not literal nor actual. Coleridge's neologism, 'tautegorical', is designed to express that state, for his definition of a symbol is that it 'always partakes of the Reality which it renders intelligible'.[2] All Wordsworth's hopes of

---

[1] When Coleridge set down his 'Order of the Mental Powers' (*M* V 798) he put 'Sense' and 'Reason' at opposite ends of the scale; but those extremes meet, and I suggest that Wordsworth is attempting to find the power that would infuse sense with Reason, and thus make the world of mere appearance real or intelligible.

[2] *LS* 30. Cf. Helen Vendler's notion of 'repossession of the world by metaphor'. She writes, 'If every object in the adult poet's eye thus becomes weighty with possible meditation, he is no longer a stranger in the world, longing hopelessly for the "imperial palace whence he came". He has become, instead, naturalized in the world' ('Lionel Trilling', p. 71). This

this kind of seeing are contained in this passage from *The Excursion*, addressing the presence of God in nature:

> By thy grace
> The particle divine remained unquenched;
> And, 'mid the wild weeds of a rugged soil,
> Thy bounty caused to flourish deathless flowers,
> From paradise transplanted: wintry age
> Impends; the frost will gather round my heart;
> If the flowers wither, I am worse than dead!
> (*Excursion* IV 51 ff.)

It was 'the particle divine' still alive in him that enabled his heart to leap up at the sight of a rainbow, apparently quenched when the rainbow merely comes and goes; but if quenched, then 'Let me die'. The frost here is like that of the deathly 'weight of custom' in the *Ode*. The possibility that in the immediate world – 'the wild weeds of a rugged soil' – one may find the 'deathless flowers / From paradise transplanted' is at heart of Wordsworth's looking, his understanding of Nature. This is the world the child knew, and the adult seeks.

Mitigating the Spell

It is an extraordinarily demanding vision, which when achieved is, in Eliot's words, 'both a new world / And the old made explicit' (*BN* II) or 'intelligible', which Wordsworth believes possible because of what he can remember from his early childhood. The loss is mourned, but the memory celebrated as suggesting a mode of revival. However, the recovery of this power depends, not only in this poem, but throughout his works, on Wordsworth's belief that we must 'mitigate the spell / Of the strong frame of sense in which we dwell', or, in other words, we must be laid asleep in body and become a living soul before we can see into

---

theory leads to some mistaken readings: 'As I see the *Ode*, Wordsworth implies ... that the acquisition of the philosophic mind depends on our participation, as we grow up, in a wedding or a funeral; on those dialogues of "business, love, or strife"' (p. 78). Quite the opposite – the philosophic mind rejects these as the weight of custom. Alan Grob thinks that the 'basic materials of 1802 undergo in 1804 a substantial shift in function, transposed from literal facts of perception into broad epistemological metaphors' ('Wordsworth's *Immortality Ode*', p. 53). As I resist Helen Vendler's 'repossession of the world by metaphor', so I resist the notion that the 'literal facts of perception' become no more than metaphors: I would rather think that they are a form of celestial light, re-apparelling the earth.

the life of things, or only when the light of sense goes out do we get a glimpse of that infinity which is our home.[3] To give any kind of primacy to sense is to obscure that power or vision. Only when infused 'with a glory scarce their own' – 'not their own' in 1850 – do we see into the life of things themselves (*1805* V 629). Wordsworth only wants to see what there is to be seen, what the senses present, but simultaneously irradiated with a glory that does not belong to them. If not so glorified the objects remain dead and spiritless, part of the repressive 'strong frame of sense'.

It is only through these objects and images that Wordsworth can convey his vision. This has the makings of a significant difficulty. For the reader, the difference between things as they appear and things imbued with power is indistinguishable. To the poet without that power the visible world remains unintelligible, a mere weight of meaningless images. The only distinction between the one condition and the other available to readers is 'the turnings intricate' of a poet's verse (*1805* V 627), coupled with the willingness to accept that whatever is declared is so. Why do we, for example, believe in the 'visionary dreariness' of Wordsworth's description of the woman with the pitcher, her garments vexed and tossed by the wind? Because he requests that belief of us, and the integrity of his verse on this and other occasions permits us to accept his request. The same is true of other writers making similar assertions: if 'The voice of the hidden waterfall' really does represent the long-sought-for 'condition of complete simplicity', then we either take the poet's word for it because his verse convinces us, or we say it is hocus-pocus, conjuring a mystical nothing out of a material something.

The source of that power or glory, and the relationship between power and object, celestial light and starry night, is the principal question that the poem seeks to answer. In the childhood vision remembered there is no distinction between the thing seen and the power by which it was seen, so the appearance of the object *is* the experience of the power, or as he said in Tintern Abbey, it is without the 'need of a remoter charm, / By thought supplied'.[4] This sense of power invested in the object informed many of Wordsworth's early experiences, and he had no cause to

---

[3.] This truth, of endless importance to Wordsworth, is at the heart of the Fenwick note on the *Ode*, and is frequently asserted throughout his verse: for instance, speaking of the Convent of Chartreuse under threat from the Revolution, Wordsworth pleads, 'be the house redeemed / With its unworldly votaries, for the sake / Of conquest over sense, hourly achieved / Through faith and meditative reason, resting / Upon the word of heaven-imparted truth, / Calmly triumphant' (*1850* VI 456-62).

[4.] This power will be separated out in stanza IX, as he had made a comparable distinction between he who finds his life in 'unimagineable things' and then paints this life 'in all / The visible imagery of all the worlds' (*1798-9* p. 126).

differentiate the object from the power. Nature thus appears a power and a good in itself, the power residing in the object, the power not separable from the object. When the adult Wordsworth came to look on the world he expected to find the power, and was aghast to realize that it is no longer inherent in the object, although the object remains 'beautiful and fair'. He wants to see around him the Eden-like world that he remembers from his early childhood, and the whole impetus of the poem is the recovery of that vision. By celebrating the splendour of a spring morning in the first four stanzas he is attempting to revive the quality of vision in which object and power are one. But, however beautiful, 'this majestic imagery, the clouds, / The ocean, and the firmament of heaven' have become unintelligible, 'a barren picture on the mind' (*MW* 679).

The first glimmering of potential recovery, of moving on beyond the lost sense of childhood unity, is his questioning of the origins of that lost power: has it left me, or has it fled the earth? When Coleridge wrote, 'In our life alone does Nature live', he was answering that question. If Coleridge's answer was unequivocal, it was also hopeful – that power belongs to us as human beings and therefore, if lost, is recoverable. Quite possibly Wordsworth picked up that hope, because in the latter part of the *Ode*, particularly in stanza IX, he looks for the source of power in himself, in the human heart. The revelation of that fugitive power, however, is oppressed by the relentless notices of sense, working 'Against, or with our will'. It is only when he realizes that the childhood vision is a guide forward, not a route back, that he is able to celebrate 'those obstinate questionings / Of sense and outward things'. The poem oscillates between belief in these two sources of power – in himself or in nature – and never comes to rest in either, by contrast with Coleridge's declaration. Only if we are able to follow the flux and reflux of Wordsworth's mind through the poem, conscious of this division, will the *Ode* become emotionally and intellectually intelligible.[5]

Lamentation and Celebration

Aware of these competing forces within himself, Wordsworth believed they influenced the structure of the poem. After suggesting that to the attentive and competent reader the *Ode* will explain itself, he added, 'but there may be no harm in adverting here to particular feelings or

---

[5.] 'I have said each of these poems has a purpose … it is to follow the fluxes and refluxes of our mind when agitated by the great and simple affections of our nature.' Preface to *Lyrical Ballads* (1802), *MW* 598. Cf. *BL* II 147.

experiences of my own mind on which the structure of the poem partly rests'. He then speaks of how as a boy he internalized the objective world, seeing all external things 'as something not apart from, but inherent in my own immaterial nature', adding:

> At that time I was afraid of such processes. In later periods of life I have deplored, as we have all reason to do, a subjugation of an opposite character & have rejoiced over the remembrances, as is expressed in the lines 'obstinate questionings & c.' (*FN*)

The 'subjugation of an opposite character' is that of the mind by the world or the senses. Setting aside Wordsworth's interpretation of those childhood experiences here, in a nutshell, is a central feature of the *Ode* – a counterpoint of competing forces, of lamentation ('I have deplored') and celebration ('[I] have rejoiced') that informs the whole: the lamentation for a power lost, the celebration for that power remembered and, through the act of remembering, looking to means of restoration; a power of which he was once afraid – 'before which our mortal Nature / Did tremble like a guilty thing surprised' – but later subjugated by the 'earthly freight' of custom. It is the 'subjugation' by the senses of that childhood power that has given the visible and natural world an independent existence, which has allowed it to claim a life and reality of its own, no longer part of Wordsworth's 'immaterial nature' (*FN*). Wordsworth recognizes the goodness of that life in such declarations as 'No more shall grief of mine the season wrong' – the season speaks just as much as the mind. There is an implicit conflict here: that as an adult, recognizing the separation of the world from himself, nonetheless he is trying to re-envision it as he did as a child. What he finally realizes is that, though he may long to travel back, only a 'forward motion' will enable any kind of restoration. That he cannot return is what he initially deplores, inferring either a lost glory or a lost power. Because he expects the power to be in the object, at the outset he's not sure what he's lamenting – the lost glory or the lost power. He nevertheless comes to a decision in stanza IX, and it is significant that Wordsworth points to that stanza, much of which many critics find obscure, as the principal grounds of his celebration and not to any qualities or appearances of the natural world. The power he seeks is initially independent of the world of sense, and therefore barely expressible.

Three Parts – Loss, Analysis and Recovery

The poem begins with the poet conceding that power is lost and only sense remains. The search for power in the later stanzas will turn the failed recovery of the first four stanzas into a poem that at least offers some promise, a progression from an undoubted loss to a hesitant restoration. Although critics do not agree on the quality of the outcome, there is some consensus as to how that progression is achieved. Harold Bloom sets out the agreed template in a sentence as neat as it is terse: 'The poem's initial four stanzas state the problem; the next four embody a negative reaction to it; the final three positive.'[6] Those three stages can be further developed. The first four stanzas assert a loss and conclude with two closely related questions – 'Whither is fled the visionary gleam?/ Where is it now the glory and the dream?' Stanza V begins by providing an answer to those questions, and then the rest of that stanza and those following, through to the end of stanza VIII, work out the consequences and collaterals of that answer, a history of the soul's divine origins and the child's mortal life, ending on a very downbeat note – 'Full soon shall thy Soul shall have her earthly freight, / And custom lie upon thee with a weight, / Heavy as frost, and deep almost as life!' – as if the life we are born to risks destroying the life we remember.[7] Stanza IX begins in a quite different mood: gone is the sense of the soul oppressed almost to the point of death, immortality lost; instead there is a celebration of the fugitive, shadowy recollections of past years, because those memories point the way forward to a further union, a deeper and more sustainable communion. This mood is maintained, in varying degrees, to the end of the poem, and works towards 'the faith that looks through death, / In years that bring the philosophic mind'.

The restoration of the lost power is never complete, despite, in stanzas III and IV, initial declarations to the contrary, so the lamentation is not quite silenced, its principal cause never fully resolved. As one progresses through the poem, it is often difficult to be confident whether one is witnessing lamentation or celebration; sometimes a celebration asserted is an ineffective pushing away of doubt, which returning clouds or

---

[6.] Bloom, *Visionary Company*, p. 167. Vendler ('Lionel Trilling', p. 76) agrees that there is a tripartite structure, but disputes Trilling's analysis of it. Curtis (*Experiments* 115) supplies a further list of critics who agree that it is tripartite but not quite on how it is constituted.

[7.] Wordsworth is happy to live with the paradox that one form of life, this life, which is where we have our happiness or not at all, good in itself, competes with another form of life, the soul, perceived as the greater or ultimate good. See also *F* II 338: 'Were we to grow up unfostered by this genial warmth [Reason], a frost would chill the spirit, so penetrating and powerful, that there could be no notions of the life of love.'

obscures the preceding celebrations. What is sought is a new though comparable power; and yet this potential gain, this sense of recovery, is vitiated by a continuing sense of loss.[8] In the end there is an emotional compromise between lamentation and celebration, but because they are antithetical, one essentially precluding the other, it is a complex compromise, reflected in the poem's tentative and tender conclusion.

---

[8] Cf. the DCMS fragment 44, quoted in Chapter 6: 'The lyric spirit of philosophy / Leads me through moods of sadness and delight.'

Chapter 12

Stanzas I–IV: The Statement of Loss

'I believe in pure explication de texte.
This may in fact be my principal form of piety.'[1]

THE FIRST TWO VERSES are emotionally lucid, in that they state the loss unequivocally, though the conclusion of each verse suggests a different cause – either loss of vision in the poet, or loss of glory from the earth, and this is the first indication of his divided vision. In the third verse, the poet looks up from his sense of loss to observe the loveliness of a spring morning,

>   Now, while the birds thus sing a joyous song,
>   And while the young lambs bound
>   As to the tabor's sound,

That 'Now' marks a wish to participate in the Maytime celebrations, to look outward on the immediate world, not backward or inward to a sense of loss.[2] It represents an attempt to unite time past and time present. Nevertheless, the spirit of this looking, the kind of looking that he brought or wanted to bring to the rainbow, is compromised by 'a thought of grief' – probably, but not certainly, the loss lamented in the first two verses – a grief singularly at odds with the 'joyous song' that all nature is otherwise singing. The very next line suggests an immediate recovery, confirmed in the following line, 'And I again am strong.'

[1.] Wallace Stevens to Bernard Heringman, 21 July 1953: *Letters of Wallace Stevens*, ed. Holly Stevens (London, 1967), p. 793, quoted by Jim Mays, 'Reading Alice du Clós, and for the Birds', *The Coleridge Bulletin*, NS Vol. 45 (Summer 2015), pp. 1-21.
[2.] *Experiments* 121-22: 'the first four stanzas ... establish the basic conflict between "then" and "now" over which the poet broods. ... The force of "now" is literal: not "nowadays" but "exactly at this moment."'

> To me alone there came a thought of grief:
> A timely utterance gave that thought relief,
> And I again am strong:

The sources of that strength are identified in the lines that follow:

> The Cataracts blow their trumpets from the steep,
> No more shall grief of mine the season wrong;
> I hear the Echoes through the mountains throng,
> The Winds come to me from the fields of sleep

Like many of Wordsworth's lines, their potential significance is suppressed by the simplicity of their syntax and the brevity of their reference. Cataracts, echoes and winds have more than walk-on parts in Wordsworth's poems, and it is possible that he is expecting readers to have picked up hints on what these lines signify from poems in this volume, as well as the earlier *Lyrical Ballads*.

'The Cataracts blow their trumpets'

The first of those lines might be considered a good example of the bombast of which Montgomery, Coleridge and others complained. Trumpets traditionally announce the arrival or return of power, but the metaphor is unusual, an unlikely association of two very different types of sound. Cataracts are noisy, a dense and continuous roar, nothing like the cracking or blaring of trumpets. Southey, who used every relevant verb to describe how the falls come down at Lodore, makes no association with trumpets or any kind of horn. So this military or regal metaphor seems inaccurate and hyperbolic, out of place in a poem intimating the immortality of the soul. Whatever the accuracy of his observation, Wordsworth was conscious not just of the sound itself, but some quality in himself thus disclosed – 'The sounding cataract / Haunted me like a passion', as he puts it in Tintern Abbey (77-78) – the passion itself undefined.[3] But he suggests the quality of that passion, using the river as a metaphor, in To a Skylark: 'Happy, happy Liver, / With a soul as strong as a mountain river / Pouring out praise to the Almighty Giver' (March-July 1802).[4] That passion is comparable to the

---

[3.] Wordsworth remarks in the 'Preface' to *Poems* (1815), that these lines 'represent implicitly some of the features of a youthful mind, at a time when images of nature supplied to it the place of thought, sentiment, and almost of action' (*MW* 629).

[4.] See also On the Power of Sound (1828-29): 'The headlong Streams and Fountains / Serve Thee, Invisible Spirit, with untired powers' (ll. 17-18). Wordsworth's headnote to the

experience described in Chapter 8, in To H.C., when 'a gentle shock of mild surprize / ... carried far into' the boy of Winander's heart 'the voice / Of mountain torrents' (1805 V 405-8), De Quincey seeing in that 'far' Wordsworth's attribution of 'space and its infinities' to the human heart. That he was right in making a connection between the voice of mountain torrents, and a sudden impression of the infinite is confirmed by what follows Wordsworth's disappointment after he realizes that he has crossed the Alps.

He pauses, and then pours forth his great tribute to the imagination. That uttered he continues on his way, but the power is still with him, and colours all he sees as he walks down 'a narrow chasm'. The features of the immediate landscape 'Were all like the workings of one mind.../ Characters of the great apocalypse, / The types and symbols of eternity', prominent amongst which are 'The stationary blasts of waterfalls, /... torrents shooting from the clear blue sky,' and 'the sick sight / And giddy prospect of the raving stream' (*1805* VI 556-72). The power of the imagination alive in him, Wordsworth connects cataracts, waterfalls and raving streams with the ideas of infinity or eternity. And those ideas he links to the Apocalypse, the traditional herald of which is The Last Trumpet. Thus it is possible that cataracts blowing their trumpets from the steep announce the return of that imperial power, the lost vision – what perhaps we might call an intimation of immortality. It is perhaps worth repeating a quotation from the first chapter: if he manages to retain a faith 'That fails not ... / ... the gift is yours / Ye winds and sounding cataracts! ... / ... O Nature! Thou hast fed / My loft speculations;' (*1850* II 447-51). A faith that looks through death to immortality may be the loftiest of speculations, but a belief that such a faith has been fed by the features of nature, including cataracts, justifies, whatever one may make of such a belief, what would otherwise be no more than an extravagant and bombastic metaphor.

'I hear the Echoes'

Celebrating the coming of spring, 'The Idle Shepherd-Boys', composed in 1800 some two years before the first stanzas of the *Ode*, begins, 'The valley rings with mirth and joy, / Among the hills the Echoes play / A never, never ending song / To welcome in the May'. The nature of that song is undefined, just as the passion associated with the 'sounding cataract' of Tintern Abbey is undefined, but it is emphatically endless.

---

poem begins, 'The Ear addressed, as occupied by a spiritual functionary... This "Invisible Spirit" is "Harmony", a form of immortality.'

Could it also be a song pouring forth some kind of recognition of or praise for 'the Almighty Giver'? The two poems on the cuckoo offer such a reading, and the first, To the Cuckoo, from which that quotation comes, considered in Chapter 8, was probably written just before the first four stanzas of the *Ode*, and like 'My heart leaps up', is much more optimistic than the *Ode*, as he is able to beget again the golden time of childhood. The second, 'Yes! full surely 'twas the echo', belongs to 1806, two years after completion of the *Ode*. The cuckoo is heard not seen, and upon this Wordsworth builds both poems. The progress of the 1804 poem, from a natural observation to the visionary world of childhood revived, is the progress Wordsworth sought in the *Ode*, although it left the question of where our home is – heaven or earth – unresolved.

In the 1806 poem the cuckoo's original call is distinguished from its echo, and the cuckoo is puzzled – 'Whence the Voice? from air or earth? / This the cuckoo cannot tell'. What the poet can tell, however, is that the cuckoo's echo is like 'her ordinary cry, / Like – but oh how different', and the rest of the poem depends upon this perceived difference. The two worlds, material and immaterial, are more closely related in this poem than that of 1804. The cuckoo's cry is mortal; its puzzling echo points to the immortal and, in our mortality, although 'Slaves of Folly, Love, or Strife', we can still can hear 'Voices of two different Natures'. Although the idea is clear, the language and verse are strange, intense – each question and answer almost rough, the syntax hectic and disordered, pulling in different directions:

> Hears not also mortal Life?
> Hear not we, unthinking Creatures!
> Slaves of Folly, Love, or Strife,
> Voices of two different Natures?
>
> Have not We too? Yes we have
> Answers, and we know not whence;
> Echoes from beyond the grave,
> Recognized intelligence?
>
> Such within ourselves we hear
> Oft-times, ours though sent from far;
> Listen, ponder, hold them dear;
> For of God, of God they are!

Like the cuckoo, we hear 'answers' or echoes to our material calls – but initially we do not know where these echoes come from. In the next line, however, that not knowing is replaced by an assertion that they are 'from beyond the grave' and that they come in the form of a 'Recognized intelligence' – that intelligence which makes the world intelligible – a surprisingly latinate phrase, almost out of place in this otherwise lexically simple poem, yet suggesting the seriousness of Wordsworth's affirmative questions. The final verse is steadier, an assertion in which doubts are replaced by certainties. If we question De Quincey's evaluation of 'far', then here the word is used again in much the same way – the echoes are sent to us 'from far' by God: unlike the child, we are no longer close to the source, but that source is still in touch with us. The distance is implicit in the penultimate line – though perhaps not seeming such to us, the echoes must be taken as divine utterances. The final line not only declares this conviction boldly, it does so in a way that conveys its emotional truth. The surprising repetition, 'of God, of God' is a rising note of discovery, (inversely matching the call of the cuckoo?) a rhythm in which the joy of knowing the source is as much felt as spoken.

To return to The Idle Shepherd-Boys: it is a pastoral and the springtime celebrations are forgotten in the poet's saving of a lamb. Yet the voice of mountains and their echoes, used instinctively here, have a particular resonance for Wordsworth, often speaking of a power that lives beyond the immediate, beyond mortality, as does the cuckoo's cry.[5] In *Home at Grasmere* Wordsworth recalls an 'awful voice' that

> ... I in my walks have often heard,
> Sent from the mountains or the sheltered fields,
> Shout after shout – reiterated whoop
> In manner of a bird that takes delight
> In answering to itself   (*HG* B 407-12)

That awful voice speaks of a mysterious power, a power 'sent' to remind the poet that behind appearance is a life issuing from and constituting the being of nature, a power in which fear and awe are close companions. Here the 'Shout after shout – reiterated whoop' might be that of shepherd boys, but is more like the 'restless shout' of the cuckoo, also restless in the 1806 poem. 'Whence the voice... /.... the Cuckoo cannot tell', but goes on shouting, puzzled. The boy of Winander mimicked the hooting owls, and when they ceased to answer, the ensuing silence 'carried far into his heart / The voice of mountain torrents' (*1805* V 408-9), which is

---

[5.] There are a few lines in The Idle Shepherd-Boys that look forward to the springtime celebrations of the *Ode*: 'A thousand lambs are on the rocks, / All newly born! both earth and sky / Keep jubilee, and more than all / These boys with their green Coronal'.

a little odd, in that he would have more likely heard the echoes of his or the owls' hootings. Unlikeliness is often associated with Wordsworth's hearing of mountain voices: in his boat-borrowing, 'an act of stealth / And troubled pleasure' he remembers that 'Not without the voice / Of mountain echoes did my boat move on' (*1805* I 389-90). No cause is assigned to these echoes, but they are certainly not the splash of oars, however 'lustily' dipped. They might have been sounds unheard arising from the guilt and fear which invested 'the huge cliff' that 'like a living thing / Strode after me'.

Even when a 'jocund din' is the source of an echo, the end is almost always awe or fear. With a laugh Joanna mocks the poet's 'ravishment' at the beauty of an early morning. It is some laugh, even from a 'wild-hearted Maid', for first it echoes from the rock that would be named after her, and then is taken up by Helm-crag, Hammer-Scar, Silver-How, Loughrigg, Fairfield, Helvellyn, Skiddaw, Glamara and Kirkstone. Wordsworth wonders, justifiably, whether this was 'A work accomplished by the brotherhood / Of ancient mountains, or my ear was touched / With dreams and visionary impulses', adding 'It is not for me to tell'. If the word 'brotherhood' suggests they are close to each other, it also suggests that their echoes are in some way alive. Joanna's scepticism is happily punished because she finds this 'loud uproar in the hills' not a 'jocund din', but a source of fear: 'to my side / The fair Joanna drew, as if she wished / To shelter from some object of her fear'.[6] If the hills are not alive with the sound of music, they are certainly alive with a mysterious and awful power.

At the time of publication, only very close readers of Wordsworth's poetry would have been able to pick up the reverberations that substantiate 'I hear the Echoes through the mountains throng'. With the publication of his works and manuscripts completed, current readers are in a position to understand just how significant that simple sentence might have been to Wordsworth.

'The Winds come to me from the fields of sleep'

The final line of these four has proved the most difficult to interpret, if interpretation is required: what are the winds that come to him, and what 'the fields of sleep' from which they come? Early comments tend to the literal, taking Wordsworth as a poet of nature; referring to such lines as 'The green field sleeps in the sun', (Lines written in March), Helen

---

[6.] Poems on the Naming of Places II – To Joanna.

Darbishire suggests that he is simply remembering 'The yet reposeful country-side' and that that 'The echoes come from the mountains, the winds from the sleepy fields'. She records Professor Dowden first thinking that the winds refer to the blowing of the west wind, because the west is where the sun sets, and is thus emblematic of sleep.[7] Dowden then adds that the fields of sleep may be the shadowy parts of our own souls that lie out of the view of consciousness. That interesting idea, not followed by Derbishire, moves the phrase beyond the literal, and is comparable to Frank Kermode remarking that 'The basic meaning, I suggest, is "sleep, or inactivity – a fallow period – has refreshed me; out of it blows the wind of inspiration: as in the opening lines of *The Prelude*"' – in other words, a correspondent breeze.[8]

George Whalley takes up a version of that reading, believing that the phrase '"the fields of sleep"… is linked with … the notion of a lost Paradise', pointing to the passage, 'Fortunate Fields – like those of old / Sought in the Atlantic Main', from the Prospectus to *The Excursion*, variations on it from earlier manuscripts, and another passage from *A Tuft of Primroses*, which all associate Paradise with islands in the Atlantic.[9] Nonetheless, as in the opening of *The Prelude*, he begins with a literal reading akin to Dowden's – that the winds blow into Grasmere from the west, from the Atlantic, and thus from the fields of Paradise. Still, his most interesting insight is to connect this line with a passage from Book V of *The Prelude*:

> Visionary Power
> Attends upon the motions of the winds,
> Embodied in the mystery of words:
> There darkness makes abode, and all the host
> Of shadowy things work endless changes there,
> As in a mansion like their proper home;
> Even forms and substances are circumfused
> By that transparent veil with light divine,
> And through the turnings intricate of Verse,
> Present themselves as objects recognis'd,
> In flashes, and with a glory scarce their own.
>   *1805* V 619 ff; (*1850* 'not their own')

---

[7] Helen Darbishire, *Wordsworth, Poems published in 1807* (Oxford, 1914), p. 452.
[8] Kermode, *Romantic Paradox* (London, 1962/2016), p. 78, and M. H. Abrams, 'The Correspondent Breeze: A Romantic Metaphor', *The Kenyon Review*, Vol. 19, no. 1 (Winter 1957).
[9] Whalley, 'The Fields of Sleep', *Review of English Studies*, Vol. 9, no. 33 (February 1958), pp. 49-50.

As the lines from the *Ode* are presented as an illustration of renewed strength, the winds are those of a recovered visionary power, of a kind with 'Such feelings' as pass into an infant's 'torpid life / Like an awakening breeze'.[10] Whalley suggests that the winds here and in the *Ode* are both actual and inspirational, literal and metaphorical, or, to use Coleridge's word again, 'tautegorical' – partaking of the truth they symbolize.[11] Were it not for the third line, 'Embodied in the mystery of words', the winds would be little more than the wind that 'rav'st without' in 'Dejection', initially one of the sounds that might 'their wonted impulse give' to 'startle this dull pain', but finally dismissed with other natural phenomena by the question 'what can these avail, / To lift the smoth'ring weight from off my breast?' Had they contained any visionary power, that is what they would have done.

Words work (like the Word) in 'a mansion' – the mind, his purer mind – comparable to the 'proper home' of words – heaven, infinitude or God – and imbue the objects of sense with a glory 'scarce their own'. The winds are thus endowed with 'light divine' by which 'forms and substances are circumfused' and via 'the turnings intricate of verse' become 'objects recogniz'd' or made intelligible, transfigured from a type of sensation into a symbol of glory and power, a process that could be described as creation or recreation. Nonetheless, we are left with a residual doubt as to whether these winds really are themselves, or have been given a life 'not their own'.

If the winds are those of visionary power, 'the fields of sleep' provide a metaphor for the conditions under which that power comes upon him. The sleep is that of the senses, the escape of a mind 'beset with images' from immediate sensory input – sleep a symbol of the 'conquest over sense' (*1850* VI 446) that Wordsworth repeatedly insists is required for the realization of the power he seeks. This method as part of process of rendering the world intelligible is first evident in Tintern Abbey, which follows the growth of 'that serene and blessed mood', the effect of which is to make the eye quiet, not roving restlessly over disparate objects, and so laid asleep in body, the senses conquered, the deep power of joy is released, and we are enabled to 'see into the life of things'.

Therefore, what we see is less the things themselves, more the immanent power that sustains them. The very process of realizing the immanent life of nature, seeing into the life of things, is also a realization

---

[10] *The Prelude*, 1798-99, II 274-75.
[11] Wordsworth seemed to be emphasizing that point in *1850* by describing the winds as 'viewless'.

that that informing power is ultimately separate from nature. Thus, after his disorientation in the Alps,

> to my soul I say
> 'I recognise thy glory.' In such strength
> Of usurpation, in such visitings
> Of awful promise, when the light of sense
> Goes out in flashes that have shewn to us
> The invisible world, doth greatness make abode,
> There harbours whether we be young or old.
> (*1805* VI 531-37)

The visible world is separate from the invisible. This double vision is more easily discerned in this description than in Tintern Abbey, where the power gained seems to irradiate the visible world. He proceeds down 'a narrow chasm' of which all the features are 'like the working of one mind', 'Characters of the great apocalypse'. Not, one might argue, the things in themselves, but things invested with a glory other than their own.

To sum up: visionary powers ('The winds come to me') are only revived under certain conditions ('the fields of sleep'), and those powers enable two potentially conflicting forms of experience: 'Voices of two different Natures' – one which speaks of infinity or eternity and has sight of 'that immortal sea / Which brought us hither'; and one which can see 'into the life of things'; one looking beyond the world and the other looking into the world, one recognizing the soul or mind, human and divine, with a separate life of its own; at times claiming to be the life of the object, at others asserting that the glory of the object is not its own. Perhaps these are theoretically reconciled in the idea of Paradise, but as Wordsworth grew older the more certain he was of the source of power, the less certain he was that it informed the visible world. That doubt infuses his elegy Ode Composed Upon an Evening of Extraordinary Splendour and the assertion that only one life is real concludes On the Power of Sound, where the 'Voice' that 'to Light gave being' shall 'sweep away life's visionary stir' – finally declaring of Platonic Harmony:

> No! though Earth be dust
> And vanish, though the heavens dissolve, her stay
> Is in the WORD, that shall not pass away

The sentiment is echoed in Emily Bronte's Last Lines:

> Though earth and man were gone,
> And suns and universes ceased to be,
> And Thou were left alone,
> Every existence would exist in Thee.

'No more shall grief of mine the season wrong'

However much the three lines considered may reflect Wordsworth's aspirations, this, the second of the quartet betokens doubt, a grief still needing to be resisted. It is one of several lines in the first four stanzas that cast a shadow over a previously asserted joy. The visible and audible energy spring has revived in the outer world – 'while the Birds thus sing a joyous song' – is almost immediately countered by 'To me alone there came a thought of grief', a tension between the positive energy pervading all forms of nature and the singular and isolating lack of power he feels within himself. The deeply felt loss, freely acknowledged in the first two verses, is inadequately represented by the brief and simple 'a thought of grief', and so the reader is left wondering whether they are one and the same, or the second has come upon him just then. Whatever the nature of that grief, it is succinctly dispatched in the next line by 'a timely utterance', the nature of which is not disclosed, a sudden switch that belittles the preceding loss or grief. The reader is unsure of what has or hasn't happened, but whatever it is it enables Wordsworth to declare 'I again am strong' and rediscover the power of cataracts, echoes and winds, so obviously lacking in the rainbow, rose and moon of the second stanza. However, the assertion that his grief will no longer wrong the season comes between the lines on cataracts and echoes – as if that grief is still troubling him. After the 'Winds' have come to him for 25 lines the poet finds that he is as full of joy as the rest of nature, and appears to have moved from a sense of loss to a participative rejoicing. One phrase still betrays a residual doubt: 'Oh evil day! if I were sullen / While the Earth herself is adorning...'

Finally, in line 51, after what George Whalley calls 'the deliberately "jolly" element' becoming increasingly 'insistent, artificial, and "literary"' (p. 49), and Cleanth Brooks describes as 'the poet... straining to work up a gaiety that isn't there' (p. 110), the truth suddenly breaks back in again. Some power is missing. The passage beginning 'But there's a Tree', speaks frankly and magically of the poet's unresolved condition, lines that captivate many readers as the preceding haven't. The stanza ends summarizing the conclusions of the first two: 'Whither is fled the visionary gleam? / Where is it now, the glory and the dream?' If we are back in an emotionally credible place, we are also more or less back where we started, the recovery abandoned. Yet not quite, because instead of closing with an assertion of irreversible loss, the question offers the possibility of an answer.

Like the Leech-gatherer, Wordsworth waited patiently.[12] In the Fenwick note he remembers Archimedes' declaration that he could move the world 'if he had a point whereon to rest his machine', and then asks, 'Who has not felt the same aspirations as regards the world of his own mind?' Perhaps this is an acknowledgement that his mind was 'stuck' with the unanswered questions of 1802, for he goes on, 'Having to wield some of its elements [of his own mind] ... I took hold of the notion of pre-existence'.[13] If the first four stanzas conclude in a question, then the rest of the poem, the next seven stanzas, provides the answer to that question. Nevertheless, the pattern set in the first part – loss, recovery and then one competing with the other – is also the pattern of the second part, except that instead of a complete and alternating dominance of one by the other, there is a process of moderation in which both are able to speak. By March 1804 Wordsworth had found his fulcrum, and felt able to move his mind onwards.[14]

[12.] What parts of the *Ode* were composed when is debated. Wordsworth says he composed the first four stanzas in 1802, and then waited 'two years at least' before adding 'the remaining part' (*FN*). Dorothy records that on 17 June, 'William added a little to the *Ode* he is writing', which Mark Reed suggests refers to stanzas V-VIII. Wordsworth had a good memory, particularly for the composition of his own poems, and what Dorothy records him as adding may have been part of the first four stanzas.

[13.] Most critics pass by what I see as a significant metaphor, but Simon Jarvis stops, unsympathetic: 'Moving the world of one's own mind is not much like moving the world, so it is hard to see why Archimedes had to be introduced' (*Wordsworth's Philosophic Song*, p. 15). Surely such a comparison tells us how significant Wordsworth believed his 'taking hold' of that idea was.

[14.] What Alan Grob (Wordsworth's *Immortality Ode*, p. 33) calls the 'adoption of an enlarged metaphysical framework'.

Chapter 13

Stanzas V-VIII: The Analysis of Loss

THAT HE FELT HE COULD move his mind onwards is suggested by the bold opening of Stanza V, almost a cry of 'eureka!': 'Our birth is but a sleep and a forgetting / The Soul that rises with us, our life's Star, / Hath elsewhere had its setting, / And cometh from afar'.[1] This is Wordsworth's solution to why childhood memories seem to have faded and lost their glory, and this single thought both informs the rest of the poem, and is the basis of the subsequent hopes of revival.[2] Finding ourselves alive on earth, we realize we have left behind the heaven to which our soul once belonged and from which it came – its 'setting'.[3] Mortal or temporal life gradually obliterates the memories of our soul's divine origins, and 'the vision splendid' fades 'into the light of common day'. Yet after our arrival, if remembering where we came from, we remain at least partly clothed in celestial light – 'not in utter nakedness'.

The explanation opening stanza V has an intellectual clarity that answers the emotional clarity of the fourth stanza. However, intellect and emotion begin to work against each other as this section progresses, confusing the reader's response. As soon as 'Shades of the prison-house / Begin to close upon the growing Boy' we are on a path of deepening regret, moving ever further 'From God, who is our home'. An

---

[1.] 'Some extraordinary revaluation of his childhood experiences clearly occurred between the initial composition of the first four stanzas and the later completion of his poem' (Vendler, 'Lionel Trilling', p. 81). Note also 'afar' in relation to De Quincey's comment above (*Recollections*, p. 161).

[2.] Paul Magnuson expresses a comparable idea: 'The 1804 stanzas offer a consolation for loss, but they also offer a new direction for the poem and introduce a myth that is nowhere implied in the opening stanzas' (*Coleridge and Wordsworth*, p. 279).

[3.] Alan Grob ('Wordsworth's *Immortality Ode*', p. 44) writes that Wordsworth assumed 'the existence of a component of self whose being must extend beyond life's temporal boundaries. Hence any claim for continuity in man's spiritual nature was also inevitably a claim for immortality.'

emotional ambivalence then starts to counter this lucid explanation of loss, arising principally from Wordsworth's indecision as to whether the world is a place of joy, or a place of distraction, whether nature acts as a vernal impulse, teaching us, or whether that kind of impulse must proceed from us in order to let nature live, to see the rainbow aright. This uncertainty begins to appear towards the close of the fifth stanza:

> The Youth, who daily farther from the East
> Must travel, still is Nature's Priest,
> And by the vision splendid
> Is on his way attended;

The uncertainty is introduced in the phrase 'Nature's Priest'. This youth, though attended by the original 'vision splendid', is not looking back to the heaven his home, but out on the world – the priest of a deified Nature. This charming picture of a young itinerant priest, surrounded by the nimbus of a pristine and innocent vision, moving on through a bright pastoral landscape, runs counter to the intention of the stanza. We have to remind ourselves that this priest, who travels daily 'farther from the East', is in fact travelling relentlessly westward, like John Donne on Good Friday, away from the 'celestial light', the source of his vision. There is something here that is not regret, not presented as loss, in a verse explaining the very cause of loss. This is a picture of celebration painted upon a canvas of lamentation, just as, in stanza III, a declaration of joy is unsuccessfully superimposed upon the larger song of loss. With the bathos of the stanza's closing lines yet to come, the emotional paradox of travelling away from the source of light, but still surrounded by it, hardly strikes us.

This confusing duality or ambiguity of emotion – should we look back to Heaven or forward to Nature? – is given a significant twist at the beginning of stanza VI, which introduces the idea of earth as a place of benign distraction. Almost unnoticed, what was 'Nature' in the previous verse becomes 'Earth' in this. Are we supposed to register this distinction, and if so what are we to make of it? Michael O'Neill distinguishes the two (O'Neill, 'Tremble', p. 77) in order for 'Nature' not to meet the strictures applied to 'Earth', possibly a synonym for 'world', or even 'society'. This is a nice and potentially useful distinction, but the negative implications associated with 'Earth' – capitalized – are ambiguous, and part of the poem's emotional conflict. In the fourth stanza Wordsworth, feeling the fullness of the bliss in 'Ye blessed Creatures', declares that 'My heart is at your festival /... While the Earth herself is adorning'. In stanza VI, that same Earth 'fills her lap with pleasures of her own', surely a form of goodness, but countered by the earth's seeking to make her 'Foster-child, her Inmate Man / Forget the glories he hath known'. The idea of 'fostering' is in itself benign, as the earth's inmate, man, is being cared for – with 'a Mother's mind' – a universal metaphor of goodness; but it implies a previous loss. In the very act of caring, the 'earth' initiates the process of loss that is the wellspring of the poem. Yet, almost every phrase of this short verse has an air of cheerfulness, and what is done is done with the best of intentions. Nonetheless the aim and end of all this goodness is to divorce mankind from that imperial, or empyrial, palace, 'whence he came'.[4] What we are asked to think conflicts with what we are asked to feel.[5] O'Neill's distinction might be read another way: the 'Earth' is the source of 'ready wealth', of forms ready to be imbued with power, and Nature is that power or 'lore', the 'Youth' its dying vicar. Wordsworth is looking for a life prior to and underpinning that of 'the beauteous objects of Nature' – lacking which they become 'solitary objects still beheld / In disconnection dead and spiritless', returning us to the opening stanzas of the poem.

Stanza VII might be a development of stanza VI, in that it provides a particular example of how a child moves away from the imperial palace; or, if not a development, it might be a distinction, in that the distractions of VI are of sense, of earth and nature, and the distractions of VII of the world and society, the child gradually adopting the normal patterns of human life.[6] Whatever, both are distractions, both betrayals of our divine origins. The emotional ambiguity continues. Although To H.C., Six Years Old celebrates the child as something strange – 'Thou Faery Voyager' – in contrast to the worldly activities of the child in the *Ode*, Lucy Newlyn makes a good case for Hartley Coleridge as the subject of stanza VII. This would account for the feeling of family fondness in the opening lines – 'A four year's Darling... / Fretted by sallies of his Mother's kisses' – a cheerful picture of a boy trying to escape the attentions of an

---

[4.] *MW* 679 RC MS D, additions, pp. 373-4). Vendler ('Lionel Trilling', p. 72) suggests the word 'empyrial'.

[5.] Cf. T.S. Eliot's Animula, which begins, quoting and translating Dante, 'Issues from the hand of God, the simple soul', thus fully in accord with Wordsworth's declaration, 'we come / From God, who is our home'. Unlike Wordsworth, Eliot believes that the soul gives up all its power upon its 'temporal reversion' (*VMP* 56-57).

[6.] Peter Manning regards the role of the mother and father in this process as 'a satiric dismissal of the parents', freeing 'the child from any obligation to them' ('Wordsworth's Intimations Ode', p. 529). Perhaps that is to forget that Wordsworth means what he says when he says 'the simple creed / Of Childhood' 'is most worthy to be blest', even though there is a deeper goodness which this goodness obscures.

over-fond mother.[7] 'With light upon him from his Father's eyes!' could be a reference to Coleridge's delight in his first-born – though it could also be a nod to the source of celestial light still attending the boy. This child is surrounded by 'his new-born blisses' (evoking by contrast 'The fullness of your bliss' in stanza IV?), and the happy chaos of a nursery implicit in 'See, where mid work of his own hand he lies'. Thus, although this stanza sets out to be a particular example of the process by which the child forgets his imperial origins, the opening lines present a goodness to be glad of.[8] All that follows is, paradoxically, both an evocation of a happy childhood, and a detailed account of the continuous distraction that such a life entails. The warmth and affection of this stanza is thus emotionally confusing: which side is Wordsworth really on? As he says elsewhere, in this, the very world, we have our happiness, or not at all – and yet our home is in the abyss of infinity.[9]

The boy of the *Ode* is unlike Hartley in that he is losing his vision as he becomes enthralled and blinded by his parents' lives (*Centuries* III 8), putting on the inevitable yoke of custom, and so at strife with his blessedness. By contrast, Hartley – 'O blessed Vision! Happy Child!' – does not give up that blessedness and rather than fitting his tongue to 'dialogues of business, love or strife' 'fittest to unutterable thought / The breeze-like motion and the self-born carol' – two very different 'fittings'. In the *Ode*, the nursery is a place of imitation that prepares the boy for life in the world; in refusing this process of imitation, but rather following his 'fancies from afar', 'glorious in the might / Of untamed pleasures' – pleasures untamed by custom – Hartley unfits himself for the world. Not 'doomed to jostle with unkindly shocks' of adult life – 'among the full-grown flocks' – even a minimal contact with this visionless world – 'at the touch of wrong' – he is likely to slip 'in a moment out of life'. Hartley retains his visionary power by not being doomed to bear his earthly freight, 'sorrow / Or the injuries of tomorrow'.

Amidst the warmth of stanza VII it is easy to overlook the implicit condemnation. The subtext of what we see as the play of childhood, the 'fluttering' from one activity to another – 'But it will not be long / Ere

---

[7] *Language of Allusion*, pp. 141 ff. Newlyn also thinks 'fretted by sallies' a poor pun, referring to Hartley's mother, Sara (Sally) Coleridge, and her husband's tasteless 'Sally Pally' (*CL* II 888).

[8] The depth of Wordsworth's division of mind is evident in a celebrated passage from Book II (*1805* 237 ff.) of *The Prelude*, beginning 'Blest the infant babe', the very health of whose life is dependent upon his or her mother, and who is described as 'An inmate of this *active* universe', with a soul free of any alienation from this world caused by divine origins.

[9] *1805* X 727-28; and VI 538-39.

this be thrown aside' – is inconstancy, taking to no final form of being, the endless imitation of the different modes of adult life, which know nothing but the light of common day.¹⁰ The child's is a 'dream of human life' and this is not an echo of 'the glory and the dream', but a comment on the quality of the life that the child seeks to imitate, appearing to know no better. Although this progress might be an echo of Jacques's seven ages of man, the advertised quotation in the two lines, 'The little Actor cons another part, / Filling from time to time his "humorous stage"', is from the first line of Daniel's dedication of his *Musophilus* to Fulke Greville. Daniel associates 'this hum'rous Stage' with 'these times of dissolution' in which poets write verse 'transformed... / With others passions, or with others rage; / With loves, with wounds, with factions furnished', that is with imitations. By contrast, what Daniel offers Greville is 'modelled' in 'the forme of mine own heart: / Where, to revive my selfe, my Muse is led / With motions of her owne, t'act her owne part'.¹¹

To revive himself by considering the form of his own heart, with motions of his own, is the task that Wordsworth has set himself, in distinction from the child conning part after part, comparable to Daniel's decadent poets, putting on the passions, loves and rages of other people. That the child's activity, charming in itself, is nonetheless a superficial, socialized form of existence, is further suggested by Wordsworth's presenting his vocation as imitating all 'That Life brings with her in her Equipage'. This is a subtle image, easily passed over. An equipage is, or was, a coach and four, and 'Life' is personified ('her') and so we glimpse a woman of society gliding through town in a horse-drawn coach, accompanied by a dazzling variety of people. 'As if' begins the closing couplet of this stanza – as if this were all of life the implicit comment, though how it is said, with love or scorn, or a mixture of both, is again difficult to tell.¹²

If stanza VII describes the life of the child in this world, then turning aside from what Eliot more derisively calls 'this stony rubbish', Wordsworth sets out his credo in stanza VIII, describing the child's

---

[10.] Cf. *CN* V 6487, Coleridge's positive take on imitation: 'it is ... an instinct of our human nature, to pass out of our *self*'.

[11.] On 24 November 1801, Mary Hutchinson read aloud a poem 'on Learning' by Daniel. Mark Reed thinks this was probably *Musophilus* (*Reed* 130). 'Motions of her own' and 'moods of his own mind' are much of a kind. See also Gill, 'Meditative Morality', p. 577, for a passage of similar import in *Musophilus*.

[12.] Cf. *MY* I 145: Think, he asks Lady Beaumont, of 'the thoughts, feelings, and images, on which the life of my Poems depends ... what have they to do with routs, dinners, morning calls, hurry from door to door, from street to street, on foot or in Carriage'.

still living powers lost to the adult, one life warring with the other. This stanza is the only one in which the child is directly addressed, the poem developing from the observational 'Behold ...' of stanza VII, to the 'Thou' opening VIII, to the 'we' and 'I' of stanza IX. It begins with a distinction between appearance and reality: 'Thou, whose exterior semblance doth belie / Thy Soul's immensity', the visible playing of child in the nursery, to the hidden reality of his inner life. Although the nature of that 'immensity' is not unfolded, the word puts us in touch with the kind of language Wordsworth uses when discussing the qualities of immortality – 'abyss', 'infinity', 'mighty influx' in his prose, 'the eternal deep' in this stanza, and in the next 'that immortal sea' and 'mighty waters'. This quality of being gives the child the right to several surprising titles – 'Thou best Philosopher', 'Mighty Prophet!', 'Seer blest!' – which Wordsworth stood by, despite the fierce criticism of Coleridge.[13]

This stanza is again full of the kinds of paradox arising from the conflict between the life of the soul and the life of the senses – akin to the heaven and earth conflict – whether focused on nature or society. The child is an 'Eye among the blind', and we suppose 'the blind' are adults who can only see things of sense – so whatever kind of sight the child has, it is something other than physical sight. That same child is 'deaf and silent', incapable of communication, perhaps still unlettered, but nonetheless 'read'st the eternal deep, / Haunted for ever by the eternal mind'. Yet, in the previous stanza, this child is apparently oblivious to the condition of his soul; and clearly not haunted 'for ever', as growing up he will become one of the blind, knowing only the light of common day. What is 'for ever' is therefore not a condition of time, has priority over sense, and allows the deaf, blind and silent child to rest 'in the being / Of the eternal silence' of the next verse. Whatever the child knows, whatever heritage he keeps, whatever the nature of 'those truths' with which he is invested, they are not part of his articulate consciousness – and may even be opposed to it: they are unutterable thoughts, 'far hidden from the reach of words'.[14] As previously noted, Traherne, in

---

[13.] See Chapter 6, 'Recollections'. David Duff, 'The Romantic Ode and the Art of Brinkmanship', Études Anglaises (April-June 2020), p. 144, points out that 'Seer blest' is 'Milton's epithet for the archangel Michael (*PL* XII 553)'. He also notes that the 'other rhetorical figures – personification, paradox, hyperbole' congregating around 'the wonder-rousing apostrophe' (*BL* II 140) opening stanza VIII, underline 'the apostrophe's strategic importance, making it a focal point of lyric utterance, a place where the most powerful emotions are expressed, where the imagination is most forcefully engaged and the greatest linguistic risks are taken' (p. 147). Duff's paper has many such rewarding insights.

[14.] *1805* III 182 ff.

Dumnesse, believed that 'the accursèd Breath' of language was the first step in his apostasy:

> For nothing spoke to me but the fair face
> Of Heaven and Earth, before myself could speak,
> *I then my Bliss did, when my silence, break.*[15]

The child knows – 'On whom those truths do rest' – what adults 'are toiling all our lives to find', and yet these are different modes of truth, for the child cannot articulate them, cannot even be said, in some sense, to know them. They are truths resting *on* him; but adults, other than those forever subject to distractions, seek to make the child's accidental investiture a deliberate form of consciousness – the first moment in the poem when a recovery is considered possible. How the condition of immortality relates to the child is expressed in lines that have proved controversial:

> Thou, over whom thy Immortality
> Broods like the Day, a Master o'er a slave,
> A Presence which is not to be put by;

The appropriateness of the metaphor is not the question. Much more significant is that the child is subject to another and superior power – the day, a master or a presence – a power which is separate from but 'above' the child. Wordsworth uses the word 'brood' to describe this – which we may or may not like (Coleridge didn't) but it does give an air of moody, uncertain, almost uncontrolled power exerted upon another – a power 'not to be put by' or dismissed as a servant might be dismissed, but to be acknowledged as dominant. That may be fitting, for it is an indication of how self is related to immortality or eternity in Wordsworth's thinking.

Following the two lines, 'On whom those truths do rest / Which we are toiling all our lives to find', in 1815 Wordsworth inserted, 'In darkness lost, the darkness of the grave'. Those truths lost, the frost gathering round our hearts, the light of immortality not brooding over us, we are as good as in the grave, despite all our toiling. Almost immediately, this image is reversed, and contrasted with the child's consciousness of immortality, for although not a very comfortable place, the grave is associated not with fear or loss, but patience:

---

[15] *TPW* 23. Traherne's italics.

> To whom the grave
> Is but a lonely bed without the sense or sight
> Of day or the warm light
> A place of thought where we in waiting lie;[16]

Waiting for what? Divine reversion to the pre-natal condition? Coleridge was horrified by the idea of lying awake in one's grave, and these lines are sometimes linked to William and Dorothy's habit of lying on gravestones or in ditches; but to think of the horror of being buried alive, or the morbidity of that mode of relaxation, is to be diverted from Wordsworth's intention. He is imagining a child, in bed at night, all sensory input shut off, as if in the grave; but unlike the adult, the child has no fear of what the grave brings – the absence of any sense or sight of the light of day, the lack of the warmth from the sun – because the child, 'deaf and silent', is alive in 'thought'. It is this 'thought', preceding sense in order to make sense of sense, which the adult no longer has and which makes the grave, for an adult but not a child, a place of loss and darkness. The child is bound in a nutshell, counting himself king of infinite space. If the senses are dead, thought or intellect, the supersensual, is alive in the child, who can thus look through death back to the place of birth, to that pre-natal condition which is bodiless and without the faculties of sense. He is in touch with 'the eternal spirit', and the grave is then, as in an earlier version, 'A living place' (*P2V* 367, l. 123).

One word is more puzzling than all the rest – 'lonely'. If Wordsworth didn't want to express something negative, there are other words he might have chosen: 'lonely' points to lack of society, to something wanting. At its most general that lack must be the world of sense that this child is absented from, and which Wordsworth hopes to make one with the lost celestial light, the world evoked at the opening of the last stanza, the 'Fountains, Meadows, Hills, and Groves'. There is companionship and society in that, and he would share an unshared power, move from what is singular, lonely and without sense to the forms of temporal being. This movement parallels that change in the *Ode* from lamenting the lost celestial light to the attempt to celebrate and participate in 'This sweet May-morning', between consciousness of a singular power, to that

---

[16.] Cf. *DWJ* 29 April 1802: 'We then went to John's Grove ... William lay, & I lay in the trench under the fence – he with his eyes shut & listening to the waterfalls & the Birds ... he thought it would be as sweet thus to lie so in the grave, to hear the *peaceful* sounds of the earth & just to know that ones dear friends were near'. Cf. 'These chairs...': 'Oh! who would be afraid of life? / The passion the sorrow and the strife, / When he may lie / Sheltered so easily? / May lie in peace on his bed, / Happy as they who are dead'.

power painting itself into the visible imagery of the natural world.[17] The word or idea that Wordsworth wants is something like 'incarnation', an idea which, facing a similar problem, Eliot adopted.

Stanzas VII and VIII should be read as concurrent, coexisting, rather than consecutive – for the two different kinds of life each describe are going on in the child simultaneously. The first is this life in all its stages and the second his original and divine life still alive in him. If Wordsworth is divided about the real nature of home, he is equally divided about the real nature of childhood. Stanza VIII's description, some seventeen lines, of the qualities of immortality brooding over the child, is a long clause setting out the conditions of a question: why does this epitome of a child, still 'glorious in the might / Of heaven-born freedom', choose to 'provoke / The years to bring the inevitable yoke, / Thus blindly with thy blessedness at strife?' If so divinely blessed, why so eager to lose that blessing in this world? Wordsworth provides no answer, for he has no answer, here or elsewhere.[18] All he can record is that it happens, and custom freezes the child's immortal life. However, something more important has happened – by raising the question Wordsworth has remembered and thus partially revived the experience in himself.

[17.] *1798-9*, MS JJ 122-29.
[18.] *Experiments* 128, notes the 'long formation' of stanza VIII – four 'thou's, followed by 'prophet', 'seer', two more 'thou's and finally 'Why?' He notes that this construction 'is a sign of the poet's difficulty even in phrasing the question'.

Chapter 14

Stanzas IX-X: Recovery

Stanza IX

THE LONG RHETORICAL ASCRIPTION of power to the child in stanza VIII has brought back some life to what Wordsworth feared was lost, and stanza IX begins with a celebration of this rediscovery, reigniting the hesitant real rather than the forced ebullient joy, which he had earlier persuaded himself was fitting to this summer day: 'O joy! that in our embers / Is something that doth live /... The thought of our past years in me doth breed / Perpetual benedictions'. Hidden behind its latinate wording, this last phrase is an oblique expression of a Puritan belief that grace once experienced was ineradicable. In *God's Englishman* Christopher Hill reminds us that a 'man knew when he was saved because he felt, at some stage in his life, an inner satisfaction, a glow that told him he was in direct communion with God'. Hill then adds, 'Cromwell was said to have died happy when assured that grace once known could never be lost: for once he had been in a state of grace.'[1] This memory or reminder induces the same happiness in Wordsworth, but unlike Cromwell he wants to rediscover the power he had once known.

So the joy, at this stage, is for that celestial light still alive in him, or the 'particle divine' that has 'remained unquenched', not yet an expression of delight in the external world.[2] For Wordsworth is at pains to define the source and function of that continual blessing, and his very determination to be precise in this stanza leads to some awkward syntax. Many phrases criticized either for their bombast or lack of precision – 'delicate vatic vagueness' in Hartman's words (*Unremarkable Wordsworth*, p. 152), 'references without a referent' in Richard Gravil's

---

[1] Christopher Hill, *God's Englishman, Oliver Cromwell and the English Revolution*, (Harmondsworth, 1970), pp. 212-13.
[2] *Excursion* IV 51.

('Sunless Land', p. 127) – are in this section, a problem that I consider inherent in the nature of the experience he is trying to describe: that inter-relation outlined earlier, in which the 'unimaginable things' of the mind, disowned by memory, almost lost by the accursèd breath of language, inform the 'beauteous objects' of nature. Wordsworth is therefore quite consistent in declaring that his 'song of thanks and praise' – or his 'loftier song' – is *not* for what is most worth blessing: not for all the qualities we normally associate with childhood, not with delight and liberty and new-fledged hopes, *but*... – and two verse paragraphs, both beginning 'But', try to define what it is that has been revived in him. The repetition of 'But' is clumsy, and makes the reader initially think that the second 'But' is taking exception to the first, whereas they are in fact repeated attempts to define the obscure sense of power that Wordsworth always has difficulty in capturing. He is making room for 'Breathings for incommunicable powers', summarized elsewhere as the 'imagination', a word he resorts to only because of 'the poverty of language'.[3]

He raises his song of thanks and praise for these fugitive powers, the glowing embers of his once visionary fire, because they throw doubt on reality being derived from the uninvested notices of sense, and they do so with a repeated determination: 'those obstinate questionings / Of sense and outward things' challenge a mind 'intoxicate / With present objects, and the busy dance / Of things that pass away', challenge a mind that could be held 'In absolute dominion' by the 'most despotic of our senses' – the eye, master of heart or mind, which thus creates a legislature from 'the laws of vulgar sense', ruling only this world, 'a universe of death, / The falsest of all worlds'.[4] Powers though they may be, they are fugitive, almost nothing compared to the light of common day, and they are recognized only as 'Fallings from us, vanishings; / Blank misgivings of a creature / Moving about in worlds not realiz'd', conscious that there is a world or worlds not this world, inward not outward, but moving as if in darkness, unable to see the world that is there, lost the celestial light by which it was once illuminated. However, these fallings and vanishings are also 'High instincts, before which our mortal Nature / Did tremble like a guilty Thing surpriz'd'. The natural is afraid of the supernatural. There is a barely noticeable but possibly significant change of tense, praising what had happened – 'did tremble'

[3.] *Preface* (1815), *MW* 686. See also *1850* VI 592-93.
[4.] *1805* XIII 135 ff. Cf. T.S.Eliot, Marina: 'Those who sit in the sty of contentment, meaning Death', etc.

not 'does tremble' or 'trembles' – by contrast with the still continuing fallings and vanishings. This might look back to a particular event, possibly the boat-stealing episode, composed in January 1804, close to the completion of the *Ode* in early March. After more borrowing than stealing a shepherd's skiff on Ullswater, he saw, looking back to the lake's edge, a 'huge cliff / As with voluntary power instinct,' rising up between him and the stars, then seeming to stride after him 'like a living thing'. Taking the boat was 'an act of stealth / And troubled pleasure', so no doubt a sense of guilt catalysed his fear of being pursued. With 'trembling hands' he turned and 'stole' his way back to where he had found his boat. Thus he 'Did tremble like a guilty Thing surpriz'd'.

However, that was more the beginning than the end of the experience:

>   after I had seen
>   That spectacle, for many days my brain
>   Worked with a dim and undetermined sense
>   Of unknown modes of being. In my thoughts
>   There was a darkness – call it solitude
>   Or blank desertion – no familiar shapes
>   Of hourly objects, images of trees,
>   Or sea or sky, no colours of green fields,
>   But huge and mighty forms that do not live
>   Like living men moved slowly through my mind
>   By day, and were the trouble of my dreams.
>   (*1805* I 412 ff.)

His mind ceased to work with the notices of sense, with what is deducible and rational, but instead with 'unknown modes of being', a working that emptied the mind of all immediate impression, the known world lost in darkness, without the 'images of trees / Or sea or sky'. In one sense, Wordsworth felt abandoned, suffering a 'blank desertion', perhaps of a kind with the 'Blank misgivings of a Creature / Moving about in worlds not realiz'd'. However, that desertion is co-ordinate with an access of power, not quite his, yet realized in him, 'huge and mighty forms' moving slowly through his mind, quite different from the experiences of daily life, not living like living men.[5] The quality of these forms is uncertain: they are disruptive, trouble his dreams, but are they to be welcomed or dismissed? If these two passages do speak to each

---

[5.] These forms might be a more frightening version of the Pedlar's 'ideal stores, his shapes and forms' (*RC* E 138-40).

other, then these might be the 'High instincts' before which our mortal nature trembles, as the boy surprised had trembled. And if the mortal trembles, the implication is that it trembles before the immortal. That is not confirmed by either passage, but in *The Prelude*, the lines above are immediately followed by an acclamation, 'Wisdom and spirit of the universe / Thou soul that art the eternity of thought', as if he had felt its presence in those huge and mighty forms. The second phrase is easily passed over: but the soul or principle of thought – that thought or thinking which is the source of all thoughts and thinking – has an eternal being, and is therefore a form of immortality. Wordsworth then goes on to thank this spirit – an everlasting motion, the breath of forms and images – for intertwining the passions of his youth 'with high objects, with enduring things' (*1805* I 436). High instincts and high objects are surely of a kind, the objects not material, and 'enduring' points to the immortal.

Then beginning with the second 'But' he redescribes 'those obstinate questionings' and 'High instincts' as 'those first affections, / Those shadowy recollections' originating in his childhood – reminding us of a key word in the poem's subtitle. If as suggested these recollections can be associated with Wordsworth's more substantial descriptions of similar powers, then their often-criticized referential uncertainty has at least been diminished. From here to the end of the stanza there is none of the emotional confusion that has so far created a sense of uncertainty in the reader. The 'blank misgivings', 'high instincts', 'first affections' and 'shadowy recollections' are all summed up as 'a master light of all our seeing', 'truths that wake / To perish never' – which may be comparable to Cromwell's idea of grace: once woken, nothing, however inimical to their existence, nor man nor boy, can abolish or destroy them. A platform, delicate though it may be, has been established for a looking forward, not just a looking back. In such a mood the stanza concludes: 'Hence' (from here), 'in a season of calm weather' (undistracted by distractions) / 'Though inland far we be' (surrounded by Earth's natural pleasures) / 'Our Souls' (the soul thus distinguished from self, or the 'we' of the previous line) 'have sight of that immortal sea' (the infinite abyss) / 'Which brought us hither' (to this earth from heaven our home) / 'And see the Children sport upon the shore' (able to look back to our childhood) / 'And hear the mighty waters rolling evermore' (alive to the presence of that immortal power).[6]

[6.] John Worthen (*Life*, p. 277) suggests that Wordsworth's sonnet, 'It is a beauteous evening, calm and free', written while at Calais visiting Annette Villon and their daughter Caroline, may inform these lines.

If one takes stanza VIII as an extended 'thought of grief', the burden of custom lying like frost upon the soul, then stanza IX might be considered an unpacking of the latent substance of the 'timely utterance', which had immediately answered the initial thought of grief in stanza III. We do not need to look outside the poem to discern what Wordsworth meant by that phrase, revealed in the emotionally unequivocal assertions, conditions and caveats of this later stanza.[7] It is the most confident in the poem, laying out the foundations of his power and his vision – the perpetual benedictions which are the expressions of a grace that cannot be extinguished, however little of the original power is left – 'truths that wake / To perish never'. This sense of waking is significant, for it introduces the idea of the permanent, and is associated with a movement from intuition in the child to conscious truth in the adult – that is, with a growth of faculties, of the philosophic mind, discussed below.

Stanza X

His careful delineation of the nature of the perpetual blessing removes his sense of disparity between the child's two modes of being that end stanza VIII, and in stanza X enables him to return to the immediate world. The similarities of this stanza to stanzas III and IV suggest a comparable recovery of joy and power, but here not wholly lost again. At the beginning of this stanza, a renewed inner confidence enables the poet to look outward, and celebrate the renewed glory of the immediate world, 'the gladness of the May!'[8] That both utterances are of the same kind is signalled by the repetition of earlier phrases, such as 'the young Lambs bound / As to the tabor's sound!' of stanza III. Yet following the earlier pattern, after a brief celebration of the rekindled joy (just seven lines) the sense of loss returns: 'What though the radiance which was once so bright / Be now for ever taken from my sight'. The syntax ('What though') and the absence of a question mark let the reader know that now the loss is relative not absolute, that something still remains,

---

[7.] Not, for instance, to 'Resolution and Independence', which is Lionel Trilling's suggestion: *The Liberal Imagination* (London, 1951), p. 139. For a list of critical ideas on the 'timely utterance' see https://www.jstage.jst.go.jp/article/elsjp/37/1/37_KJ00006939443/_article.

[8.] However, there is a change from the earlier celebration, which Curtis notices, 'We *in thought* will join your throng', which he believes 'contains the knowledge that the light is gone' (*Experiments* 134). But, remembering Tintern Abbey, until image becomes thought it remains unintelligible, and so part of his progress from the immortality investing the child to that disclosed by the philosophic mind. This developing consciousness justifies his renewed rejoicing.

moderated by the active knowledge absent in the earlier stanza.[9] In declaring that 'nothing can bring the hour / Of splendour in the grass, of glory in the flower', Wordsworth may also be marking the connection between the two stanzas by a tacit reference to the loss epitomized in the single field and the pansy. The renewal after this readmitted loss is modest, and only tentatively asserted, but its presence marks the second of the major differences between the two parts of the poem. In Tintern Abbey, after the discovery of power that concludes with 'We see into the life of things', there is a reprise that begins with his casting some doubt on what he has just declared – 'If this / Be but a vain belief'. This is followed by an admission that the love that 'had no need of a remoter charm, / By thought supplied, or any interest / Unborrowed from the eye' belongs to time past, and 'all its aching joys are now no more'. But 'other gifts / Have followed'. The revival is much lengthier and more complex in the *Ode*, but as in Tintern Abbey, it begins with a looking back and ends in feeling again the 'might' or power of the meadows, hills and groves, and a petitioning of the beloved by the lover not to think of separation. Whether or not the later utterance succeeds in ways the earlier hadn't is what decides the reader as to whether the poem is an elegy for lost powers, or a celebration of renewed vision.

The similarity of pattern continues. The words of stanza III, 'I again am strong…/ No more shall grief of mine the season wrong', find their echo in 'We will grieve not, rather find / Strength in what remains behind' and although the confidence at the end of stanza IX is here reduced, it is not wholly removed.[10] It is perhaps more real in being more modest. The pattern common to these two stanzas was earlier evident in Tintern Abbey:

> That time is past,
> And all its aching joys are now no more,
> And all its dizzy raptures. Not for this
> Faint I, nor mourn nor murmur; other gifts
> Have followed, for such loss, I would believe,
> Abundant recompence.[11]

[9.] Cf. the lost 'hour of splendour in the grass' and the man who looked at 'the common grass from hour to hour' of 'Within our happy Castle there dwelt one'. Although critics agree that this is a poem that describes Coleridge and Wordsworth, who is represented by which character is by no means evident.

[10.] The importance of revived 'strength' is also evident in Wordsworth's reflections after revisiting the mouldering gibbet with Dorothy and Mary: 'diversity of strength / Attends us, if but once we have been strong' (*1805* XI 320 ff.).

[11.] The 'Not for this' of Tintern Abbey is echoed in the 'Not for these' of the *Ode*. Both assert that whatever has been lost has its compensation in the development of another power.

In the *Ode* recompense is more residual than abundant, but the last six lines of stanza X describe or define some of those 'other gifts', unspecified in Tintern Abbey. Just as he had illuminated the nature of the 'timely utterance' in some detail, so now, rather than just saying 'I again am strong', Wordsworth offers a full if condensed account of where his remaining strength is found:

> In the primal sympathy
> Which having been must ever be,
> In the soothing thoughts that spring
> Out of human suffering,
> In the faith that looks through death,
> In years that bring the philosophic mind.

That strength has four discrete sources: in the primal sympathy, in the soothing thoughts, in the faith of a life beyond life and in the coming of the philosophic mind. The primal sympathy is, as the phrase implies, the first and also the foundation of the other three, a succinct summary of the obscure powers, 'be they what they may', that are the 'master light of all our seeing'.[12] It is 'primal' because it points to the power Wordsworth described as 'the eternal spirit' which, finding its life in 'unimaginable things', then paints itself into the visible imagery of the world.[13] That spirit appears as 'the soul / Of our first sympathies' or 'those first affections' of the *Ode*. Part of the development here is an acceptance that what is no longer a matter of experience remains 'truths that wake, / To perish never', truths 'Which having been must ever be'. 'Must' is a carefully chosen word, and upon that 'must' we can act if the original experience is still credible. That those truths are no longer felt as a power does not invalidate the original experience, a reversal of the presumption of the first four verses. Wordsworth is not now looking back, but looking forward to a means of recovering that power.

The list appears progressive: from primal sympathy to philosophic mind. The link between the two appears explicit in Book II of *The Prelude*:

> I deem not profitless those fleeting moods
> Of shadowy exaltation; not for this,

[12.] In a variant reading that light can 'mitigate our spell / Of that strong frame of sense in which we dwell', a light comparable to the power enabling 'those obstinate questionings / Of sense and outward things' (P2V 276).

[13.] *1798-9* 126. For a more detailed discussion of these lines and the following passage from *The Prelude*, see the conclusion to Chapter 5, 'Intimations'.

> That they are kindred to our purer mind
> And intellectual life; but that the soul,
> Remembering how she felt, but what she felt
> Remembering not – retains an obscure sense
> Of possible sublimity, to which,
> With growing faculties she doth aspire,
> With faculties still growing   (*1805* II 331-38)

The 'shadowy exaltation' in this passage is the 'shadowy recollections' of the *Ode*, and both are 'kindred to our purer mind' – 'my purer mind' of Tintern Abbey. That is, intuitions speak to intellect, but the intuitions of 'the purer mind', that mind not subject to sense, are principally those exemplified by geometry, intuitions of reason rather than of Reason. The 'not for this', followed by 'but that the soul', also associates 'those fleeting moods' with another distinct form of being – 'the soul': that is, 'intellectual life' and 'soul' are not synonymous, but are both substantiated by the same experience of 'shadowy exaltation'.[14] It is the soul, and not the intellectual life or the purer mind, that can aspire to a conclusive sublimity.

However, if the list from primal sympathy to philosophic mind is progressive, it moves through the intermediate stage of 'soothing thoughts that spring' (so cheerful a word) 'Out of human suffering'. As we have seen, Wordsworth's progress towards something 'more sublime', is habitually preceded by a recognition of the suffering of mankind – the 'woes / Which thou endur'st'; but they are only a stepping stone, a 'weight, albeit huge', which he then charms away. Nonetheless, to reach that stepping stone the love of nature must first lead to the love of man. In principle these six lines follow that pattern: a love of nature – the primal sympathy – leads to the recognition of human suffering, and that temporal suffering is then resolved by 'something more sublime' – 'the faith that looks through death' – a transcendent peace beyond space and time. Such peace is the source of soothing thoughts, which succeed (or spring from) mortal suffering. Uncomfortable stuff for many of us, but one of the principal structures of Wordsworth's thought.

Such a progress also concludes the Pedlar's intellectual history, whose 'whole figure breath'd intelligence'. Age...

[14.] The 'Not for this / Faint I' of Tintern Abbey introduces a comparable distinction: 'other gifts have followed'. The editors of the Norton edition suggest that in effect 'intellectual' means 'spiritual'. However, that would conflate 'intellect' and 'soul' – two words which Wordsworth has carefully distinguished.

> had not tam'd his eye, which, under brows
> Shaggy and grey, had meanings which it brought
> From years of youth, which, like a being
> Made of many beings, he had wondrous skill
> To blend with knowledge of years to come,
> Human or such as lie beyond the grave.   (*RC* E 372-75)

His untamed eye brought meanings from his earlier years – from the 'little Child, yet glorious in the might / Of untam'd pleasures' – which he was able to combine with the knowledge later acquired in adulthood, though requiring wondrous, perhaps philosophical, skill. He was not divided from his past, so that his 'many beings' – child, boy, youth, man – form one being, the child the father of the man. His knowledge is prophetic, 'of the years to come', and follows the pattern described above that knowledge is first of nature, then of the human and human suffering, and finally of what is beyond the grave.

The infant vision or primal sympathy is the paradigm of the lost power – 'eager to combine / In one appearance all the elements / And parts of the same object, else detached / And loathe to coalesce' (*1805* II 247-50). The sublimity to which the faculties aspire will be an expression of that unity. As we saw in Chapter 6, Traherne says of his childhood: 'I knew by intuition those things which since my Apostasy, I collected again by the highest reason' (*Centuries* III 2). The distinction implicit in Traherne's declaration, that there are higher and lower forms of reason, Wordsworth makes explicit when he discusses geometry and poetry, differentiating between 'the adamantine holds of truth / By reason built, or passion (which itself / Is highest reason in a soul sublime[)]' (*1805* V 40). For both poets 'highest reason' denotes an ultimate power, and presumably that and 'the philosophic mind' are to all intents one and the same. Passion may seem an unlikely word to describe that power, but it indicates the presence of feeling: the absence of feeling was the original impetus of the poem. That passion is principally love, as discussed at the end of Chapter 5, summed up in Traherne's 'For he that delights not in Love makes vain the universe', and which finds its place at the end of the *Ode*.

Just as in Wordsworth's ambiguous world nature as lore is the source of power – 'Thence did I drink the visionary power' (*1805* II 331) – so it is the source of feeling. 'From Nature doth emotion come' (*1805* XII 1), that emotion at one with 'our first sympathies'; and in Nature he 'had been taught to reverence a power / That is the very quality and shape / Of right reason' (*1805* XII 25 ff.), presumably at one 'with high objects, with enduring things' which were intertwined with the passions of his youth (*1805* I 436). In such experiences lie further intuitions of 'the primal sympathy', the foundations upon which the growing years will build the philosophic mind. The foundations may cease to be visible, but 'having been must ever be', each continuous with the other.[15]

[15.] But not for every one: in Book II of *The Prelude* Wordsworth notes 'the first / Poetic spirit of our human life' is in some 'by uniform controul [or custom]... / ... abated and suppressed'; but in others, 'Through every change of growth or of decay / Preeminent till death' (*1805* II 275-80).

Chapter 15

Stanza XI: Resolution

IF WE DIDN'T HAVE THE final stanza of the *Ode*, we might think the last lines of stanza X – finding strength 'In the faith that looks through death, / In years that bring the philosophic mind' – a fitting conclusion. Stanza IV opened with a renewed celebration of the spring, but closed with an unmitigated sense of loss. Stanza X opens with a reprise of that celebration, which is followed by an acknowledgment of loss, which the long reparative stanzas V-VIII had attenuated, rendering it partial, not absolute. Yet unlike stanza IV, the conclusion to stanza X identifies what had been lost, what had not, what could be regained, and how. The radiance once so bright was still glowing quietly, and is now co-ordinate with faculties growing in the adult, consistent with the lost intuitions of the child. Past, present and future have reached a tentative union. That balanced, complex pattern, of loss and recovery, of sadness and delight, is rehearsed in a fragment in the Dove Cottage Manuscripts:

> I look into times past as prophets look
> Into futurity a [?thread ?trail] of life runs back
> Into dead years, the [?faculty ?fantasy] of thought
> The lyric spirit of philosophy
> Leads me through moods of sadness to [?and] delight.[1]

The *Ode* is Wordsworth's finest expression of the lyric spirit of philosophy, and moves from dead years and sadness to a feeling of power ('might'), having all his delights but one intact. This most lyrical of poems has a coherence that grows out of, and could only have grown out of, a mind profoundly organized. He had what by and large Eliot thought the Victorians poets didn't have, a 'hold on permanent things,

---

[1.] *DCMS* 44.84, from *Experiments* 42, also quoted in Chapters 6 and 11.

on permanent truths about man and God and life and death' (*SE* 337); and, we could add, a hold on what the soul was, its relation to human nature, and to God, and a hold on Love as the greatest of all powers. These were the solid, unshaken foundations of his poetry.

If philosophy or metaphysics is a form of knowledge, poetry is an expression of power, and however mature the philosophic mind, for a poet it is nothing if it cannot find expression, if it cannot, as a lyric spirit, unite itself with experience. The last stanza is a tentative manifestation of that renewed power, an auxiliar light, which if not bestowing new splendour, partially recovers the celestial vision, allowing mind and nature to be at one, each able to speak to the other.[2] The evidence of recovery is felt in the fear of separation that opens the final stanza: 'And oh ye Fountains, Meadows, Hills, and Groves, / Think not of any severing of our loves!' – that love, perhaps, the absence of which 'would make vain the universe' (*Centuries* II 65). As Stanza IX was a reprise with variations of stanza IV, so the opening line of this stanza looks back to the first words of the poem – 'There was a time when meadow, grove, and stream' – reminding us of that initial divorce between seeing and feeling. That severance has been partially repaired, and he is more at one with the landscape he looks upon.[3] In 'our loves' we can see his belief in a shared consciousness, worried by the continuing risk of separation, as if they were a pair of lovers having a difficult conversation. This is already a falling off from much more confident but comparable lines in *Home at Grasmere*, which open by bringing the two lovers together, 'Embrace me then, ye Hills, and close me in', and then goes on,

> But I would call thee beautiful, for mild
> And soft and gay and beautiful thou art,
> Dear Valley, having in thy face a smile
> Though peaceful, full of gladness.   (*HG* B 129-36)

Fear that the fragile restoration of 1804 might fail deepened as the years passed. If 'Think not of...' is an earnest request between equals, from 1836 onwards it became the more ominous 'Forbode not ...', a phrase

---

[2.] 'An auxiliar light / Came from my mind, which on the setting sun / Bestowed new splendor' (*1805* II 387-89).
[3.] The distinction between the opening observation that 'There was a time when meadow, grove and stream', and the apostrophe of the final stanza – 'And oh ye Fountains, Meadows, Hills and Groves' – matches that of 'Behold the Child ...' of stanza VII and 'Thou best Philosopher ...' of stanza VIII. Both move from a detachment to an engagement. See Duff, 'Romantic Ode', p. 144, fn. 13.

that may reflect Wordsworth's increasing anxiety that the hiding places of his power had closed.

Nevertheless, with that reunion, however frail, also comes an experience of a return of power in nature – 'Yet in my heart of hearts I feel your might' – the power noticeably absent from rainbow, rose and moon.[4] Here the 'might' is attributed to the objects of nature working on the poet, but stanza IX describes the recovery of strength and power from within the individual, distinct from any external stimulus. That the poet rediscovers the power in nature only after having recovered the power in himself and then attributing that power to nature, is the paradoxical truth Coleridge saw as enabling such restoration: 'we receive but what we give / And in *our* Life alone does Nature live' (*VL* 296-97). The emphasis is his, countering Wordsworth's uncertainties about the origins of power. If not evident in the *Ode*, Wordsworth takes on Coleridge's dictum in Book XI of *The Prelude*, probably written in the spring of 1805 (*Reed* 14): 'but this I feel, / That from thyself it is that thou must give, / Else never can receive' (*1805* XI 331-33). But he had given and he has received.

The 'might' that Wordsworth feels here is of a kind with the power of the 'mighty mind' he witnessed on Snowdon, able to thrust forth upon the senses 'a genuine counterpart / ... of the glorious faculty / Which higher minds bear with them as their own' (*1805* XIII 85-90). Both the 'lore' or mind of nature and the intellect or imagination of man meet each other through the medium of the senses. If power, whatever its source, is invested in an object, then that object becomes a thing of power itself. Such a union Wordsworth thinks of as a marriage, and his poetry 'the spousal verse / Of this great consummation'. The potential outcome of this 'blended might' of world and mind is not '*a*' but '*the* creation', the world made or remade – Paradise restored (*HG* D 800-24).

In the *Ode* the 'might' of the meadows, hills and groves, revived by the reunion of 'our loves', is a power moderated by the experience of previous loss. The declaration, 'I love the Brooks which down their channels fret / Even more than when I tripp'd lightly as they', is quieter and more credible than the restoration first asserted as cataracts blowing their trumpets from the steep.[5] If more modestly expressed, his love is now more assured than in his youth, an achievement also recognized in *Home at Grasmere*:

[4.] This pattern is also evident in Tintern Abbey, in which the unifying spirit is evoked, followed by, 'Therefore am I still / A lover of the meadows and the woods, / And mountains'.

[5.] Dorothy records that 'Wm showed me the little mossy streamlet which he had before loved when he saw its bright green track in the snow' (*DWJ* 16 April 1802).

> ... in my day of childhood I was less
> The mind of Nature, less, take all in all,
> Whatever may be lost, than I am now. (*HG* B 94-96)[6]

The loss is admitted, but the gain is that he has become more 'the mind of Nature'. He has learned to look on nature 'not as in the hour / Of thoughtless youth', but with the remoter charm that has been supplied by thought: The participative 'We in thought will join your throng' echoes and reverses the isolating 'To me alone there came a thought of grief'. If joining the throng by 'thought' is taken as a very limited mode of participation, then we need to remember that some form of thought or thinking, a faculty still growing, underpinned by Reason, provides the resolution to Wordsworth's problems, as it did for Traherne (*Centuries* III 2).

One word more on brooks as cataracts in a minor key, which might underlie his simple expression of love. In two poems composed in 1802 – 'Brook, that has been my solace days and weeks', and 'Dear Native Brooks your ways I have pursued' (*MW* 274-75) – Wordsworth finds a significance only implicit in the mountain streams of the *Ode*. In the first, whenever he visits the brook he feels a rainbow-like delight: 'I come to thee, thou dost my heart renew / O happy Thing!' and rather than anthropomorphize it as did the Greeks, he gives it an incarnational significance: 'It seems, the Eternal Soul is clothed in thee / With purer robes than those of flesh and blood'. Here, perhaps, is another example of the idea of the soul running through the landscape as through a person, from the abyss to eternity, which is developed in the Essay on Epitaphs. In the second, a much more boisterous stream 'Comes roaring like a joyous multitude', reminding him 'of life and its first joys'. Those memories, 'a tender chain / Of flowers and delicate dreams' enable the man to trace his life back to that of the boy – that is, establish a continuity between them. One might have expected a reflection on how the boy became a man, but Wordsworth reverses this, and finds that these memories 'entertain / Loose minds when Men are growing into Boys': the child is becoming the father of the man. The word 'loose' suggests lax or undisciplined, but Wordsworth probably meant 'free', as the poem ends, 'My manly heart has owed to your rough noise / Triumphs and thoughts no bondage could restrain.' What triumphs we are left to imagine, but connecting the man to the child is part of the process of renewal in the *Ode*, and it is possible that the ideas outlined

---

[6.] The loss of childhood vision followed by restoration through thought or reflection is a structural part of Tintern Abbey, *Home at Grasmere* and the *Ode*.

in these poems returned to Wordsworth as he completed the poem in 1804, so brooks find their place in the closing of the poem.

'One delight'

The tentative renewal is oddly compromised by the suggestion that this relationship has been established through the sacrifice of another: 'I only have relinquish'd one delight / To live beneath your habitual sway'. There is no indication what this one delight is. His decision to retire to Grasmere, to abandon any profession and seek out a purity of being, was troubled: 'And did it cost so much, and did it ask / Such length of discipline, and could it seem / An act of courage, and the thing itself / A conquest? Shame that this was ever so…' (*HG* B 64-67). He says goodbye to the world, but he also says goodbye to a certain kind of poetry: 'Then farewell to the Warrior's deeds, farewell / All hope, which once and long was mine, to fill / The heroic trumpet with the muse's breath!' (*HG* B 953-55), an abandoned aspiration he considered at much greater length in *The Prelude* (*1805* I 157-228), and which concludes 'Then, last wish – / My last and favorite aspiration – then / I yearn towards some philosophic song / Of truth that cherishes our daily life'.[7] It is easy to underestimate just how troubled Wordsworth was by his decision to abandon the traditional forms of Romantic and heroic poetry and write another kind of verse, which required, as he saw it, another way of life. Those two lines reflect the final resolution behind a very great disturbance of mind and heart.

The spring morning is acknowledged rather than celebrated, for there is no forced enthusiasm in 'The innocent brightness of a new-born Day / Is lovely yet'. Is that any more an affirmation than 'The sunshine is a glorious birth' of the second stanza? This air of reservation typifies the cautious mood of the last verse. In line with the anxiety as to whether the recovery is really there, the opening of the day is immediately followed by its closing: 'The clouds that gather round the setting sun / Do take a sober colouring from an eye / That hath kept watch o'er man's mortality' – as the Pedlar and the poet kept a very sober watch over Margaret's mortality. Still, there is a determination to look through

---

[7.] Cf. *HG* B 929-33: 'I cannot at this moment read a tale / Of two brave Vessels matched in deadly fight / And fighting to the death, but I am pleased / More than a wise Man ought to be; I wish, / I burn, I struggle, and in soul am there.' Stephen Gill (*A Life*, p. 163) enlarges on Wordsworth's militaristic nature.

death. It is possible that the line 'Another race hath been, other palms are won' is a distant or disconnected reference to relinquishing 'one delight', to the untravelled path of heroic or romantic verse. Because it follows the lines on the closing of human life, it may also be read as preparatory to the final lines, and read as a setting aside of mortality. A different task has been chosen, with a different reward, which informs the epigraph, to make the boy the father of the man, to connect the life past with the life present, ensuring that his heart will always leap up at the sight of a rainbow. And so that line ('Another race hath been') introduces the final quatrain, which sums up the nature of the other race and the other palms:

> Thanks to the human heart by which we live,
> Thanks to its tenderness, its joys, and fears,
> To me the meanest flower that blows can give
> Thoughts that do often lie too deep for tears.

The 'human heart' is 'the secret spirit of humanity' – by which we live through death, and which survives 'the malice of the grave' and 'the calm oblivious tendencies / Of Nature' (*RC* D 503-5). That secret spirit also has a tenderness for the immediate and visible world, that love expressed in the opening lines of the stanza, as well as a tenderness for man's suffering and mortality – 'tears to human suffering are due' (Laodamia). We need not read 'its joys, and fears' as generalities, for in the context of the *Ode*, the principal joy is that of 'Oh joy! that in our embers / Is something that doth live', that joy which is 'the fountain light of all our day', at one with the informing spirit of nature; it is also the substance of 'the vision splendid' attending Nature's priest, and integrated into ordinary human life, it is the joy of the shouting 'happy Shepherd Boy'. There are many joys in that one word.

The fears are principally the 'High instincts, before which our mortal Nature / Did tremble like a guilty Thing surpriz'd'; and those instincts are composed of 'first affections' and 'shadowy recollections', which challenge 'Delight and liberty, the simple creed / Of childhood'. Wordsworth spoke of that quality of fear as foundational, notably in *The Prelude* – 'I grew up / Fostered alike by beauty and by fear' (*1805* I 305-6) – catalysing a consciousness of power anterior to all the forms of nature, of a 'dim and undetermined sense / Of unknown modes of being', the disturbing power without which the appearances of nature may be beautiful and fair, but not intelligible.

'Too deep for tears'

Thus the joys and fears so lightly mentioned carry the weight of profound reflection. Wordsworth is not employing words casually or sentimentally. The last two lines are more often subject to a 'feel-good' reading than most. Those for whom the idea of immortality is hardly comprehensible prefer not to define and so restrict the range of thoughts that might be too deep for tears, or ask why the meanest of flowers should enable such thoughts.

As we have seen, *The Ruined Cottage* provides a connection between thoughts that spring from human suffering and those that lie too deep for tears. In MS D, the Pedlar laments the bleakness of Margaret's death with a pitying but relentless determination:

> She is dead,
> The worm is on her cheek, and this poor hut,
> Stripp'd of its outward garb of household flowers,
> Of rose and sweet briar, offers to the wind
> A cold bare wall whose earthy top is tricked
> With weeds and the rank spear-grass. She is dead
> And nettles rot and adders sun themselves
> Where we have sat together while she nursed
> Her infant at her breast.   (*RC* D 103-11)

All these symbols of loss and decay – the bare walls, the rotting nettles, the rank spear-grass and the adders sunning themselves resonant of our loss of Eden – are carefully invested in the cottage, which might otherwise have been looked on with the aesthetic pleasure of a minor gothic ruin. In her decaying body, and in the repeated 'She is dead', we feel finality of Margaret's death – that finality Wordsworth always attributes to death. However, the spear-grass reappears at the end of this poem, in a very different guise.[8]

After advising the poet, suffering 'the impotence of grief', to be wise and cheerful, and seeing Margaret's death from a very different perspective – 'no longer read / The forms of things with an unworthy eye. / She sleeps in the calm earth, and peace is here' – the Pedlar, looking back to 'the rank spear-grass', discovers something wholly different:

[8.] The following paragraph is a variation on the ending of *The Ruined Cottage* as discussed in Chapter 4.

> I well remember that those very plumes,
> Those weeds, and the high spear-grass on that wall,
> By mist and silent rain-drops silver'd o'er,
> As once I passed did to my heart convey
> So still an image of tranquility,
> So calm and still, and looked so beautiful
> Amid the uneasy thoughts that filled my mind,
> That what we feel of sorrow and despair
> From ruin and from change, and all the grief
> The passing shews of being leave behind,
> Appeared an idle dream that could not live
> Where meditation was.[9]

The most serious mistake in reading this passage would be to think that Wordsworth believes that an aesthetic response might somehow soothe away all the troubles of the world. The perceptual change from 'the rank spear-grass' to something beautiful 'silver'd o'er' by 'mist and silent rain-drops' has either catalysed or been effected by 'meditation' – which is but another name for imagination, contemplation or faith – all the work of Reason. This transformation is comparable to that of the water-snakes in *The Ancient Mariner* from 'slimy things' that 'did crawl with legs / Upon the slimy sea' to 'happy living things' whose beauty – 'Blue, glossy green, and velvet black' – no tongue might declare. This is the prelude to the mariner's ability to pray and as here it precedes, at least in order of description, the realized power of meditation. The process, tightly compressed, is that love of nature – the revisioned spear-grass – leads to a love of mankind and sympathy for all the 'sorrow and despair' which is the burden of human existence; and then moves through and beyond nature – just as the Pedlar's eye could look beyond the grave (*RC* E 372-75).

That of course is why the meanest of flowers – the spear-grass in this instance but any flower in fact – can give thoughts too deep for tears. Tears are shed for our mortality, as they were shed in Laodamia, and in the beautiful elegies for Margaret, for John, for Catherine. However,

---

[9.] Similar reflections occur twice before this conclusion: once, when the Pedlar speaks of musing on the cottage 'As on a picture, till my wiser mind / Sinks, yielding to the foolishness of grief' (*RC* D 118-19). And further on, less certainly: 'Why should we thus with an untoward mind / And in the weakness of humanity,/ From natural wisdom turn our hearts away,/ To natural comfort shut our eyes and ears,/ And feeding on disquiet, thus disturb / The calm of nature with our restless thoughts?' (*RC* D 193-98).

earth destroys both mortal raptures and mortal sorrows. If there were nothing but mortality, there could be nothing but tears. Wisdom runs deeper: mortality has been dismissed, and so tears can be dismissed. Be wise and cheerful. Meditation – that living power which is at one with the imagination or 'Reason in her most exalted mood' – enables the transition from the sorrows of human life to the happiness beyond the grave.

So here at the end of the poem, the human heart by which we live, if not leaping up, is at least stumbling to its feet. Whatever the precise qualities of those 'thoughts', they point to the mysterious power of the primal sympathy evoked in stanza IX, and the philosophic mind of stanza X. That power is the nearest thing Wordsworth knows to immortality, a power, and not a condition nor a belief, with which he has finally, if temporarily, reinvested or re-apparelled the appearances of nature – father and child almost at one, bound to nature by love and natural piety, both 'wedded to this goodly universe'. After our reading of the poem, Wordsworth encourages us to turn away, as did the Pedlar, and walk along our road in happiness.[10]

[10.] It is less marked, but there is a similar pattern at the end of Tintern Abbey: he first looks to Dorothy's potential suffering, which, when she remembers him, he imagines relieved by 'healing thoughts / Of tender joy'. His experience, shared with her, will supercede her suffering. He has returned to Nature and the Wye with 'far deeper zeal / Of holier love' - deeper and holier, presumably, than on his first visit. (The two visits might be comparable to the two attempts to revision nature in the Ode, the second succeeding.) This 'love' is of a kind with the reciprocated love of the opening of Stanza XI, a love that here informs 'this green pastoral landscape', as it had the fountains meadows, hills and groves of the Ode. If, in his absence, Dorothy remembers this landscape and their experience of it, then, implicitly, all will be well for her, even if he is no longer here. The last lines wrap all these kinds of love together. Dorothy will not forget that 'these steep woods and lofty cliffs, / And this green pastoral landscape, were to me / More dear, both for themselves, and for thy sake.' Then in happiness they begin their walk back to Bristol.

Part V
Looking Forward into History

Chapter 16

Poems Published and Unpublished

'Imagination having been our theme'[1]

A Misreading

WORDSWORTH HAD COMPLETED the *Ode* by early March 1804 (*Reed* 247), and the thirteen-book *Prelude* by late May 1805 (*Reed* 15). That is a substantial volume of work to produce in so short a time: what had all that work achieved? A full and mature expression of his vision in lyrical and narrative forms is a possible answer. A resolution was achieved in the *Ode* that enabled him to marry the intuitions of a 'Mighty Prophet!' and 'Seer blest!' to the insights of a philosophic mind, comparable to the tracing of the imagination from its hidden and wordless source to its articulation in the light of Reason in the *Prelude*. Each follows much the same pattern – the realization of an intuitive vision lost, its association with childhood, tracing the causes of loss, searching for a means of recovery, learning that the answer is not in beating a path back, but trusting the truth of those memories and looking to the growth of faculties to which the soul aspires (*1805* II 338-39), faculties at one with the philosophic mind. The lost power is thus revived, however faint it might seem by comparison with its original. In Wordsworth's estimation, this progress represents something like the full or ideal course of human life, which is the business of those undistracted by everything that 'Life brings with her in her Equipage' – a course which he felt he could best pursue in retirement. If his 'dear Imaginations' did not quite reach 'their highest measure', nonetheless in the *Ode* and *The Prelude* he achieved what was only proposed at the conclusion of *Home at Grasmere*.[2]

---

[1] *1805* XIII 185.
[2] *HG* B 127-28.

As is fitting, probably the finest expression of that achievement begins the last book of the *Prelude*, after his vision from the top of Snowdon. The 'meditation' that rose in him saw there the 'perfect image of a mighty mind'; and at the heart of that mind 'had Nature lodged / The soul, the imagination of the whole'. Those in whom 'the express / Resemblance' of that power lives:

> ... build up greatest things
> From least suggestions, ever on the watch,
> Willing to work and to be wrought upon,
> They need not extraordinary calls
> To rouze them – in a world of life they live,
> By sensible impressions not enthralled,
> But quickened, roused, and made thereby more fit
> To hold communion with the invisible world.
> Such minds are truly from the Deity,
> For they are powers; and hence the highest bliss
> That can be known is theirs – the consciousness
> Of whom they are, habitually infused
> Through every image, and through every thought,
> And all impressions; hence religion, faith,
> And endless occupation for the soul,
> Whether discursive or intuitive;
> Hence sovereignty within and peace at will ...[3]

The imagination works in man as in Nature. To see what Wordsworth means by building up the greatest from the least, we might look to many of his 'short' or 'small' poems, particularly of 1802, exemplified in the daisy poems. Their lightness of touch, the very modesty of their subject matter, belies their seriousness. As described in Chapter 8, the Bright Flower, for instance, 'suffering all things from all' thus fulfils its 'function apostolical'. There could hardly be a more serious purpose for one of the smallest and most ordinary of flowers. Wordsworth is 'ever on the watch', willing to use the power of his imagination to inform or work on even very modest forms of nature, as well as to allow nature to inform him, a reciprocity of power central to his poetry. In a world

---

[3.] *1805* XIII 98-114. In *1850*, 'peace at will' is developed as 'that peace / Which passeth understanding'. This is not the mark of Wordsworth's turning Tory Anglican, but a recognition that a power he has discovered is of a kind with one of the most mysterious of Christian promises.

of life such minds live, because its objects are not disconnected, dead and spiritless, but all infused with the one life, of mind and of nature. Paradoxically perhaps, although they allow the impressions of nature to speak to them, yet simultaneously they are 'By sensible impressions not enthralled' – the difference between impressions empowered and not empowered: subsequently he describes such power as infused through 'All impressions'.

Minds in whom the imagination is alive are thus not restricted to understanding life solely through the senses but are fit to 'hold communion with the invisible world'. In this plain statement Wordsworth unreservedly recognizes the existence of such a world, just as Coleridge had in the epigraph to *The Ancient Mariner*. What's more, that world, realized by minds descending directly 'from the Deity', substantiates this world, not merely making and then abandoning what they have made. It is not making but creation, a continuing, unremitting process, to be part of which is the ultimate or perfect mode of being, 'hence' the highest form of bliss, 'consciousness / Of whom they are', a complete confidence of their identity, which they discover in 'every image, and through every thought, / And all impressions'. From that state derives another: 'hence religion, faith'; religion is inherent in such minds – a binding of our being to the non-sensory – as Wordsworth said in a letter, 'all great Poets are ... powerful Religionists' (21 January 1824); faith that the invisible is actual and real; but most significantly an 'endless occupation for the soul' – from those minds issues a power immanent in the creation they sustain; and that power is allusively identified as 'discursive or intuitive' – the twin functions of Reason in Milton's great chain of being, co-ordinate with what both Wordsworth and Coleridge mean by the Imagination. As Reason is a 'crown, an attribute of sovereign power' (*The Excursion* V 502-4), 'Hence sovereignty within', that active power enables full control of 'the world of life' in which such minds live.[4] It is also a world of which Wordsworth says, addressing himself, 'Thou, thou art king, and sole proprietor'.[5] Traherne's design is show Susanna Hopton that she is not only the heir but 'the possessor of the whole world' (*Centuries* I 3). There is sovereignty within and sovereignty without, and so, unsurprisingly, 'peace at will'.

It is an extraordinarily encompassing vision. Wordsworth has come full circle: 'Blest the infant babe' for whom 'there exists / A virtue which

---

[4.] In the passage ll. 98-119, 'hence' occurs four times, indicating the consequential interconnectedness of its several stages.
[5.] *WPW* V 347. See *HG* 12 for the provenance of this extract.

irradiates and exalts / All objects through all intercourse of sense. / No outcast he, bewildered and depressed' (*1805* II 237 ff.),

> For feeling has to him imparted power
> That through the growing faculties of sense
> Doth like an agent of the one great Mind
> Create, creator and receiver both,
> Working but in alliance with the works
> Which it beholds.   (*1850* II 255-59)

No outcast, but at home in the world of which he is the created, the creator and the sovereign lord.

The Prelude and the *Ode* are the two greatest poems, in that strand of his genius, that Wordsworth would write, but it is far from certain whether either he himself or Coleridge recognized what he had so early achieved. If it now seems self-evident that *The Prelude* is a history of the imagination – a power central to two key moments in the poem, and at the heart of Wordsworth's summary – neither man at any time, in verse or in prose, chose that word to describe the poem either in part or in whole. Until published in 1850, its household title was The Poem to Coleridge, and Wordsworth frequently described it either as 'a Poem on my own earlier life' (*EY* 436, 440, 447), or as that and on 'the growth of my own mind' (*EY* 518), and even published in 1850, retained that idea in the subtitle, thus keeping the focus on *The Excursion* as his principal work. Coleridge described it in very similar terms. Commenting on *The Excursion*, he says to Lady Beaumont, 'I do not think, I did not feel, it equal to the Work on the Growth of his own spirit' (*CL* IV 564); and writing to Wordsworth he called it first 'the Poem on the growth of your own mind' (*CL* IV 573), and then 'the Poem on the Growth of your own Support' (*CL* IV 576). Both therefore misread the poem as a personal rather than public work

Coleridge's poem, To William Wordsworth, Composed on the Night after his Recitation of a Poem on the Growth of an Individual Mind, tells a slightly different story. The title is in line with the other descriptions, but the substance less clearly unique. For example: 'Of the foundations of a Human Spirit thou has dared to tell / What may be told', although uncertainty about its universality remains in the indefinite article. Reason gets a mention – 'Of smiles spontaneous, and mysterious fears / (The first-born of Reason and twin-birth)' – but not in a context that either makes much immediate sense or illustrates its relationship to the Imagination, a word absent from the poem, and yet occasionally implicit, as in 'moments awful, / Now in thy inner life, and now abroad, /

When power streamed from thee, and thy soul received / The light reflected as a light bestowed – '. There are other lines that indicate this is not just a personal development: 'From the dread Watch-Tower of Man's absolute Self' the poet looked 'Far on ... to behold, / The Angel of the vision!' Again it is difficult to determine what Coleridge actually means. The poem declines into a lament for his own lost powers, but it is evident that he is speaking both of a power potentially more than personal, and that his conception of that power fails to connect Nature, Reason and the Imagination as *The Prelude* does. Yet Wordsworth's association of the growth of the mind with the imagination is asserted in a near contemporaneous manuscript of *The Pedlar:* 'many a legend, peopling the dark woods, / Nourish'd imagination in her growth / And gave the mind that apprehensive power / By which she is made quick to recognize / The moral properties and scope of things' (*RC* E 159 ff.). It is as if both poets could not formulate what they intuitively realized.

Their emphasis therefore fell not on the universal power that he and Coleridge claimed as fundamental to our humanity, Reason or Imagination, but on the growth of a singular and private mind, 'his divine Self-biography' (*CN* I 1801). Wordsworth believed that this focus, 'a frightful deal to say about oneself' (*EY* 470), its 'alarming length' (*EY* 586) and the fact that it would be 'a tributary to a larger and more important work' (The Recluse), made it unsuitable for publication in his lifetime – a decision made even before he finished the five-book version for Coleridge to take to Malta (*EY* 454; 6 March 1804). The extraordinariness of his task fell upon him a year later, when he felt it 'a thing unprecedented in literary history that a man should talk so much about himself' (*EY* 586; 1 May 1805). In literary history perhaps, but not if he had compared his poem to Puritan confessional narratives, as some have.

Progress on *The Excursion* and Consequent Publication Decisions

So his primary document on the relations between Nature, Reason and the Imagination was locked away for 45 years, partly from a scrupulosity that doesn't bear examination, and partly because neither he nor Coleridge appear to have understood what he had achieved. The latter kind of failure also applies – at least initially, and therefore much less disastrously – to the *Ode*. Probably completed in early March 1804, it was immediately followed by the astonishing burst of creativity which enabled the completion of another eight books of *The Prelude* in little more than a year. In some 450 surviving letters of William and Dorothy written between April 1802 and the end of December 1820, *The Prelude* and *The Recluse* are mentioned frequently, but, according to the index, the *Ode* only twice, in May 1809 (*MY* I 334), and in January 1815 (*MY* II 189).[6] There is no celebration of its completion – to be expected given how long it had lain dormant – nothing comparable to the doleful announcement of the completion of *The Prelude*;[7] nothing at that time indicating his sense of its future importance. Coleridge doesn't refer to its completion in his letters, but it went with him to Malta, together with the five-book version of *The Prelude*. He recited 'this sublime ode' to Humboldt in Rome in late 1805 or early 1806.[8] It is possible that he recognized its sublimity before Wordsworth did, who, although placing it, with its significant and distinguishing epigraph, at the end of *Poems in Two Volumes*, first made reference to it, as 'the grand ode', in 1809 (*MY* I 334). In 1804, the sequence of events simply suggests that its completion was linked to progress with *The Prelude*.

Completion of *The Prelude* – always and variously described in relation The Recluse as 'an appendix' (*EY* 440), as 'supplementary (*EY* 470), 'a tributary' (*EY* 454), 'an introduction' (*EY* 456), 'a sort of portico' (*EY* 594) – enabled progress on The Recluse; from which all other work, certainly in Coleridge's eyes, and in Wordsworth's self-estimation as a poet, was a distraction. Its subject was to be all encompassing – 'Indeed I know not any thing which will not come within the scope of my plan' – designed 'to give pictures of Nature, Man, and Society', (*EY* 212), or whatever he finds 'most interesting' about this triumvirate. Regularly announced thus in his letters, in The Preface to *The Excursion* it is reversed to 'Man, Nature, and Society' – perhaps because the Wanderer's intellectual history opens the poem.

However, his progress was painfully slow. If it took him a year to complete some eight books of *The Prelude*, it took him six years to finish eight of the nine books of *The Excursion* – the first, *The Wanderer, The Ruined Cottage* by another name, was already written. The causes were various, and the first was the loss of his brother John in the wreck of the

---

[6.] Hard to believe, and I expect to be corrected.

[7.] 'I was indeed grateful to God for giving me life to complete the work, such as it is; but it was not a happy day for me. I was dejected on many accounts; when I looked back upon the performance it seemed to have a dead weight about it' (*EY* 594). Compare this with his unstinted belief in *The Excursion*. History has reversed his opinion, but Hazlitt got it right at the time, describing *The Excursion* as a 'dead weight', using Wordsworth's own phrase by accident or design.

[8.] *F* I 509-10. *The Five Book Prelude* is in *DCMS* 44, a collection of Wordsworth's poems which William, Dorothy and Mary transcribed for Coleridge to take to Malta.

Abergavenny in February 1805. Although Dorothy records his return to The Recluse in April (*EY* 576), at the end of October she writes of the need for leisure so 'that my Brother may begin in good earnest with his important Task' (*EY* 634), still not taken up by the end of November (*EY* 650). This pattern of stopping and starting continued throughout its composition.

For Wordsworth, there was another and perhaps more deep-seated problem, going further back. As early as 1798, he and Coleridge had planned his great work – into which Wordsworth intended to pour 'most of the knowledge of which I am possessed' – and of which some 1,300 lines then existed (*EY* 212). How much the idea for the poem was the child of Coleridge's brain and how much of Wordsworth's is a matter of conjecture, but at the end of March 1804, two days after Coleridge had left for Portsmouth on his way to Malta, and hearing of Coleridge's 'late attack', Wordsworth wrote to him in near panic, declaring that it was severest shock he had ever received (*EY* 464). His primary concern was less for Coleridge's mortality, more that he might depart this life without him having received 'your Letter on The Recluse', for which he would gladly have given '3 fourths of my possessions'. As long as Wordsworth got his letter, Coleridge was free to die: 'I cannot say what a load it would be to me, should I survive you and you die without this memorial left behind. Do for heaven's sake, put this out of the reach of accident immediately.' This apparent dependence on a framework designed by Coleridge marks a fundamental difference between the two modes by which *The Prelude* and *The Excursion* were composed. In *The Prelude* to all intents Wordsworth looked into his heart and wrote; in *The Excursion* he was trying to write to a systematic plan not entirely his. No wonder that *The Excursion* is much the stodgier poem, of which Hopkins said, 'Now judging from my own experience I should say no author palls so much as Wordsworth; this is because he writes such "an intolerable deal" of Parnassian'.[9]

Coleridge claimed he responded but, he told Wordsworth, 'my Ideas respecting your Recluse were burnt as a Plague-Garment'.[10] Was Coleridge finding an excuse for what he had never done? Such ideas could easily have been revived and rewritten, which in effect they were when Coleridge told first Lady Beaumont and then Wordsworth why he thought *The Excursion* a lesser poem than *The Prelude* (*CL* IV 564). Two other contemporary letters mention the same event, and the loss of travel

---

[9.] *GMH Letters* III 218; 10 September 1864.
[10.] *EY* 607 and *CL* II 1169.

letters to Beaumont, but not notes on The Recluse, and Wordsworth continued to feel the want of Coleridge's ideas or conversation.[11] In December 1805, Dorothy records that he is anxious to get on with The Recluse, doing some preparatory reading 'for the nourishment of his mind', but unable 'to do much more until we have heard of Coleridge' (*EY* 664). In August 1806 he has taken up The Recluse again, but with the caveat that, should 'Coleridge return, so that I might have some conversation with him on the subject, I should go on swimmingly' (*MY* I 64).

Poems, in Two Volumes

In the end he went on without Coleridge's conversation, but not swimmingly. His confidence was sufficiently eroded by June 1806 for him to have 'some thoughts of publishing a little Volume of miscellaneous Poems, to be out next Spring' (*MY* I 41), what in November he called 'small pieces in Verse' (*MY* I 89). The little volume proved to be the substantial *Poems, in Two Volumes* published in May 1807. As noted above, Wordsworth acknowledged that these poems, 'short' or 'small':

> were chiefly composed to refresh my mind during the progress of a work of length and labour, in which I have for some time been engaged; and to furnish me with employment when I had not resolution to apply myself to that work, or hope that I should proceed with it successfully.
>
> (*P2V* 527).

Coleridge had let him down: his resolution was failing, his uncertainty growing. This stop-gap had precedence, however – the *Lyrical Ballads*. In Wordsworth's vacillating mind that publication – 'a considerable collection of short poems' – was on the one hand comparable to and so justified these two volumes; on the other he 'did not wish to add these to the number, till after the completion of my larger work', deciding to deny that wish because he had no idea of a completion date. He added, rather weakly, that he thus thought it better 'to send them forth at once' because some had already circulated in manuscript (*P2V* 527).

From a preface wisely not published, these are the words of a man being pulled in two directions: aware how much both his wife and Coleridge denigrated small poems, believing that they thwarted progress

---

[11.] *CL* II 1159, 1169.

on The Recluse, he was also conscious that he had published nothing new since the two-volume edition of the *Lyrical Ballads* in 1802, revised and reordered in 1805, and foresaw that he might well drop out of public sight long before he finished *The Excursion*. The ballads had established him as a poet – almost all the reviews collected by Robert Woof have some praise or at least approval, recognizing that he was attempting to write a different kind of poetry. Wordsworth was conscious that he was a success in the public eye, and therefore another volume along the same lines would maintain his status until he could complete his larger work. Under his name on the title-page is the conspicuous 'AUTHOR OF *THE LYRICAL BALLADS*', guiding readers' expectations. To further salve his conscience he added an epigraph, 'Hereafter shall our Muse speak to thee in deeper tones, when the seasons yield to me their fruits in peace' (*P2V* 26), pointing towards The Recluse. Revising the final proofs, Wordsworth recognized that the final poem did speak in those tones, and so the *Ode* gained its own epigraph, echoing that of the whole (*P2V* 27).

As much as the *Lyrical Ballads* had been a success, *Poems in Two Volumes* was a failure. The reviews were almost uniformly negative – 'puerile', 'namby-pamby' and 'drivelling' are words each occurring two or three times in different reviews. The Redbreast and the Butterfly, and Lines Written in March are singled out more than once for mockery. The collection is compared unfavourably to the *Lyrical Ballads*, Tintern Abbey often admired, but its counterpart, the *Ode*, rarely mentioned and then only in terms of its incomprehensibility. The reviewers also had some fun with the epigraphs: Byron regrets that Wordsworth has confined 'his muse to such trifling subjects; we trust his motto will be in future, "Paulo majora canamus"', although he otherwise ignores the *Ode* (*Woof* 170). His barb is a minor prick compared to the shafting of *Le Beau Monde*, which quoted the title-page epigraph, and then commented 'But this muse really seems to be in her dotage … which has now shifted into that second childhood, in which, though *sans* eyes, *sans* ears, and *sans* teeth, she unluckily is not *sans* tongue.'[12]

There is plenty of such knockabout stuff – amusing to read and selling reviews – but a larger point emerges. What *is* it all about? What is the purpose behind these two volumes? One review, otherwise slight and brief, opens 'As neither preface, address, or advertisement informs us why these poems are published, we are unable to inform our readers of the author's design in so doing' (*Woof* 176). Another much more substantial review by James Montgomery – always fair to Wordsworth

---

[12.] *Woof* 178; see also pp. 203, 230.

and full of carefully modulated praise for the *Lyrical Ballads* – decides that it 'would be in vain to attempt to characterize all the contents of these incomparable, and almost incomprehensible volumes' (*Woof* 210), and concludes his piece by noting that the poet:

> says, in the preface to his former volumes, that 'each of the poems' contained therein 'has a *worthy purpose.*' Of the pieces now published he has said nothing: most of them seem to have been written *for* no purpose at all, and certainly *to* no good one. (*Woof* 213)

From a fellow-poet willing to see the best in Wordsworth's poetry, this is a stern judgement. In his Preface to the *Lyrical Ballads* in 1802 Wordsworth had declared that his purpose was 'to follow the fluxes and refluxes of the mind when agitated by the great and simple affections of our nature', employing a poetic diction based on 'the real language of men'.[13] This provided the reviewers with a very clear topic for debate, one which largely redounded to his credit. It was well-focused in the poems he selected, and the critics got the point, even if they didn't always appreciate the results.

He may have thought his indication of the likeness of the *Poems, in Two Volumes* and the *Lyrical Ballads* a sufficient guide to his intentions, but if so the selection and arrangement of the poems in that respect offered more confusion than clarity. Many were clearly not in such a language – all the 46 sonnets for instance – and those that were the reviewers often took as slight in themselves, nothing, as an example, that matched The Idiot Boy.[14] The first three poems of the first volume – To the Daisy, Louisa and Fidelity – had no apparent connection, either with each other or with their group title – The Orchard Pathway – and all got a hammering from one critic or another. Fidelity was particularly subject to unfavourable comparison with Scott's version of the same subject, Helvellyn.[15] Compared to the 1798 *Lyrical Ballads*, which opened with The Rime and ended in Tintern Abbey, and in 1802 found

---

[13.] Coleridge uses the first phrase in the *Biographia* (*BL* II 147), but 'Wordsworth's Preface is half a child of my own Brain / & so arose out of Conversations, so frequent, that with few exceptions we could scarcely either of us perhaps positively say, which first started any particular Thought' (*CL* II 830).

[14.] Montgomery thought The Blind Boy the 'younger brother to Mr. W's own inimitable *Ideot Boy*, but very far behind him in merits and accomplishments' (*Woof* 211).

[15.] Jared Curtis does not agree: 'The autobiographical source and resulting intimacy implied by the title and motto fit the first eight poems well' (*P2V* 37).

them together closing the first volume, this was not a strong start. As some reviewers remarked, simpleness was replacing simplicity.¹⁶

Searching for Order

Wordsworth had described his proposed volume as a collection of short or small or miscellaneous poems 'culled' from his manuscripts. Their presentation in seven separate sections attempts to impose an order on that miscellany, but with what success? Neither the titles themselves nor their arrangement are encouraging, for it is difficult not to feel that both are arbitrary, and also that Wordsworth is insensible to potential connections: composition on foot is a feature common to three sections, but only in the first is it recognized, and by a jejune epigraph – '*musa pedestris*' as one critic unkindly declared.¹⁷ Jared Curtis made a valiant attempt to elucidate Wordsworth's ordering, deferring to Wordsworth's comment that one cannot form 'a true estimate of a Vol of *small* Poems by reading them all together; one stands in the way of another' (*MY* I 95). To mitigate this ghettoization of poetical types, Curtis believes that Wordsworth dispersed 'both narratives and lyrics ... more or less evenly through the two volumes' so that the sections 'define meaningful contexts that support and widen the range of each individual poem' (*P2V* 38). Each group, Curtis says, 'must create its own context or fall into miscellany'.¹⁸ All the evidence, both of reviews and of private opinions, denies the success of that endeavour. None of his contemporaries saw the two volumes so structured, nor has it been convincingly defended since. What always was a miscellany remains a miscellany, by which Wordsworth's real achievements to that date were then and still are obscured. The order reveals no design, is planned to no discernible purpose.

That Wordsworth himself doubted the success of his ordering is evident in his planning of a different kind of order some two years later, set out in a long letter to Coleridge (*MY* I 33-36). This was his claimed template for the arrangement of his 1815 poems – a combination plus

---

16. A pointed, stinging and well-researched parody was titled *The Simpliciad* (Woof 262-69).
17. The Orchard Pathway; Poems Composed During a Tour Chiefly on Foot; Miscellaneous Sonnets; Sonnets Dedicated to Liberty; Poems Written During a Tour in Scotland; Moods of My Own Mind; and The Blind Highland Boy, With Other Poems.
18. *P2V* 37. Richard Matlak also notes, neutrally, that Wordsworth 'said that he gave a great deal of attention to arranging and grouping short poems so that they would gain a cumulative weight in the context of their sections' *Poems, in Two Volumes, 1807*, ed. Richard Matlak (Ontario, 2015) p. 15).

additions of the *Lyrical Ballads* and *Poems, in Two Volumes* – and all subsequent collections. He finally divided his poetry into Poems Written in Youth, Poems Referring to the Period of Childhood, Poems Founded on the Affections, Poems on the Naming of Places (oddly placed), Poems of the Fancy and Poems of the Imagination. But then follow various miscellanies that subvert his plot. The *Ode* is indeed the final poem as always planned, but widely separated from the poems of imagination by the vast array of often incidental verse; even Tintern Abbey is neither first nor last in the Poems of Imagination, and Wordsworth was sometimes uncertain to which category a given poem belonged – Coleridge thought that in his 1815 Preface Wordsworth had muddled or conflated fancy and imagination. Reading through Poems of the Imagination, it would be very difficult to deduce what Wordsworth meant by the term, particularly compared to the magnificent declarations of *The Prelude*. When he did pick out a passage from *The Prelude* to include in that category he did not choose, say, that beginning 'Imagination! lifting up itself …', one of the two or three great paeans to that power, but the visionary apocalyptic landscape consequent upon its manifestation. That looks like a perfect opportunity missed to present the Imagination, by name, in all its greatness. The subtitle of Books XII and XIII of the 1850 *Prelude*, 'Imagination and Taste, How impaired and Restored', implies an extraordinary and misleading reversion to eighteenth-century ideas about the imagination.

The Victorians

It would only be a modest exaggeration to say that by 1815 Wordsworth had published most of his minor poems and, bar the *Ode* and *The Excursion*, very few of his major ones. The Victorians therefore grew up on *The Excursion* (1814) and, still using the *Lyrical Ballads* as their advertisement, the 1815 poems and their obfuscatory organization.[19] Stephen Gill notes that '*The Excursion* was published in August 1814 to general indifference', but he also says that Jeffrey's was 'the most devastating critique Wordsworth was ever to suffer' (*A Life*, p. 347) – which, at least, is not indifference. In the 1830s it would be taken up mostly by novelists, socialists, moralists and theologians, all able to turn to *The Excursion* as supplying either some fuel for their fires or something

---

[19] The full title: *Poems by William Wordsworth: Including* Lyrical Ballads *and the Miscellaneous Pieces of the Author. With Additional Poems, a New Preface, and a Supplementary Essay.*

onto which they could pour cold water.[20] It was, to all intents, a moral and philosophical treatise. Hazlitt, both perceptive and just, described it as 'a philosophic pastoral poem' adding that Wordsworth's 'thoughts are his real subject ... The common and the permanent, like the Platonic ideas, are his only realities ... the tendency of his mind is the reverse of dramatic ... It is as if there were nothing but himself and the universe. He lives in ... the deep silence of his thought' (*Woof* 370-71). By and large the Victorian poets turned away from both *The Excursion* and the *Poems* of 1815, not finding what they wanted – had they but known it – neither understanding what Wordsworth meant by the Imagination, nor its importance as the power behind a coherent metaphysics, which might have given them solid ground for their poetry. Among the poets Hopkins is the notable exception – a 'powerful Religionist'. As it was, the metaphysical confidence of most Victorian poets evaporated, and if Reason, Imagination, Meditation, Contemplation and Faith were Wordsworth's key words, reason, doubt, scepticism and despair were some of the central markers of Victorian poetry. Nature was divided from nature: at the mercy of empirical thought, the Victorians were on the cusp of that extraordinarily successful process of 'vexing' nature in order to reveal her secrets, but failing to understand that, for Wordsworth and Coleridge, Nature was a unitary power, able to bear comparison to the powers of the human mind. Consequently, on the one hand, nature was, in Arnold's words 'cruel', and on the other it offered us 'the flowery lap of Earth'. Arnold's only positive response to nature was aesthetic, to appearance, to the impressions about which Wordsworth was so wary.

Arnold, as the principal mediator of Wordsworth's poetry to the modernists, saw, in making his selection, no virtue in Wordsworth's ordering, and made his own – to no better purpose. This had the pernicious effect of tending to further denude Wordsworth of his metaphysics, making him instead into a consolatory nature poet. Thus without his magic cloak about him Wordsworth entered the twentieth century and into the consciousness of the modernists. Much of their work earned the contempt of a rising star, Eliot, who saw Wordsworth, via Arnold, as responsible for the sentimentalizing of nature, so producing 'the annual curse of the Georgian anthology'. As a result Eliot didn't see Wordsworth at all, merely a mirage partly of his own making, partly of

---

[20.] Cf 'the George Eliot of *Adam Bede* and *Silas Marner* and other novelists ... are Wordsworth's true heirs in the Victorian period' (Gill, *A Life*, p. 15). For a fuller and more nuanced account of the Victorians' understanding of Wordsworth, see Stephen Gill's *Wordsworth and the Victorians* (Oxford, 1998), esp. the chapters on George Eliot and on Arnold and Tennyson.

Arnold's, and partly of Wordsworth's himself, whose failure to publish and original ordering obscured his most substantial achievements.

An Idea of Order

So what is the ideal order, revealing the poet as he might have been? William Knight, in 1882, was the first to choose the chronological as the most fitting, and one that has yet to be superseded. His reasons are eminently sensible:

> The chief advantage of a chronological arrangement of the Works of any author – and especially of a poet who himself adopted a different plan – is that it shows us, as nothing else can do, the growth of his own mind, the progressive development of his genius and imaginative power. By such a redistribution of what he wrote we can trace the rise, the culmination, and also – it may be – the decline and fall of his genius.[21]

But there are difficulties. The first is the most obvious: was anyone really going to plough through Knight's eight volumes, or any equivalent, in order to trace this progressive development and possible decline? Even if one did so, shouldn't the chronology be considered the foundation rather than the building (or cathedral) itself? For a chronology per se is simply poem piled on poem, not a structure but a heap. There's no guarantee, lacking a conceptual framework, that one would necessarily see anything but a mound of undressed stones. Similarly, if one reads a chronologically ordered selection, it always has been editorial protocol to keep conceptual opinions out of sight, to make a selection as little interpretative as possible, even if the very process is bound to break that rule more or less. Therefore the only certain advantage of a selection is a smaller pile of stones. Then there is the question hanging over revised poems – first or final? – and long poems in particular – when were they actually composed? *The Ruined Cottage*, for example, was begun in 1798 and went through several iterations until published in 1814, and then

---

[21.] William Knight, *The Poetical Works of William Wordsworth* (London, 1896). Knight first adopted the chronological order in his edition of 1882. https://www.gutenberg.org/files/10219/10219-h/10219-h.htm. Ernest de Selincourt retained Wordsworth's order on the grounds that 'it is, in a measure, illuminative of his mind', while recognizing that 'it will not stand logical examination' (*WPW* I ix).

only as part of *The Excursion*, not as a separate poem, or poems, as it originally was.[22]

If chronology is the foundation, then some act of interpretation must provide the structure.[23] Wordsworth chose a structure not based on the chronology of composition, but to exhibit 'the three requisites of legitimate whole, a beginning, a middle, and an end', arranged 'according to an order of time, commencing with Childhood, and terminating with Old Age, Death, and Immortality' (Preface, 1815). Even though that scheme was at least partially consistent with the growth of his own spirit, it created two problems: it was an order imposed on a body of work that did not reflect the complex creative impulses by which it was realized; and, as already discussed, his choice of classes by which to group the poems along that road further obscured the marks and patterns of his genius.

[22.] Coleridge distinguished it from *The Excursion*, describing it as 'the finest Poem in our Language, comparing it with any of the same or similar Length' (*CL* II 564).

[23.] To achieve a reliable method of interpretation, one must, in principle, test a thesis, a *prudens quæstio*, against the poetry (*F* I 489). Yet how can formulate such a thesis except by reading the poetry? Presumably that is the task of professional critics for the benefit of general readers.

Chapter 17

What if? A Counterfactual Reading

IN SUM, THE NEED TO find an order in a miscellany originated in Wordsworth's decision to publish an interim collection of poems in 1807, a decision developed and carried through to the 1815 collection, setting the structure for all subsequent editions, from which followed all the consequences considered above, the most important of which, at least in the history of English poetry, was the failure of the Victorian poets to understand his work and the impetus behind it; and as a direct consequence the failure of the modernists to think of Wordsworth as much more than a nature poet, to which Eliot's early reactions were a comic venom – nonetheless accepting the appellation and so totally failing to grasp either the language or the spirit in which Wordsworth wrote. Coupled to Wordsworth's obscure ordering is his failure to publish many of his most substantial poems at the time of their writing. As Francis Jeffrey rightly said, 'the world could only judge by what the world was allowed to see'.[1]

So, to speculate: consider first what poems Wordsworth had completed or could have completed but had not published by late 1808: *Salisbury Plain, The Borderers, The Ruined Cottage, Home at Grasmere, Peter Bell, Benjamin the Waggoner, The Tuft of Primroses* and, looming over them all, *The Prelude*.[2] Consider then a publication plan loosely based on their chronology in conjunction with what Wordsworth had already published.[3] Had the earliest version of *Salisbury Plain* (1793-94)

---

[1] Gill, *A Life*, p. 305.
[2] Dates of approximate completion and publication: *Adventures on Salisbury Plain* 1794, as *Guilt and Sorrow* 1842; *The Borderers* 1796-1842; *Peter Bell* 1798-1819; *The Ruined Cottage* 1803-1814; *Home at Grasmere* 1806-1888; *Benjamin the Waggoner* 1806-1819; *The White Doe of Rylstone* 1808-1815; *The Tuft of Primroses* 1808-1949; *The Prelude* 1805-1850; and the 1805 *Prelude* 1926.
[3] This is the plan followed by Stephen Gill in his selection, *The Major Works*.

appeared, say, in late 1795, it would have introduced Wordsworth to the reading public as a very different kind of poet to that of *Descriptive Sketches* (1793), wearily reviewed by Holcroft as 'More descriptive poetry! ... Have we not yet had enough?' (*DS* 11). Holcroft didn't recognize what Coleridge did, qualities in Wordsworth's language so striking that 'seldom, if ever, was the emergence of an original poetic genius above the poetic horizon more evidently announced' (*BL* I 77).

In *Salisbury Plain* Holcroft would have found a fellow radical, a Godwinian poet deeply concerned with the effects of war on the poor, as he would also have found in Wordsworth's dangerously polemical *Letter to the Bishop of Llandaff* – had that been published.[4] It was a time of considerable social and political disturbance, of hope and anxiety.[5] In the same year, 1793, William Frend was put on trial by Cambridge University for publishing his pamphlet, *Peace and Union Recommended to the Associated Bodies of Republicans and Antirepublicans*, which contained an appendix titled The Effect of War on the Poor. The trial was widely reported, so Wordsworth would have seen in Frend a companion spirit at least as radical, and more openly so. His trial was attended by Coleridge who enthusiastically if cautiously supported Frend, and also by Southey, who though making no political comment, endorsed his rhetoric.[6] There was a potential nest of radical friendships out there, into which Wordsworth might have happily fallen. Had he published *Salisbury Plain* in 1794, which he considered, if only for 'some pecuniary recompense' (*EY* 120), discerning readers, also aware of *An Evening Walk* and *Descriptive Sketches*, would have been conscious of a strong mind working with different but developing emphases – landscape descriptions alone in *An Evening Walk*, those and some political concerns in *Descriptive Sketches*, concerns that became dominant in *Salisbury Plain*. If the first two poems were largely ignored, *Salisbury Plain*, given the climate of the times, would have been much more widely and positively noticed, certainly by the radical community, and Wordsworth would have had a much stronger and more confident start to his career. He had hoped that the first two poems 'might shew that I could do something', having achieved nothing at university (*EY* 120). Their reception gave him no such confidence. Had he published *Salisbury Plain*, he would have been positively noticed, and could have

---

[4.] For Wordsworth's attempts to get it published, see *SP* 7-8. Had he succeeded he might well have been imprisoned.
[5.] For an indication of just how dangerous, see Gill, *A Life*, pp. 73, 88-89.
[6.] See https://romantic-circles.org/editions/southey_letters/Part_One/HTML/letterEEd.26.49.html. My thanks to Tim Fulford for providing this reference.

seen himself as having done something. As it was, and as it was so often to be, instead of ploughing on and publishing, in his slightly bitter disappointment Wordsworth shot himself in the foot.

Consequently, none of those who might then have endorsed Wordsworth's radical poetry knew of it, and by the time some of those friendships were established, radicalism was no longer at the forefront of his mind. Having done his best 'to probe / The living body of society / Even to the heart', he had 'Yielded up moral questions in despair', turning 'towards mathematics, and their clear / And solid evidence'.[7] Coleridge remarked that, when they first became neighbours, Wordsworth's 'conversation extended to almost all subjects, except physics and politics; with the latter he never troubled himself'.[8] That is, by 1796, he had turned inwards, to the intuitive truths of the self-sufficient mind, and in 1797-98 met Coleridge on his own ground in the main subject of their conversation – the imagination (*BL* II 5).

After *Salisbury Plain*, *The Borderers* might have been published in 1796 or 1797, a five-act tragedy in blank verse, admired by Coleridge. It is a remarkable psychological study of the growth of evil, as Wordsworth described in his prefatory note to its publication in 1842:

> in the trials to which life subjects us, sin and crime are apt to start from their very opposite qualities, so there are no limits to the hardening of the heart, and the perversion of the understanding to which they may carry their slaves. During my long residence in France, while the Revolution was rapidly advancing to its extreme of wickedness, I had frequent opportunities of being an eye-witness of this process.

There are, as Coleridge 'the subtle-souled psychologist' put it, '*profound* touches of the human heart'.[9] If the play grew out of radical sympathies, it found an entirely different focus. Instead of looking outward on the human condition, it looked inward, perhaps signifying that change more or less complete by the time he and Coleridge began their conversation.

[7.] *1805* X 874-76, 900. The Norton editors note that this internal battle took place in the spring of 1796.

[8.] *BL* 1 I88. Coleridge also noted that 'on one subject we are habitually silent' (*CL* I 410, May 1798). The editors of the *Biographia* suggest the subject is politics. It is unlikely to be religion as in the same letter he remarks 'he loves & venerates Christ & Christianity – I wish, he did more', so not a subject on which they were silent.

[9.] *Shelley's Poetry and Prose* (New York, 1977), p. 379; *CL* I 325, 603.

That would have been a pretty strong publication record, four long works, all significantly different over some four years. Readers would, or should, have seen enough to make them sit up and think who this poet was and what he was about. They might also have noticed his rapidly developing poetic confidence: from the safe conventional rhymed couplets of the first two poems, to the Spenserian stanzas of *Salisbury Plain*, and then the strong, lucid blank verse of *The Borderers*. There were no 'short' or 'small' poems.[10] In 1798, his readers would have found in Wordsworth another and a different kind of poet, not only employing the much-vaunted, but inconsistent, simplicity of language, but also writing in various forms of rhymed verse, in a variety of moods – the light as serious as the sombre – and with a variety of subjects.[11] A second volume was added in 1800, the 1798 volume rearranged and two more editions would follow in 1803 and 1805. Any reader familiar with the preceding works would have found many poems profoundly empathetic to the sufferings of the poor, the dispossessed, the betrayed and the simply unfortunate, all offering some continuity with the radical concerns of *Salisbury Plain*. There are what might be termed psychological studies such as The Thorn, The Mad Mother, The Idiot Boy and Goody Blake and Harry Gill, perhaps prepared for by *The Borderers*. The reader would also meet shorter, simpler and yet more mysterious poems, such as those we now associate with Lucy, or the always paired Expostulation and The Tables Turned, which grew in importance for Wordsworth for he moved the pair to the head of Volume 1 of the 1800 edition. Even in a poem as apparently simple as Poor Susan, there are the lineaments of the heaven and earth distinction that so troubles the *Ode*.

Then, to end with, there is the wholly different vision of Tintern Abbey, personal, written in structurally complex blank verse, very far from 'the language of conversation in the middle and lower classes', all Wordsworth's political and social concerns apparently abandoned.[12] It was the fruit of a very different and growing vision, and was distinguished in the same way the *Ode* would be distinguished from the preceding poems – by being placed last both in the 1798 *Lyrical Ballads* and

---

[10.] Wordsworth himself said of *An Evening Walk* and *Descriptive Sketches* that they were 'juvenile productions, inflated and obscure, but they contain many new images, and vigorous lines' (*EY* 327).

[11.] Readers would have been unable to distinguish Wordsworth's poems from Coleridge's until the publication of *LB* 1800. Yet if *LB* has a lack of unity similar to *P2V*, it mattered much less because the critics had a topic for debate – the claim of a new form of poetic diction.

[12.] Not true of course from the point of view of a new historicist. See Chapter 3, fn. 8, for a consideration of that approach.

the first volume of 1800: Wordsworth was singing his greater song. Coleridge recognized this distinction when he described the majority of the *Lyrical Ballads* as experiments, to which Wordsworth 'added two or three poems written in his own character, in the impassioned, lofty, and sustained diction, which is characteristic of his genius' (*BL* II 8). As noted earlier, this was a muted version of his 'hostility towards the plan of several of the Poems in the L. Ballads'. Even in 1798, because *The Recluse* was under way in various guises, Coleridge felt that Wordsworth had 'deserted his former mountain Track', perhaps seeking the same kind of refreshment wandering 'in Lanes & allies' that he would seek when unable to proceed with *The Excursion* (*CL* II 1013). Given this remarkable if putative publishing record, by late 1798, and certainly some fifteen months later, there could have no doubt in the mind of attentive readers that 'A Voice' was speaking, powerfully: but the question would still have remained – what really was the theme?[13]

If in 1804 *The Ruined Cottage* came next – that version containing both the intellectual history of the Pedlar and Margaret's story (*RC* E) – readers might well have wondered why these two stories were set side by side. What have they really to do with each other? Margaret's story is simple, relentless and tragic; and, as with Michael, it seems to point to the unredeemable nature of human life, to the sufferings of the poor, deranged or dispossessed. That had been the theme of *Salisbury Plain* as it is of several of the *Lyrical Ballads*. A first experience of either Michael's or Margaret's narrative has the reader hoping and believing that their sufferings will be resolved. They never are, and one arrives at the end disappointed, surprised, conventional sensibilities confused, almost shocked. If Margaret's story is all to do with the circumstances of her life, by contrast, the Pedlar's is an intellectual history, the growth of his own mind, in which circumstance is minimalized and even then focussed on his natural surroundings and the effects of nature, the relentless journey towards death ignored. At first sight they are utterly heterogeneous narratives and, had they stood together as a single poem, its earliest readers might have recognized, with *Salisbury Plain* on the one hand and Tintern Abbey on the other, comparable to the juxtaposition of *The Ruined Cottage*, that they were looking at two major threads of Wordsworth's poetry, two very distinct modes of thinking and feeling, their relationship to each other obscure. If the stories of Margaret, of Michael, of The Discharged Soldier, of The Leech-gatherer, of the Old Man Travelling, of The Cumberland Beggar and of many others – stories

---

[13.] 'A Voice shall speak, and what will be the theme?' (*HG* D 753).

of dispossession, of irresolvable suffering, of stoicism in the face of that suffering – had all been brought close enough together to impress the consciousness of readers, this would have reinforced the difference between the two kinds of poetry that Wordsworth had by then written. That is, at least two themes would have emerged, that of radical human sympathy, and that of a poetry transcending human suffering, a relationship he sought to resolve in 'the 'addendum' to *The Ruined Cottage*. Similarly, in *Peter Bell*, they might have noticed Wordsworth's belief that the power of nature can redeem a wayward soul – or the love of nature leads to the love of man, as he would subtitle Book VIII of *The Prelude*. Mock *Peter Bell* one might, and many have, but the first duty of any reader is to find the spirit in which the poet wrote. One might even argue that *Descriptive Sketches* preceding *Salisbury Plain* is the first subconscious workings of that progress.

Organizing our Reading

The above is a speculation on how Wordsworth might have been received had he published in approximately chronological order all he had and might have completed until the final edition of the *Lyrical Ballads* in 1805. It is also a suggestion of how we might see significant patterns of thought emerging in his poetry. What follows moves on from there to suggest a how-to: how should we organize our reading and interpretation of Wordsworth's subsequent work up to, say, 1810, prior to *The Excursion* and *Poems* 1815?

My first suggestion would be to defer many of the *Poems, in Two Volumes* (1807) to *Poems* (1815), with the kind of exceptions considered below, to allow a miscellany its place after an idea of order had been achieved. Imagine then, say in 1807, a volume in three parts, the first opening with selected passages from *Home at Grasmere*, which contains some of Wordsworth's most wonderful and striking poetry, ordered so as to reflect his retirement from the world, his arrival in Paradise, some description of it, and concluding with what 'must be done' – the purpose of Paradise – which is, in effect, to recreate Paradise, to marry mind and nature.[14] Unfinished, containing passages seemingly of disproportionate

---

[14.] The last poem in the *Lyrical Ballads*, Tintern Abbey would thus abut *Home at Grasmere*, where his 'thoughts of more deep seclusion' and retirement are realized. The selection from *Home at Grasmere* might begin with the first 170 lines of MS B, adding a completed and edited version of lines 171-215, ending with 'A habit of Eternity and God'. Missing out the two swans, and missing out all that goes on in 'Yon cottage' (MS B 469 ff.), I would incorporate the very tender passage that points to Wordsworth's struggle with

length to the intended whole, *Home at Grasmere* sets down his principal theme with a magnificent clarity. However, it ends with an intention, not with an achievement, and the hope of its realization seemed to recede in the years following.

When he felt that union quite out of reach, and he could find no way forward, Wordsworth wrote his *confessio* – the first four verses of the *Ode*.[15] Part II of this proposed volume would in principle follow Jared Curtis, and select poems describing that crisis and its consequences, largely consisting of those discussed in Chapter 8, 'Heaven and Earth' and a few others, including the first four verses of the *Ode*. Part III might be nothing but the completed *Ode*, offering a muted resolution to the crisis – done, to some degree, what had to be done, the marriage of mind and nature.

Finally, in this imagined trajectory of his earlier work, the publication of the 1805 *Prelude* in, say, 1809, would have rehearsed *in extenso* the achievement of the *Ode*, incorporating, as well as subordinating, his human and moral sympathies to 'something more sublime'.

That is only the barest and most tentative of suggestions. The leading idea would be to bring into focus the two principal strands of Wordsworth's poetry, and thus his purpose, even if that purpose remains divided at the core. On the one hand readers would have seen narrative poems with a strong and continuous concern with the sufferings of ordinary people, but frequently a suffering that pursues the protagonist unrelieved to the grave – what Wordsworth implicitly believed becomes of others. On the other, a lyrical impulse that would look through death, depending on a power, considered as one, issuing both from the poet and from Nature, a power he described variously as Imagination, Reason or Meditation. It is a power Wordsworth found near impossible to integrate into a narrative. *The Prelude* might be considered an exception, but it is both lyrical in spirit, and only a story of himself. That is, Wordsworth failed to find a story that spoke for all, an unsung romantic tale, with which to integrate his metaphysics, a failure to which *The Excursion* is a principal witness.

---

the still, sad, circumstantial music of humanity – lines 607-45 of MS B. For something of the particular qualities of this Paradise, describing his 'habit of Eternity', possibly lines 471-531 of MS D, though I could not omit 'those humbler sympathies / That have to me endeared the quietness / Of this sublime retirement' of MS B 721-23. Finally, to answer the question of what must be done, lines 665 to the end of MS D, missing out lines 703-44.

[15.] The last section of *Home at Grasmere*, proposing the marriage of mind and nature, was published in 1814 as the Prospectus to *The Excursion*, and it made an impression, parts much quoted by Arnold; but placed out of context as the beginning of one rather than as the conclusion of another poem, it loses its presence and its force as soon as the reader begins to plod through *The Excursion*.

Imagination was Wordsworth's theme, but the chance of his contemporary readers realizing that, or what he meant by Imagination, was negligible in the absence of *The Prelude*, the only work in which these connections are explicit. Neither Imagination nor Reason are words present in the *Ode* – 'the philosophic mind' the nearest – and in *Dejection* Coleridge names the power 'wedding Nature to us' as 'Joy', which makes for an easier rhyme, but if that is not the function of the Imagination, what is? The expression of Joy is the outward and visible sign of the Imagination at work – with feeling comes power. But, bizarre as it may seem, in their prose neither poet makes any reference to the imagination as other than poetic, always failing to mention the much greater power and its connection to Nature and Reason. The nearest Wordsworth gets to it is in his 1815 Preface, asserting that the function of the Imagination is 'to incite and support the eternal'.[16] Coleridge intended to connect Reason and Imagination in the *Biographia*, but abandoned the attempt, saying it would take him at least 100 pages. The imagination he does define at the end of Chapter 13 is singular, puzzling, and isolated from all other discussions, and without any reference to *The Prelude*. Given the centrality and the power ascribed to the Imagination in that poem, the failure of both poets to build on and present Wordsworth's insights in their prose works would have made it very difficult for contemporary readers to grasp the insights behind his major achievements, the groundwork of his metaphysics.

Had *The Prelude* been published in, say, 1809, this would not have been impossible. Even if it had retained its subtitle, as the growth of the poet's intellect or spirit, rather than the more accurate 'growth of the imagination', unique in kind and length, it would have received much closer scrutiny, and to much more effect, than it did in 1850 – when to all intents it fell dead in the water. It is therefore possible that, combined with the publication of some version of *Home at Grasmere*, Wordsworth's insights into the Imagination, essentially a power newly discovered, or an old power rediscovered, would have made a significant impression on the next generation of poets. They might have at least asked themselves what he meant by the term, and weaned themselves off Coleridge's highly rhetorical but not very substantial accounts of the poetic imagination,

---

[16.] Commenting on this and Wordsworth's preceding remarks on the imagination, Stephen Gill writes, 'The distance between the first and last definition marks out the whole range of eighteenth century uses of this most protean of terms. In the first, Imagination is a creative faculty associated with the making of works of art. In the last it is a function of man's spiritual being' (*A Life*, pp. 268-69). Indeed, and in Coleridge's terms, it is the essential difference between the secondary and the primary imagination. Neither man ever consolidated this distinction, and so it was lost to their successors.

his illustrations of which fell far short of his ideals – as do almost all actual poems. Had that been so, it is possible that a different Wordsworth would have come through to the twentieth century, who would have been seen to address the divorce between mind and nature, and who found in the Imagination the power to effect a reunion.

Coleridge put that divorce down to Descartes, 'the first man who made nature utterly lifeless and Godless' (*LHP* 565). As noted in the Introduction, Eliot described the same divorce as 'the Copernican revolution', pushing the tragedy further back, describing the consequence as a dissociation of sensibility. He, Wordsworth and Coleridge ascribed the principal problem, and the consequent task, to much the same cause. Eliot who, surprisingly, didn't have much time for Plato, refused to face the consequences of the divide, choosing instead to adhere to the Trecento – to Dante, Aquinas and Aristotle – his thinking, as he put it, largely ontological. Wordsworth and Coleridge accepted the Cartesian division, their minds less in the service of doctrine, more willing to explore the mind's own powers – a freedom Eliot despised and believed dangerous, not having, for instance, a good word to say about Freud. They remained on this side of the rift, and looked to Plato and to the Neoplatonists and Cambridge Platonists as their conscious or subconscious models of a unified sensibility. Needless to say, Eliot, blinded by both Wordsworth's and Coleridge reception histories, was entirely unaware of what either had achieved, and invented straw men, which he then exulted in knocking over.

The consequence was probably inevitable in some form or other. To solve the common problem, Eliot reinvented an ontological version of the psychological metaphysics of Wordsworth and Coleridge, at the heart of which was the Logos or the Word 'that shall not pass away'.[17] The *Four Quartets* have two epigraphs, both from Heraclitus. One reads 'Although the Word is common to all, most men live as though they had each a private wisdom of their own'. Eliot was extremely hesitant to translate the Greek, and when he did one can see why: he suggests that 'Logos' can also mean reason, but the reason he then describes is the reason of Coleridge's Understanding. This muddled two powers that both

---

[17.] Wordsworth, On the Power of Sound. The difference between ontology and psychology in Eliot's lexicon appears to be that ontology is based on doctrinal beliefs that are a secure form of knowledge; and that psychology is a permission of the mind to explore every kind of thought and experience. Some may assume that Wordsworth's and Coleridge's psychological investigations came to match Christian beliefs because neither could free themselves of that heritage. Not necessarily so: it just might be that those beliefs represent the profoundest truths of the human mind.

Wordsworth and Coleridge had clearly distinguished. Eliot therefore associated, but uncomfortably, the Logos with one mundane power when he meant another divine power, hence his reluctance to translate. Had he been familiar with *The Prelude* or even had an awareness of Coleridge's distinction between Reason and Understanding, he could not have made that mistake, and he would have seen that Reason shares many of the properties of the Logos, is fundamental to our humanity and so very much common to all. In other words, Reason, as imagination, is 'a repetition in the finite mind of the eternal act of creation in the infinite I AM'. It is a power that recreates, that unites idea and image, mind and sense impression, wedding the discerning intellect of man to this goodly universe, reviving the prospect of Paradise. As both Coleridge and Wordsworth understood the terms, the power of the Logos is of a kind with the power of the Imagination. Consequently, Eliot rewrote the logo-centric Romanticism of Wordsworth and Coleridge in a minor key, producing his own version of semi-intelligible odes, beginning with a dejection ode that had glimmers of a saving light, and then salvational odes in which the 'moments' in and out of time were moments of unified sensibility, moments of incarnation, pointing to a world not this world. Also like Wordsworth, Eliot struggled to see how he could decouple his insights from the 'egotistical pursuit of sublimities', to understand how a power experienced in oneself can also be a power in others.[18] He could not convincingly transpose his own, lyrical, forms of redeeming experience into other voices, and wrote dramatic narratives that did little more than gesture towards the timeless or transcendental. It is, I think, therefore an open question as to whether, a little less than 150 years after Wordsworth had finished *The Prelude*, ignorant of the work of his predecessors, Eliot didn't hoist himself on his own petard, doomed to rehearse what had long been achieved.[19]

* * *

From love, for here
Do we begin and end, all grandeur comes,
All truth and beauty – from pervading love –
That gone we are as dust. Behold the fields
In balmy springtime, full of rising flowers
And happy creatures ...

[18.] Tim Fulford, *Wordsworth's Poetry, 1815-45*, (Pennsylvania, 2019), p. 249. Fulford suggests that Wordsworth achieved this decoupling in some measure in his later poetry.

[19.] The epigraphs are from *1805* XIII 149-184; *BN* V; *EC* V.

> ... thou call'st this love,
> And so it is, but there is higher love
> Than this, a love that comes into the heart
> With awe and a diffusive sentiment.
> Thy love is human merely : this proceeds
> More from the brooding soul, and is divine.
>
> This love more intellectual cannot be
> Without imagination, which in truth
> Is another name for absolute strength
> And clearest insight, amplitude of mind,
> And reason in her most exalted mood.
> This faculty hath been the moving soul
> Of our long labour ...
> ... from its progress we have drawn
> The feeling of life endless, the one thought
> By which we live, infinity and God.
>
> Love is itself unmoving
> Only the cause and end of movement,
> Timeless ...
>
> Love is most nearly itself
> When here and now cease to matter.

Bibliography

Abrams, M.H. 'The Correspondent Breeze: A Romantic Metaphor'. *The Kenyon Review* 19, no. 1. (Winter 1957), pp. 113-30

Abrams, M.H. *Natural Supernaturalism: Tradition and Revolution in Romantic Literature*. Oxford, 1971

Barfield, Owen. *Romanticism Comes of Age*. Letchworth, 1966

Beer, John. *Against Finality*. Cambridge, 1993

Bloom, H. *The Visionary Company: A Reading of English Romantic Poetry*. London, 1962

Bromwich, David. *Disowned by Memory: Wordsworth's Poetry of the 1790s*. London, 2000

Brooks, Cleanth. *The Well Wrought Urn: Studies in the Structure of Poetry*. New York, 1970

Carr, Julie, and Jeffrey C. Robinson, eds. *Active Romanticism: The Radical Impulse in Nineteenth-Century and Contemporary Poetic Practice*. Alabama, 2015

Coleridge, Samuel Taylor. *Aids to Reflection*. Edited by John Beer. Princeton, NJ, 1993 (*AR*)

Coleridge, Samuel Taylor. *Biographia Literaria*. 2 volumes. Edited by Sara Coleridge. London, 1847

Coleridge, Samuel Taylor. *Biographia Literaria*. 2 volumes. Edited by James Engell and W. Jackson Bate. Princeton, NJ, 1983 (*BL*)

Coleridge, Samuel Taylor. *Coleridge: Early Family Letters*. Edited by James Engell. Oxford, 1994 (*EFL*)

Coleridge, Samuel Taylor. *The Collected Letters of Samuel Taylor Coleridge*. 6 volumes. Edited by Earl Leslie Griggs. Oxford, 1956-71 (*CL*, by vol. and page no.)

Coleridge, Samuel Taylor. *The Collected Notebooks of Samuel Taylor Coleridge*. 5 volumes. Edited by Kathleen Coburn and Anthony Harding. Princeton, NJ, 1957-2002 (*CN*, by vol. and entry no.)

Coleridge, Samuel Taylor. *The Friend*. 2 volumes. Edited by Barbara E. Rooke. Princeton, NJ, 1969 (*F*)

Coleridge, Samuel Taylor. *Lectures 1795 on Politics and Religion*. Edited by Lewis Patton and Peter Mann. London, 1971 (*LPR*)

Coleridge, Samuel Taylor. - *Lectures 1808-1819, on Literature*. 2 volumes. Edited by R.A. Foakes. Princeton, NJ, 1987 (*LL*)

Coleridge, Samuel Taylor. *Lectures 1818-19 on the History of Philosophy*. 2 volumes. Edited by J.R. de J. Jackson. Princeton, NJ, 2000 (*LHP*)

Coleridge, Samuel Taylor. *Letters, Conversations and Recollections of S.T. Coleridge*. Edited by Thomas Allsop. London, 1864

Coleridge, Samuel Taylor. *Logic*. Princeton, NJ, 1981 (*Logic*)

Coleridge, Samuel Taylor. *Marginalia*. 6 volumes. Edited by George Whalley and Heather Jackson. Princeton, NJ, 1980-2001 (*M*, by vol. and page no.)

Coleridge, Samuel Taylor. *On the Constitution of the Church and State*. Edited by John Colmer. Princeton, NJ, 1976 (*CS*)

Coleridge, Samuel Taylor. *Opus Maximum*. Edited by Thomas McFarland and Nicholas Halmi. Princeton, NJ, 2002 (*OM*)

Coleridge, Samuel Taylor. *The Poetical Works of Samuel Taylor Coleridge*. 3 volumes, each 2 parts. Edited by J.C.C. Mays. Princeton, NJ, 2001 (Reading Text cited as *PW* and poem no.; Variorum Text by vol., part and page no.)

Coleridge, Samuel Taylor. *Shorter Works and Fragments*. 2 volumes. Edited by H.J. Jackson and J.R. de J. Jackson. Princeton, NJ, 1995 (*SWF*)

Colie, Rosalie L. 'Thomas Traherne and the Infinite: The Ethical Compromise'. *Huntington Library Quarterly* 21, no. 1, Blake Bicentennial Issue (November 1957), pp. 69-82

Collingwood, R.G. *An Autobiography*. Oxford, 1939

Crab, Roger. *The English Hermite and Dagons-Downfall*. New York, 1990

Cudworth, Ralph. *A Treatise Concerning Eternal and Immutable Morality*. London, 1731

Cudworth, Ralph. *The True Intellectual System of the Universe*. London, 1678

Curtis, Jared R. *Wordsworth's Experiments with Tradition: The Lyric Poems of 1802*. Ithaca, NY, 1971 (*Experiments*)

Davies, John. *The Complete Poems of Sir John Davies*. Edited by Alexander B. Grosart. London, 1876

Davies, Paul. *The Mind of God: Science and the Search for Ultimate Meaning*. Harmondsworth, 1990

Darbishire, Helen. *Poems in Two Volumes*. Oxford, 1952

Darbishire, Helen. *Poems Published in 1807*. Oxford, 1914

De Quincey, Thomas. *Recollections of the Lakes and the Lake Poets: Coleridge, Wordsworth and Southey*. Edinburgh, 1862

Duff, David. 'The Romantic Ode and the Art of Brinkmanship'. *Études Anglaises* (April-June 2020), pp. 137-58

Eliot, T.S. *The Complete Poems and Plays of T.S. Eliot*. London, 1969

Eliot, T.S. *The Poems of T.S. Eliot: The Annotated Text*. vol. I, Collected and Uncollected Poems. Edited by Christopher Ricks and Jim McCue. London, 2015 (*AP* I)

Eliot, T.S. *The Poems of T.S. Eliot: The Annotated Text*. vol. II, Practical Cats and Further Verses. Edited by Christopher Ricks and Jim McCue. London, 2015 (*AP* II)

Eliot, T.S. *The Use of Poetry and the Use of Criticism*. London, 1933 (*UPUC*)

Eliot, T.S. *The Varieties of Metaphysical Poetry*. London, 1993 (*VMP*)

Emerson, Ralph Waldo. *Nature*. Boston, MA, 1836

Fairer, David. *Organising Poetry*. Oxford, 2009

Freud, Sigmund. *Civilization and its Discontents*. Translated by David McLintock. Introduction by Leo Bersani. London, 2002

Gill, Stephen. '"Meditative Morality": Wordsworth and Samuel Daniel'. *The Review of English Studies* 55, no. 221 (2004-9), pp. 565-82

Gill, Stephen. *William Wordsworth: A Life*. Oxford, 2020

Gill, Stephen, ed. *William Wordsworth, The Major Works*. Oxford, 2008

Gill, Stephen. *Wordsworth and the Victorians*. Oxford, 1998

Gill, Stephen. *Wordsworth's Revisitings*. Oxford, 2011

Gravil, Richard. '"Intimations" in America', in *The Oxford Handbook of William Wordsworth*, edited by Richard Gravil and Daniel Robinson, pp. 767-85. Oxford, 2015

Gravil, Richard. '"The Sunless Land": Intimations of Immortality from Recollections of Virgil and Ossian'. *Charles Lamb Bulletin* NS 136 (October 2006), pp. 112-30

Grob, Alan. 'Wordsworth's Immortality Ode and the Search for Identity', *ELH* 32 (1965), pp. 32-61

Hartman, Geoffrey H. *The Unremarkable Wordsworth*. Minneapolis, MN, 1987

Hartman, Geoffrey H. *Wordsworth's Poetry 1787-1814*. New Haven, CT, 1971

Hazlitt, William. *The Complete Works of William Hazlitt*. 21 volumes. Edited by P.P. Howe. London, 1930

Hopkins, Gerard Manley. *The Collected Works of Gerard Manley Hopkins: Correspondence*. 2 volumes. Edited by R.K.R. Thornton and Catherine Phillips. Oxford, 2013 (*GMH Letters*);

Jarvis, Simon. *Wordsworth's Philosophic Song*. Cambridge, 2006

Johnson, Samuel. *Lives of the English Poets*. Glasgow, 1825 (*Lives*); accessed as: https://archive.org/details/livesofenglish00john/page/12/mode/2up?ref=ol&view=theater

Johnston, Kenneth R. *The Hidden Wordsworth*. New York, 1998

Kermode, Frank. *Romantic Paradox: An Essay on the Poetry of Wordsworth*. London, 1962/2016

Lamb, Charles. *The Letters of Charles Lamb, to which are Added those of his Sister Mary Lamb*. 3 volumes. Edited by E.V. Lucas. London, 1935 (cited by letter)

Leadbetter, Gregory. 'The Lyric Impulse of Poems, in Two Volumes'. In *The Oxford Handbook of William Wordsworth*, edited by Richard Gravil and Daniel Robinson, pp. 221-36. Oxford, 2015

Levinson, Marjorie. *Wordsworth's Great Period Poems*. Cambridge, 1986

Magnuson, Paul. *Coleridge and Wordsworth: A Lyrical Dialogue*. Princeton, NJ, 1988

Magnuson, Paul. 'The Genesis of Wordsworth's "Ode"'. *TWC* 12, no. 1 (1981), p. 28

Manning, Peter J. 'Wordsworth Reshapes Himself and is Reshaped: The River Duddon and the 1820 Miscellaneous Poems'. *TWC* 51, no. 1 (Winter 2020), pp. 35-53

Manning, Peter J. 'Wordsworth's Intimations Ode and its Epigraphs'. *Journal of English and Germanic Philology* 82, no. 4 (1983), pp. 526-40

Marsh, Florence G. 'Wordsworth's Ode: Obstinate Questionings'. *Studies in Romanticism* 5 (1966), pp. 219-30

Mays, J.C.C. 'The Authorship of the "Barberry Tree"'. *The Review of English Studies* 37, issue 147 (1 August 1986), pp. 360-70

McGann, Jerome. *The Romantic Ideology*. Chicago, 1983

Merrill, L.R. 'Vaughan's Influence upon Wordsworth's Poetry'. *Modern Language Notes* 37, no. 2 (February 1922), pp. 91-96

Miller, Clarence H. 'The May-Day Celebration in Wordsworth's Immortality Ode'. *Studies in English Literature, 1500-1900* 27 (1987), pp. 571-79

Milton, John. *Paradise Lost*. Belfast, 1817 (*PL*)

Newlyn, Lucy. *William and Dorothy Wordsworth: All in Each Other*. Oxford, 2013

O'Neill, Michael. '"The Tremble from it is Spreading": A Reading of Wordsworth's "Ode: Intimations of Immortality"'. *The Charles Lamb Bulletin* 139 (2007), pp. 74-90

Patrick, Simon. *A BRIEF Account of the new SECT OF LATITUDE-MEN Together with some reflections upon the NEW PHILOSOPHY*. London, 1662

Patrides, C.A., ed. *The Cambridge Platonists*. Cambridge, 1980

Perry, Seamus. 'Coleridge, the Return to Nature, and the New Anti-Romanticism: An Essay in Polemic'. *Romanticism on the Net* 4 (November 1996)

Potkay, Adam. *The Story of Joy*. Cambridge, 2007

Rawes, Alan. 'Romantic Form and New Historicism: Wordsworth's "Lines Written a Few Miles above Tintern Abbey"'. In *Romanticism and Form*, edited by Alan Rawes, pp. 95-115. Basingstoke, 2007

Raysor, Thomas. 'The Themes of Immortality and Natural Piety in Wordsworth's Immortality Ode'. In *British Romantic Poets: Recent Revaluations*, edited by Shiv K. Kumar, pp. 45-62. London, 1968

Rea, J.D. 'Coleridge's Intimations of Immortality from Proclus'. *Modern Philology* 26, no. 2 (1928), pp. 201-13

Reader, Melvin. *Wordsworth: A Philosophical Approach*. Oxford, 1967

Reed, Mark L. *Wordsworth: The Chronology of The Middle Years, 1800-1815*. Cambridge, MA, 1975 (*Reed*)

Robinson, Daniel. 'William Wordsworth: Ode. Intimations of Immortality from Recollections of Early Childhood'. http://www.litencyc.com/php/sworks.php?rec=true&UID=34202, accessed 11 September 2014

Robinson, Henry Crabb. *Correspondence of Henry Crabb Robinson with the Wordsworth Circle*. 2 volumes. Edited by Edith J. Morley. Oxford, 1927

Robinson, Henry Crabb. *The Diary, Reminscences, and Correspondence of Henry Crabb Robinson*. 3 volumes. Edited by Thomas Sadler. London, 1869

Roe, Nicholas. *The Politics of Nature*. Basingstoke, 2002

Roe, Nicholas. *Wordsworth and Coleridge: The Radical Years*. Oxford, 1990/2018

Ruderman, David B. 'Reforming the Space of the Child: Infancy and the Reception of Wordsworth's "Ode"'. In *Romanticism and Parenting: Image, Instruction and Ideology*, edited by Carolyn Webber, pp. 103-27. Newcastle, 2007

Ruoff, Gene W. *Wordsworth and Coleridge: The Making of the Major Lyrics, 1802-1804*. New Brunswick, NJ, 1989

Ruskin, John. *Art and Life: A Ruskin Anthology*. Edited by John Alden. New York, 1886

Shelley, Percy Bysshe. 'On Life'. In *Shelley's Poetry and Prose: A Norton Critical Edition*, edited by Donald H. Reiman and Sharon B. Powers, pp. 474-78. New York, 1977

Smith, John. *Select Discourses*. Edited by John Worthington. London, 1660

Taylor, Anya. 'Religious Readings of the Immortality Ode'. *Studies in English Literature, 1500-1900* 26 (1986), pp. 633-54

Traherne, Thomas. *Centuries of Meditations*. Edited by Bertram Dobell. London, 1927 (*Centuries*)

Traherne, Thomas. 'Inducements to Retirednesse'. In *The Works of Thomas Traherne*, Vol. 1, edited by Jan Ross. London, 1995 (*Inducements*)

Traherne, Thomas. *Poetical Works*. Edited by Gladys I. Wade. London, 1932 (*TPW*)

Trilling, Lionel. *The Liberal Imagination*. London, 1951

Trilling, Lionel. 'The Immortality Ode'. In *English Romantic Poets: Modern Essays in Criticism*, edited by M.H. Abrams, pp. 149-69. London, 1975

Vendler, Helen. 'Lionel Trilling and the Immortality Ode'. *Salmagundi* 41 (1978), pp. 66-86

Vigus, James. *Platonic Coleridge*. London, 2019

Whalley, George. 'The Fields of Sleep'. *Review of English Studies* NS 9 (1958), pp. 49-53

Whichcote, Benjamin. *Moral and Religious Aphorisms*. Edited by Dr Jeffery. London, 1753

Whichcote, Benjamin. *Moral and Religious Aphorisms, with an introduction by W.R. Inge*. London, 1930

Woof, Pamela. *The Grasmere Journals*. Oxford, 1993 (*DWJ*)

Woof, Robert, ed. *William Wordsworth: The Critical Heritage*. Volume 1, 1793-1820. London, 2001 (*Woof*)

Wordsworth, Christopher, ed. *Memoirs of William Wordsworth*. 2 volumes. London, 1851 (*Memoirs*)

Wordsworth, Jonathan. *The Music of Humanity*. London, 1969

Wordsworth, Mary. *The Letters of Mary Wordsworth 1800-1855*. Edited by Mary E. Burton. Oxford, 1958 (*MWL*)

Wordsworth, William. *Descriptive Sketches*. Edited by Eric Birdsall and Paul M. Zall. Ithaca, NY, 1984 (*DS*)

Wordsworth, William. *The Dove Cottage Manuscripts*. https://wordsworth.org.uk/the-collection/ (*DCMS*)

Wordsworth, William. *The Excursion*. Edited by Sally Bushell, James A. Butler and Michael C. Jaye. Ithaca, NY, 1997

Wordsworth, William. *The Fenwick Notes of William Wordsworth*. Edited by Jared Curtis. Bristol, 1993 (*FN*)

Wordsworth, William. *The Five-Book Prelude*. Edited by Duncan Wu. Oxford, 1997 (*5BP*)

Wordsworth, William. *Home at Grasmere*. Edited by Beth Darlington. Ithaca, NY, 1977 (*HG*)

Wordsworth, William. *Lyrical Ballads and Other Poems, 1798, 1800*. Edited by James Butler and Karen Green. Ithaca, NY, 1992 (*LB*)

Wordsworth, William. *The Major Works*. Edited by Stephen Gill. Oxford, 2008 (*MW*)

Wordsworth, William. *Poems in Two Volumes, and Other Poems, 1800-07*. Edited by Jared Curtis. Ithaca, NY, 1983 (*P2V*)

Wordsworth, William. *Poems, in Two Volumes, 1807*. Edited by Richard Matlak. Ontario, 2015

Wordsworth, William. *The Prelude, 1798-1799*. Edited by Stephen Parrish. Ithaca, NY, 1977 (*1798-9*)

Wordsworth, William. *The Prelude 1799, 1805, 1850*. The Norton edition. Edited by Jonathan Wordsworth, M.H. Abrams and Stephen Gill. London, 1979 (including *The Two Part Prelude*, *The Thirteen Book Prelude*, and *The Fourteen Book Prelude*, cited by date)

Wordsworth, William. *The Prose Works of William Wordsworth*. 3 volumes. Edited by W.J.B. Owen and Jane Worthington Smyser. Oxford, 1974 (*Prose*)

Wordsworth, William. *The Ruined Cottage and The Pedlar*. Edited by James Butler. Ithaca, NY, 1979 (*RC*)

Wordsworth, William. *The Salisbury Plain Poems*. Edited by Stephen Gill. Ithaca, NY, 1975 (*SP*)

Wordsworth, William. *Selected Poems of William Wordsworth, with Matthew Arnold's Essay on Wordsworth*. Edited by Harrison Ross Steeves. New York, 1922. https://archive.org/details/selectedpoemsofw00wrd/page/94/mode/2up

Wordsworth, William. *Wordsworth's Poetical Works in Five Volumes*. 2nd edition. Edited by Ernest de Selincourt and Helen Darbishire. Oxford, 1952 (*WPW*)

Wordsworth, William, and Dorothy Wordsworth. *The Letters of William and Dorothy Wordsworth: The Early Years, 1787-1805*. 2nd revised edition. Edited by Ernest de Selincourt and Chester L. Shaver. Oxford, 1969 (*EY*)

Wordsworth, William, and Dorothy Wordsworth. *The Letters of William and Dorothy Wordsworth: The Middle Years*. 2 volumes, 2nd edition. Edited by Ernest de Selincourt, Mary Moorman and Alan G. Hill. Oxford, 1969 (*MY*)

The Wordsworth Circle, quarterly journal, Boston, 1970– (*TWC*)

Worthen, John. *The Life of William Wordsworth*. Chichester, 2014

Wu, Duncan. *Wordsworth's Reading 1770-1799*. Cambridge, 1993

Wu, Duncan. *Wordsworth's Reading 1800-1815*. Cambridge, 1996

Index of Wordsworth's Work

The Affliction of Mary 135
Alice Fell 135–36
Among all lovely things my Love had been 133
The Barberry Tree 101n1, 136, 140–41, 140n4
Beggars 135–36
Benjamin the Waggoner 242
The Borderers 119, 242, 244, 245
Brook, that has been my solace days and weeks 219

Composed in the Valley, Near Dover, On the Day of landing 132n8
Composed upon Westminster Bridge, Sept.3, 1803 131
The Cumberland Beggar 246

Dear Native Brooks your ways I have pursued 219
Descriptive Sketches 76n12, 243, 245n10, 247
The Discharged Soldier 6, 69–71, 73, 74, 246

The Emigrant Mother 135
Essay on Epitaphs 42, 219
Essay, Supplementary to the Preface 120
An Evening Walk 243, 245n10
The Excursion 19, 21, 74, 76, 79, 83, 86, 91, 97n43, 100, 108n19, 112, 116, 120, 128, 157, 180, 192, 229, 230, 232–34, 235, 238–39, 241, 246, 247, 248, 248n15
Expostulation and Reply 5, 31–34, 40, 44, 118n30, 129n4, 245
Extempore Effusion Upon the Death of James Hogg 89

Farewell, thou little Nook of mountain ground 132n8
Fenwick Notes 9, 81, 82, 88, 93, 98, 111, 134n12, 138n2, 166, 181n3, 183, 196
Fidelity 236
Foresight, or the Charge of a Child to his Younger Companion 132n8

The Glow-worm 132n8, 133–34
Goody Blake and Harry Gill 245
The Green Linnet 135, 136

Home at Grasmere 19, 21–22, 45, 47–48, 97n4, 107–8, 115–17, 119, 133n10, 135, 147, 170n17, 177, 190, 217, 218–19, 227, 242, 247–48, 248n15, 249

The Idiot Boy 136, 236, 245
The Idle Shepherd Boys 188–89, 190
I find it written of Simonides, 129
I travelled among Unknown Men 132n8
I wandered lonely as a cloud 101n1
It is a beauteous evening, calm and free 131, 209n6
It is no Spirit who from Heaven hath flown 136, 151

Laodamia 87, 90, 95, 221, 223
The Leech-gatherer 9, 146, 151, 159–61, 196, 246
Letter to the Bishop of Llandaff 243
Lines left upon a Seat in a Yew-tree 6, 74–76
Lines written a few miles above Tintern Abbey, *see* Tintern Abbey
Lines written at Small Distance from my House 129n4
Lines Written in Early Spring 88, 129n4

London, 1802 131
Louisa 132n8, 236
Lyrical Ballads 5, 34n4, 37, 88n23, 127, 129–30, 135, 136, 141, 182n5, 187, 234, 235, 236–37, 238, 245–46, 247

The Mad Mother 245
The Manciple (from the Prologue) and his Tale 127
Michael, A Pastoral Poem 69, 149
Milton! thou should'st be living at this hour 131
My heart leaps up 84, 131, 136, 156, 189

Ode, Composed upon an Evening of Extraordinary Splendour and Beauty 98n47, 177, 194
Ode: Intimations of Immortality 6, 8, 41, 42, 50, 155–224, 230, 231, 232, 235, 239, 245, 248, 249
  as attempt to connect mind and nature 2, 4–5, 7, 53, 54, 56, 58, 59, 62, 91–92, 181–83, 194, 207, 211, 212, 214–15, 216–17, 224, 251
  as ode 163–66
  childhood vision in 2, 5–6, 6–7, 54, 62, 79, 80, 81, 82–85, 93–98, 99–100, 102–3, 104–5, 107–8, 110–11, 111–12, 117, 179, 181–83, 197–98, 199–205, 206, 210, 214
  Coleridge's criticism of 6–7, 14, 50, 54n20, 80–82, 89–90, 93, 104–5, 121, 187, 203, 204
  composition of 7, 80, 155–61, 162–63, 175–76, 227
  echoes in 188–91
  epigraph to 79–80, 84, 85, 99, 179, 221, 232, 235
  grammatical simplicity in 7, 168–69, 187
  intelligibility/unintelligibility of 13–14, 27, 80–82, 84, 89–91, 92, 97, 99–100, 179–82, 190, 193–94, 210n8, 221
  loss as theme in 186–87, 195, 198–99, 199–205, 206, 210, 214
  placement of 13, 14, 79–80, 162
  reception of 6–7, 13–14, 27, 80–83, 85–86, 187
  rhyme scheme 166–68
  rivers as metaphor in 42–43, 187–88, 219
  simplicity of imagery in 7, 169–70, 176
  spontaneity of 162–63, 166–67
  subtitle to 83–85
  Tintern Abbey's relationship to 6, 40, 179, 211–12, 213
  tripartite structure of 8, 84–85
Ode to Duty 83, 135
Old Man Travelling 246
On the Power of Sound 50n15, 150, 162n1, 187n4, 194, 252n17

Personal Talk 135, 136, 140, 150
Peter Bell 143, 148, 149, 151, 158, 242, 247
Poems (1815) 6, 13–14, 20, 79, 81, 82–85, 120, 147n17, 179, 187n3, 203, 237–39, 241, 242, 247, 249
Poems in Two Volumes 13, 128, 135, 139, 232, 234–38
Poor Susan 245
Prefatory Sonnet 135
The Prelude 8, 18, 21, 29, 35, 36, 42, 43–44, 48, 51–52, 58, 64–66, 68, 75, 95–96, 99, 100, 110, 121–22, 130, 136, 144n5, 147n8, 157, 161, 178, 192, 209, 220, 221, 227–30, 231–34, 242, 248–50, 251
  1798 99
  The Five-Book Prelude 122, 232
  1805 20n17, 161, 227–28, 248
  1850 238, 249
  Book I 110
  Book II 200n8, 212–13, 215n15
  Book III 135n13
  Book V 192
  Book VI 64–66, 75
  Book VIII 68, 136, 247
  Book XI 218

The Recluse 128–31, 142, 159, 231, 232–34, 235, 246
The Redbreast and the Butterfly 235
Resolution and Independence 1, 130, 135, 141, 149, 160, 174, 210n7
The River Duddon. A Series of Sonnets 42
The Ruined Cottage 20n16, 46n9, 65–66, 71, 72–74, 127–28, 136, 149, 222–24, 232, 240–41, 242, 246
Ruth 149

The Sailor's Mother 135–36
Salisbury Plain 76n12, 242–44, 245, 246–47
She was a phantom of delight 134

Simon Lee: The Old Huntsman 6, 71–72, 73, 101n1
A slumber did my spirit seal 91
The Small Celandine ('There is a Flower, the Lesser Celandine') 144
The Sparrow's Nest 130

The Tables Turned 5, 30n2, 31, 34–36, 37, 40, 41, 47, 59, 60, 65n2, 74n11, 101n1, 118n30, 129n4, 245
There is a trickling water, neither rill 132n8
The Thorn 245
The Tinker 135, 140n4
Tintern Abbey 5–6, 9, 14, 30–31, 32, 34, 36, 37, 40–63, 67–68, 69, 70, 74, 93, 98, 101n1, 115, 129, 136–37, 141, 147, 157, 158, 179, 181, 187, 188, 193, 194, 210n8, 211–12, 213, 213n14, 218n4, 219n6, 235, 236, 238, 245–46, 247n14
To a Butterfly ('Stay near me – do not take flight!') 130, 132n8, 136, 138, 139–40
To a Butterfly ('I've watch'd you now a full half hour') 132n8, 138, 139–40
To a Skylark 83, 97n8, 136, 146, 148n13, 161, 187

To H.C. Six Years Old 136, 148–51, 188, 199
To the Cuckoo 84n10, 136, 146–48, 148n13, 156, 189–90
To the Daisy ('In youth from rock to rock I went') 136, 138, 141–43, 228, 236
To the Daisy ('With little here to do or see') 136, 138, 141–43, 174, 228
To the Daisy ('Bright Flower, whose home is every where!') 136, 138, 141–44, 174, 228
To the Same Flower ('Pleasures newly found are sweet') 138, 144–45
To the Small Celandine ('Pansies, Lillies, Kingcups, Daisies') 138, 144–45, 150n15
Travelling 132n8
A Tuft of Primroses 192, 242

The Wanderer 232
Witness thou 133, 134
Written in March 139, 140n4, 171–76, 176n29, 191–92, 235

'Yes! full surely 'twas the echo' 146–47, 189–90

General Index

Aeschylus 96
Aquinas, Thomas 250
Aristotle 2, 15–16, 16n3, 22, 250
Arnold, Matthew 173

Bacon, Francis 2, 15, 16, 19, 23
Baxter, Richard 88
Beaumont, Sir George 234
Beaumont, Lady 230, 233
Blake, William 120, 175
Boyle, Robert 15
Brahe, Tycho 15
Bronte, Emily 195
Brooks, Cleanth 195
Browning, Robert 86–87
Bruno, Giordano 22
Butler, James 127
Byron, Lord 171, 235

Cambridge Platonists 3–4, 6, 17–20, 21n19, 35, 36n7, 36n9, 165–66, 250
Carlyle, Thomas 89–90
Carver, Raymond 117, 118
Chaucer, Geoffrey 127
Clarkson, Catherine 83, 120–21, 155
Coleridge, Hartley 148–50
Coleridge, Sara 133
Coleridge, Samuel Taylor 1, 2, 3–4, 7, 8, 9, 14, 16, 17–18, 20–23, 25, 26, 27, 29–32, 35, 36n10, 40, 46, 48n11, 49n13, 50n15, 55, 64, 66, 68, 76n12, 88, 89, 91n30, 94, 96, 99, 102, 111n24, 118, 121, 128–31, 132, 134, 138–39, 142, 143, 155–61, 167n10, 168–69, 177, 179n1, 182, 211n9, 218, 230–31, 232, 233–34, 236n13, 237, 238, 241n22, 243, 244, 246, 249, 250–51
Biographia Literaria 22, 23, 81–82, 104, 129n3, 156, 236n13, 244n8, 249
Dejection: An Ode 158, 159, 161, 193, 249. *See also* A Letter to —
The Destiny of Nations 20
The Friend 81, 156
Frost at Midnight 30
Kubla Khan 46
A Letter to — 7, 82, 130–31, 148, 155–61, 167n10, 218
Opus Maximum 22
'Reason is from God, and God *is* reason, *men ipissima*' 96
The Rime of the Ancient Mariner 223, 229, 236
This Lime-tree Bower my Prison 30, 38–39, 74n11
To William Wordsworth, Composed on the Night after his Recitation of a Poem on the Growth of an Individual Mind 230–31
Collingwood, R.G. 172
Collins, William 164
Ode on the Poetical Character 164
The Passions 163, 164, 179
Congreve, William 164–65
Copernicus, Nicolaus 2, 15, 250
De revolutionibus 15
Cottle, Joseph 128–29
Cowley, Abraham 163–66
Life 164–65

The Reason, the Use of it in Divine
  Matters 165–66
Resurrection 164
Cudworth, Ralph 3, 4, 17, 18, 33,
  34–35
Curtis, Jared 128, 131, 132, 147, 174,
  237, 248

Daniel, Samuel 201
Dante 250
Darbishire, Helen 192
Davies, Sir John
  *Of the Soul of Man and the Immortalitie
  thereof* 88, 92–93
Davies, Paul 23–24, 25, 120
De Quincey, Thomas 188, 190
Descartes, Rene 2, 15, 16, 17, 18, 19, 250
  Discours de la Methode 15
Dobell, Bertram 103
Donne, John
  Good Friday, 1613. Riding Westward 198
Dowden, Edward 192
Dryden, John
  Alexander's Feast 163
Duff, David 202n13

Einstein, Albert 15
Eliot, George 239n20
Eliot, T.S. 8, 13, 15–16, 17n8, 24, 27, 41,
  46, 96, 118, 142, 163, 180, 201, 205,
  216–17, 239–40, 242, 250–51,
  Animula 199n5
  Cousin Nancy 173–74
  Four Quartets 16, 40–41
  Burnt Norton 118, 180
  The Dry Salvages 40–41
  East Coker 142, 150–51
  Little Gidding 40
Emerson, Ralph Waldo 173–74
Euclid
  Elements 6, 67, 69

Fairer, David 162, 163–64, 166
Fenwick, Isabella 81, 82, 88, 98, 166,
  181n3, 196
Fox, George 23
Frend, William 243
Freud, Sigmund 105–7, 109, 110–11,
  112, 250

Galileo 15
Gill, Stephen 5, 162, 238, 249n16
Godwin, William 243
Gravil, Richard 87, 89–91, 176n29, 206
Gray, Thomas 98n47
  The Bard 163, 164
  The Progress of Poesy 164
Greville, Fulke 201
Grob, Alan 84

Hartman, Geoffrey 206
Hayden, John 84
Hazlitt, William 14, 108n19, 232n7, 239
Heraclitus 250
Herbert, George 45, 114
Hill, Christopher
  *God's Englishman: Oliver Cromwell and
  the English Revolution* 206
Hobson, Thomas 165
Holcroft, Thomas 243
Hopkins, Gerard Manley 8, 102, 174, 176,
  233, 239
Hopton, Susanna 108, 111, 122, 229
Humboldt, Baron von 232
Hutchinson, Henry 45
Hutchinson, Mary 132, 133, 158–59
Hutchinson, Sara 151, 155, 157–58, 167

Iamblichus 18

Jarvis, Simon 107n15
Jeffrey, Francis 13, 14, 27, 80, 84n13, 91,
  238, 242
Johnson, Samuel 164n5, 165, 166, 167

Kant, Immanuel 22n20, 175
Keats, John 101–2, 150n15, 162
Kepler, Johannes 15
Kermode, Frank 192
Knight, William 240

Lamb, Charles 18, 38, 39, 133
Lamb, Mary 133
Larkin, Peter 1n4
Larkin, Philip 8
Law, William 23
Lawrence, D.H.
  Snake 106–7
Le Beau Monde 235

Levinson, Marjorie 105, 106, 110
Lowther, William 131

Magnuson, Paul 83, 99, 197n2,
Manning, Peter 85, 110n22, 199n6
Mant, Richard
  The Simpliciad 237n16
Marvell, Andrew
  The Garden 107n15, 135
Mays, Jim 140n4, 155, 161
McGann, Jerome 105, 106. 110
Merrill, L.R. 101
Milton, John 102, 135n13, 165, 169, 202n13, 229
Modiano, Raimonda 171
Montgomery, James 80, 187, 235–36, 236n14
More, Henry 88, 165
Morning Post 129, 159

Newlyn, Lucy 199
Newton, Isaac 2, 15
Newton, John 21, 66
Noyes, Russell 84

O'Neill, Michael 91, 198, 199
Ovid 87

Peat, David 24–25
Patrick, Simon 3, 16, 17, 18, 93n34
Pindar 163–64, 164n5, 166
Plato 15, 16n3, 22, 22n20, 50, 81, 250
Plotinus 18, 21, 22
Poole, Thomas 130
Pope, Alexander
  An Essay on Criticism 166
Proclus 18, 22, 163n3

Rea, J.D. 163n3
Reed, Mark 127, 196n12, 201n11, 218, 227
Robinson, Daniel 89, 89n26, 166
Robinson, Henry Crabb 13, 25, 83, 120
Roe, Nicholas 45n8
Rolland, Romain 106
Rucker, Rudy 25
Ruskin, John 85–86

Scott, Walter 80
  Helvellyn 236
Shakespeare, William 102, 169
  As You Like It 201
Shelley, Percy Bysshe 110, 147
Simonides 129
Smith, John 93n34, 97, 97n45, 98, 121n33

Smith, Patty 120
Sotheby, William 161
Southey, Robert 80, 130, 243
  The Cataract of Lodore 187
Spenser, Edmund 245
Spinoza 120
Stannard, Russell 24

Traherne, Thomas 6–7, 38, 100, 102–4, 105, 106–23, 202–3, 214, 219 229
  The Apostacy 112–13
  Blisse 112–13
  Centuries 102, 104, 108, 122–23, 214, 219
  Dumnesse 106–7, 109, 202–3
  Innocence 51n16
  The Preparative 169n15, 174n29
  The Return 106
  Salutation 103
Trilling, Lionel 110, 184n6, 211n7

Vallon, Annette 131–32, 134, 209n6
Vaughan, Henry 7, 101, 102, 106n14, 107n15
  The Retreate 85, 101
Vendler, Helen 97n43, 166, 179n80, 184n6
Vigus, James 50n15
Virgil 79, 85, 87

Whalley, George 192–93, 195
Whichcote, Benjamin 35, 36n7, 177
Woof, Robert 235
Wordsworth, Catherine 86, 223
Wordsworth, Christopher
  Memoirs of William Wordsworth 93
Wordsworth, Dorothy 7, 44, 45, 59–62, 83, 108, 115, 130, 132–35, 136, 139, 140, 142, 156–57, 158–59, 163, 172–75, 204, 232, 233, 234
  Journal 7, 9, 45n7, 127, 131, 138n2, 155, 157n2, 158n4, 172–75, 176n29, 196n12, 218n5
Wordsworth, John 86, 232–33
Wordsworth, William
  and intelligibility/unintelligibility 2–5, 18, 26, 27, 30, 36, 39, 44–45, 47–51, 55–56, 57–58, 73. *See also* Ode: Intimations of Immortality, intelligibility/unintelligibility of
Worthen John 209n6
Wu, Duncan 163

You may also be interested in:

Private Lives of the Ancient Mariner
Coleridge and his Children
by Molly Lefebure

In her last published work the celebrated Coleridgean, Molly Lefebure, provides profound psychological insights into Coleridge through a meticulous study of his domestic life, drawing upon a vast and unique body of knowledge gained from a lifetime's study of the poet, and making skilful use of the letters, poems and biographies of the man himself and his family and friends.

The author traces the roots of Coleridge's unarguably dysfunctional personality from his earliest childhood; his position as his mother's favoured child, the loss of this status with the death of his father, and removal to the 'Bluecoat' school in London. Coleridge's narcissistic depression, flamboyance, and cold-hearted, often cruel, rejection of his family and of loving attachments in general are examined in detail. The author also explores Coleridge's careers in journalism and politics as well as poetry, in his early, heady 'jacobin' days, and later at the heart of the British wartime establishment at Malta. His virtual abandonment of his children and tragic disintegration under the influence of opium are included in the broad sweep of the book which also encompasses an examination of the lives of Coleridge's children, upon whom the manipulations of the father left their destructive mark.

Molly Lefebure unravels the enigma that is Coleridge with consummate skill in a book that will bring huge enjoyment to any reader with an interest in the poet's life and times.

> '[Molly Lefebure's] insight into Coleridge's marriage is second to none. Her perception of him as a man and a poet is intellectually formidable.' – **Lord Melvyn Bragg**

Molly Lefebure (1919-2013) was a wartime journalist, novelist, children's author, writer on the topography of Cumbria, biographer, and independent scholar and lecturer. She is the author of two other works on the Coleridge family and a volume on the world of Thomas Hardy.

Published 2013

Hardback ISBN: 978 0 7188 93002
PDF ISBN: 978 0 7188 4189 8
ePub ISBN: 978 0 7188 4190 4

You may also be interested in:

The Voluble Soul
Thomas Traherne's Poetic Style and Thought
by Richard Willmott

"*The world's fair beauty set my soul on fire.*"

In this first study of the full range of Traherne's poetry Richard Willmott explains his 'metaphysical' poetry to all who are attracted by the beauty of his language, but puzzled by his meaning. He offers guidance both for the student of English, uncertain about Traherne's theological ideas, and the student of theology, put off by seventeenth-century poetic conventions and diction. Using a wealth of quotation, he examines Traherne's verse alongside that of a variety of his contemporaries, including Andrew Marvell, Lucy Hutchinson, Anne Bradstreet and Edward Taylor.

Central to Traherne's poetry and generous theology is his delight in the capacity of his soul to approach God through an appreciation of His infinite creation. This soul is 'voluble', not only because it can express its thoughts with fluency, but also because it can enfold within itself the infinity of God's creation, taking in everything that it perceives, considering the latest scientific speculations about the atom and astronomy, but also looking clear-sightedly at Restoration society's materialism and – in one startlingly savage satire – the corruption of the royal court.

> 'Alongside key Trahernian themes such as felicity, innocence and atomism, there is a surefooted discussion of Traherne's wider intellectual context, from the Psalms to Augustine to the metaphysical poets.' – **Elizabeth S. Dodd**, Sarum College

Richard Willmott is a retired headmaster of the Dixie Grammar School and Chairman of the Traherne Association. He read English at Cambridge, and took a further degree in Renaissance French drama at UEA. His previous publications include student editions of Blake's *Songs of Innocence and of Experience* and of Ben Jonson's *Volpone and The Alchemist*, and an introduction to metaphysical poetry.

Published 2021

Hardback ISBN: 978 0 7188 9568 6
Paperback ISBN: 978 0 7188 9569 3
PDF ISBN: 978 0 7188 4829 3
ePub ISBN: 978 0 7188 4830 9